Trafficking in Women and Children
Myths and Realities

About the Author

Sankar Sen, former Director General, National Human Rights Commission, New Delhi and former Director of the National Police Academy, Hyderabad, joined the Indian Police Service in 1960. He graduated from Presidency College, Calcutta, and obtained Master's degree in History from Calcutta University and LLB from Utkal University. He was allotted to Orissa cadre and held a number of posts with distinction. He joined the Border Security Force as the Inspector General in 1987 and was later on promoted as the Additional Director General. Thereafter, he was posted as the Director of the SVP National Police Academy (NPA), the premier institution for training of senior police officers in the country.

He was awarded the Police Medal for meritorious service in 1979 and President's Police Medal for distinguished service in 1986. On completion of his assignment in the NPA, he joined as the Director General of the National Human Rights Commission and later on functioned as the Special Rapporteur, in charge of custodial justice programmes of the NHRC. He has to his credit many books, including *Police Today and Human Rights in a Developing Society; Tryst with Law Enforcement and Human Rights; Law Enforcement and Cross Border Terrorism; Human Rights and Law Enforcement*, etc. At present, he is a Senior Fellow in the Institute of Social Sciences, New Delhi.

Jayashree Ahuja holds a Master's degree in Zoology from the University of Delhi. She is actively involved in the social development sector for nearly two decades. She is also a research scholar closely associated with the Institute of Social Sciences, New Delhi.

Trafficking in Women and Children
Myths and Realities

Sankar Sen
Jayashree Ahuja

CONCEPT PUBLISHING COMPANY, NEW DELHI-110 059

Cataloging in Publication Data—DK
Courtesy: D.K. Agencies (P) Ltd. <docinfo@dkagencies.com>

Sen, Sankar, 1936-
Trafficking in women and children : myths and realities / Sankar Sen, Jayashree Ahuja.
p. cm.
With reference to India.
Includes bibliographical references.
Includes index.
ISBN 13: 9788180694448
ISBN 10: 8180694445

1. Human trafficking—India. 2. Women—Crimes against—India. 3. Children—Crimes against—India. 4. Sex-oriented businesses—Law and legislation—India. 5. Forced labor—Law and legislation—India. I. Ahuja, Jayashree, joint author. II. Title.

DDC 306.362 082 095 4 22

ISBN-13: 978-81-8069-444-8
ISBN-10: 81-8089-444-5

First Published 2009

Published and Printed by
Ashok Kumar Mittal
Concept Publishing Company
A/15-16, Commercial Block, Mohan Garden
New Delhi-110059 (INDIA)

Phones : 25351460, 25351794
Fax : 091-11-25357103
Email : publishing@conceptpub.com

Dr. Justice Shivaraj V. Patil
Former Member
(Former Judge, Supreme Court of India)

National Human Rights Commission
Faridkot House, Copernicus Marg
New Delhi-110 001
Phone: 91-11-2338 7328
Fax: 91-11-2338 4863
E-mail: patilsv@nic.in

Foreword

Trafficking in human beings, more so in women and children, is one of the fastest-growing forms of transnational organized crime, next only to drugs and weapons, generating unaccountable profits annually. The reasons for the increase in this global phenomenon are multiple and complex, affecting rich and poor countries alike. India is no exception to this. We all know that till a few years back trafficking was considered coterminous with prostitution or sex trade. Trafficking, however, is carried for various other purposes too, such as, domestic servitude, labour in sweat shops and small factories, bonded and forced labour, begging, for the purposes of marriage, adoption, public sport, organ trade as well as drug peddling and smuggling. Trafficking is also closely linked to issues of migration, especially illegal and irregular migration.

Apart from the push and pull factors, trafficking takes many different forms and adopts different mechanisms, for there are different categories of traffickers and exploiters who take on different roles along the journey from vulnerability to exploitation.

Newer and more sophisticated methods of force and violence are being used to facilitate brokering, liaising, and market linkages for the sexual exploitation and enslavement of women and children. These range from international marriage alliances and the mail order bride system to use-of internet services for the global exchange of sex-related services.

Trafficking in women and children, is thus one of the worst forms of violence of human rights. This is because it gradually results in the total destruction of the victim's personal identity and his/her right to live as a free human being in the so-called civilized society. Being subjected to continuous violence and humiliation, it also violates several of their other human rights, such as, right to life, the right to liberty and security, the right to freedom from torture or cruelty, inhuman or degrading treatment, the right to a home and a family, the right to education and proper employment, the right to health care, everything that makes for a life with dignity.

The United Nations, including the Office of the United Nations High Commissioner for Human Rights has identified trafficking as a fundamental human rights violation. As a result, it has put in place several significant international agreements and treaties to address the human rights violations involved in the trafficking of human beings.

India being a country of destination, supply and transit for trafficking networks, the issue of trafficking in women and children, more so, severe violations of human rights flowing from trafficking as engaged the attention of the National Human Rights Commssion ever since it came into existence in the year 1993. So much so that, in order to give focused attention to the problem of trafficking, it designated one of its Members as the Focal Point on Human Rights of Woman including Trafficking in the year 2001. The Focal Point, in its endeavour to create an authentic database so as to strengthen the vulnerable groups in the supply zones both economically and socially as well as sensitise the public and the law enforcement agencies to the grave dangers inherent in traficking initiated an Action Research on Trafficking in Women and Children along the UNIFEM and the Institute of Social Sciences in the year 2002.

Intense efforts are needed to create awareness and enhance capacity of various institutions and individuals to make the rights of the vulnerable groups really enjoyable to which they are entitled. Mere making law and formulating schemes are not enough and they are not the solutions to the problem. Law by itself cannot protect the rights of these disadvantaged persons.

The vigilant civil society dedicated NGOs, honest and committed law enforcing agencies, independent media, pro-active judiciary and awareness of the rights and remedies in the matter of dealing with realization of the rights of the vulnerable sections of the people can really and substantially help in protecting their Human Rights. One thing is very clear that the success of any mission or movement depends on the persons engaged therein. In the final analysis, the results do depend on constructive attitude and positive mindset of the people working under legal framework however sound it may be. Will Durant says—"When one tries to change institutions without having changed the nature of men, that unchanged nature will soon resurrect those institutions."

This work "Trafficking in Women and Children, Myths and Realities" takes stock of ground realities. The "Action Research on Trafficking in Women and Children in India" report of Institute of Social Sciences (ISS), New Delhi, is voluminous one, containing analytical studies of various aspects of trafficking, survey, case studies, etc. In the present book efforts are made to bring out the main findings, analysis of voluminous data and conclusions and recommendations in condensed and abridged form with further comments and clarifications. This approach is new and needed for creating awareness, and combating the menace besides protecting and supporting the victims and sensitizing law enforcing agencies and field functionaries. Shri Sankar Sen IPS, former Director of National Police Academy and Director General (I) of NHRC (1994-1998) and now Head, Human Rights Division, ISS, knowing him as I do, is deeply committed and really concerned with issues of human rights. He with his vast and varied experience and with sincere and able assistance of

Smt. Jayashree Ahuja, has carefully and realistically drafted this book. His commitment and stupendous efforts are reflected in it. He deserves appreciation and compliments. I, hope this handy book being of good quality and substantial utility, will be well received, read and utilized by all the concerned and stakeholders besides students, teachers and general public interested in issues of Human rights. If this happens, the efforts of Shri Sankar Sen and ISS, Delhi stand rewarded and cause of human rights is well served.

Dr. Justice Shivaraj V. Patil
Former Member
(Former Judge, Supreme Court of India)

Preface

Trafficking in women and children constitutes one of the most egregious violations of human rights. It violates the fundamental right to life and dignity. It further violates the right to health and health care, liberty and security of the person and the right to freedom from torture, violence, cruelty, and degrading treatment. Over the decades, due to operation of forces such as globalization, feminization of poverty, inadequate migration and labour laws adopted by various countries, incidence of war and violence, trafficking has become a burgeoning form of organized crime.

Although men are also victimized, the overwhelming majority of those trafficked are women and children. According to official estimates over one million women and children are trafficked each year world-wide for forced labour, domestic servitude or sexual exploitation. Trafficking is now considered as the third largest source of profit for organized crime behind only drugs and guns. The International Organization for Migration (IOM) estimates that global trafficking industry generates US $8 billion annually from this *"trade in misery"*, which has also been called modern-day-slavery. Trafficking today is linked to international crime syndicates that peddle drugs, guns, false documents as well as people. It is a global public health hazard that helps spread of HIV/AIDS and other ailments. It is also a global security threat because profits from trafficking finance still more crime and violence.

Very often, trafficking is equated with prostitution, and this is one of the main reasons why human rights violation inherent in trafficking is not properly understood. There is need to demystify the term trafficking and properly understand its trends and dimensions. There is little awareness of the ramifications of trafficking as a transnational organized crime.

Again lack of reliable data on the nature and extent of trafficking both within India and across the national border hampers formulation of proper strategies to combat trafficking.

For this it was felt necessary to peer through the haze, demystify the problem and take a hard close look at it. With this end in view, the Institute of Social Sciences undertook a multi-centric research to study the problem of trafficking in all its various manifestations with the help of state authorities and NGO partners. The main objectives of the *"Action Research on Trafficking in Women and Children in India"* project was to study:

1. Broad but applicable trends that are influencing in perpetuating trafficking both in supply as well as demand side;
2. Look at vulnerability mapping and the nature of response in addressing the problem in terms of gaps in laws, gaps in law enforcement, involvement of organized mafia and agonies of the victims and so on and so forth.

The research study was sponsored by National Human Rights Commission, and funded by UNIFEM. It covered as many as thirteen States of the country. The scope and ambit of the study was challenging. Something on the scale had not been tried before. It required fruitful and constructive partnership between the Government and Non-governmental agencies.

The study highlighted the gaps in the law enforcement, vicious exploitation of women and children, lack of validated data, inadequacy of rehabilitative measures, malfunctioning of the criminal justice administration, virtual immunity of the traffickers and brothel-keepers, societal apathy and lack of political will. It also gave a loud and clear call for action. Researchers had to encounter many difficulties, overcome in many cases doubts and resentments of the respondents and traverse some untrodden paths.

Action research report of the ISS is a voluminous one

containing in-depth analytical studies of various dimensions of trafficking, survey findings, case studies, trials and tribulations of the victims of trafficking, focused interviews and extensive bibliography on the topic. More than 150 case studies were prepared as a means of spotlighting agonies of the trafficked women and children, the *modus operandi* of the traffickers and the operation of their criminal networks. The report also unveiled the close coordination of the trafficking network (though the process appears to be fragmented) and how the actors in the trafficking network collaborate and protect one another.

We have now tried to bring out the main findings of this comprehensive report, analysis of the enormous volume of data and conclusions and recommendations in an abridged form with futher comments and clarificatory details. It is hoped that this will be an useful handbook for law enforcement officers, functionaries of other social welfare agencies and NGOs and informed members of the public. It will also help wider dissemination of the findings of the action research and create a national momentum for corrective action. New norms take roots only when there is power of enforcement behind it. And in fighting for the victims of trafficking, we fight for ourselves because we cannot enforce our own dignity unless we champion the dignity of others.

I acknowledge a debt of gratitude to Smt. Jayashree Ahuja for her dedicated work and unstinted help.

Sankar Sen

Senior Fellow, Former Director, National Policy Academy
Former Director-General, National Human Rights Commission

Contents

1

Migration and Trafficking

Introduction

Migration and trafficking are two distinct but inter-related phenomena. Migration is a broad general concept and trafficking is a sub-set or category of the broader migration concept. Trafficking being a subset of migration many aspects are common to both the phenomena and appear to intersect at almost all levels. Exploitation of migration by trafficking is the dominant nature of this relationship. The relationship between these two processes suggests a possibility that trends in migration influence trafficking. Hence understanding the process of migration and influence of one on the other become very essential in order to find solutions to prevent trafficking.

Historically, migration has been an enduring component of human civilization. It has contributed to enriching societies and benefiting economies of both origin and destination countries. It is estimated that there are about 185 million people living outside their country of birth, amounting to about 2.9 per cent of global population. The dynamics of population movement has undergone fundamental transformations in the 21st century adding new dimensions, complexities and challenges. Today migration is an outcome of a set of inter-related historical, geographical, economic, social and political factors. The migration picture developed in mid-90s did not contain trafficking in persons as part of migration phenomenon. It does not mean that trafficking did not exist then. It was perhaps because of lack of understanding and knowledge of intricacies of trafficking and migration that led to the absence of recognition of trafficking as a case of population movement "gone wrong".

The movement or mobility of a trafficked person from one place to another is sometimes misunderstood as migration. The movement or mobility may be a common element of the trafficking or migration phenomena, but it is not a criterion to ascertain the difference between the two processes. Rather the presence or absence of coercion, exploitation, abuse, loss of control on life options or agency is the determining factor. Absence of some or all of these makes movement of a person migration and the presence of all these factors, make the movement trafficking.

Trafficking in persons is the "dark side" of population movement, which places people in a "harm" situation and it violates fundamental human rights. The trafficking process thrives on individual's vulnerability and it has three core elements, namely movement, deception or coercion and "harm" outcome or exploitation or slavery like practice. The interface between migration as the "bright side" and human trafficking as the "dark side" of population movement are far more complex and overlapping than our existing understanding suggests. These gaps and limitations in understanding pose a critical challenge for states and international communities to manage various types of migration effectively. In addition to the social and cultural factors, tensions between the economically rationalized integrative forces, which encourage, migration and the restrictive immigration policies that discourage such movements have further compunded the nexus between the two phenomena (Md. Shahidul Haque, 2005).

Factors which Convert Migration into Trafficking

Illegal Migration, Smuggling and Trafficking

In order to understand the nexus between trafficking and migration better understanding the concept of "smuggling in migrants" and identifying the interfaces between the concepts is very essential. Smuggling in migrants is a phenomenon in which a person acts to facilitate his/her border crossing in an irregular manner, with the help of an entity, by making financial or other material payments. The critical factor separating trafficking from smuggling is the presence of force or coercion throughout or at some stage in the process—that the force or coercion being the purpose of exploitation (UN, 2001). In a case where a person was misled about the dangers of the journey and irrespective of the treatment he/she receives at the hands of the smugglers, provided there is consent to the original transport and provided an exploitative relationship does not develop or was not envisaged between the two parties, it would be considered as smuggling in migrants. In that sense smuggling is clearly an irregular entry into a country with the assistance of a third party. Therefore, a potential migrant requests and pays a third party for assistance to cross another state, where he/she has not right of residence and the involvement of the third party goes no further than facilitating the irregular border crossing. Whereas, trafficking is a more complex concept, in that it requires consideration not only of the manner in which a migrant enters a country but also his/her working conditions (outcome). Trafficking is not single event but a process starting from the recruitment, continuing on with travel and ending with the exploitation of the person.

Although deceit and coercion are critical factors in trafficking, at times trafficking can also be a voluntary choice as noted in the Mekong region. In Mekong region, in the vast majority of cases the actual movement aspects of the trafficking are by and large 'voluntary' in the sense that the person has made the decision to travel for work by himself, within the range of choices available. In such cases the outcome—the nature, the terms and conditions of work at the destination point which define the cases as trafficking rather than the process of movement undertook by the migrated people (Phill Marshall, 2001).

Normally, smuggled migrants know to some extent the dangers and ways and means of the travel and voluntarily engage themselves in the process of irregular migration. Trafficked persons are seldom aware of the entire process. Even if they submit themselves freely to the trafficker, they cannot give consent to the abuses or exploitation or human rights violations they will be subjected to. Another difference between smuggling of persons and trafficking in persons is smuggling involves international cross-border movements, trafficking could also occur within national borders. However, there is a similarity between both smuggling and trafficking as both threaten human and state security because of the links with exploitation, organized crime and violation of national legislation in both the processes.

Interfaces between Trafficking, Smuggling and Migration

Ascertaining a clear distinction between migration, smuggling and trafficking is an extremely complex undertaking and often impossible. Cases of irregular migrants are offences themselves, but they need not be cases of trafficking. However majority of trafficked people are exploited migrants. The decisive factors in distinguishing between the two will be, the nature of consent; the intention of the agency (that is responsible for them being in that situation) involved; and in addition, the difference between the information made available at the start of the journey as compared to the journey which may then turn a contract dispute to a exploitation (ESCAP, 2003). Apart from the above mentioned factors, in trans-border migration the potential migrant is supposed to carry a lot of documents validating his/her migration to another country and consequently has to submit himself/herself whenever required for checking by concerned government officials on either side of the border. Greater resources and meticulous planning is required to take up transborder journey. In order to overcome these hurdles, many of the unskilled and uneducated migrants knowingly or unknowingly get into the trap of organized crime gangs and trafficking networks. The traffickers may then move the migrants in the destination country from place to place either by following—

—Illegal entry and exit procedures,
—Legal exit but illegal entry; or

—Legal and exit procedures as suited to their requirements.

Push and Pull Factors of Migration

The circumstances and situations that influence migration usually are examined in terms of push and pull factors. Push factors are associated with sending regions and pull, with receiving regions. These factors are interdependent. The push factors include growing inequalities in wealth between and within countries, economic decline, lack of economic opportunities and underdevelopment of an area, characterized by poverty, under-employment, landlessness and impoverishment among rural populations, discrimination, population pressure, harsh economic policies, limited access to resources, lack of opportunities for local employment, natural calamities like earthquake, famine, floods etc., and political factors such as political instability, ethnic clashes, militancy terrorism, violence etc. and lack of basic subsistence etc.

The pull factors are listed as: real or perceived differences in wages, more and better employment opportunities in destination regions, demand for female migrant workers in developed regions, and economic boom in destination areas, growing number of women and men in destinations who relegate domestic work to hired help; and increasing acceptance of the practice of prostitution, etc. The last few decades have seen a major transformation in the economies in societies of the South-East Asia region. Rapid economic growth in the newly industrialized countries including more lately Malaysia and Thailand, the graduation of the hitherto unskilled labour pool into higher working standards and declining fertility rates, have brought about labour deficit economics. This has led to need to import labour particularly for unskilled jobs such as domestic help into which irregular migrants are increasingly being drawn. The illegality of much of this migration makes migrants vulnerable to exploitation—to becoming victims of human trafficking.

A dynamic relationship between the two regions involving of various factors, results in migratory streams, patterns and flows. Some of these are most likely to provide contexts in which people become vulnerable to traffickers. For instance, trafficking is most likely to occur in the context of labour migration, as migration propelled by factors of labour demand and supply is a dominant mode of migration. Political instability, inequalities, natural disasters, discrimination and violence within the family are some of the other factors, contexts in which migration usually takes place, and in which trafficking is most likely to occur.

However contrary to popular belief, a study on trafficking found that, developed areas with improved infrastructure have invariably been the source as well as the destination of trafficking in women. However, even in these areas 79.55 per cent of trafficked people still belonged to landless households and families depending on wage labour for survival (Pandey *et al.*, 2002).

Globalization

Globalization has a mixed impact on migration and trafficking. Market integration has generated substantial economic growth on a global scale, resulting in more jobs, improved livelihoods and an overall reduction in poverty. At the same time, by bringing larger benefits to individuals and countries already possessing physical and human capital, globalization has accentuated disparities within and between countries. Among the effects of this are increase in urbanization and cross-border migration. Further, globalization is distinguished by increased focus on competitive markets. Such competitive markets tend to be characterized by considerable inequality in incomes and wealth. And it is this inequality and disparity coupled with the rise of consumerism that as much as poverty, are promoting migration. While orderly migration can forge economic, socio-cultural bonds between peoples and countries, migrants compelled or choosing to irregular forms of migration may not easily avail themselves of the socio-economic benefits of the regular migrants. Irregular migrants are also vulnerable to human rights abuses.

Globalization of the Sex Industry

Globalization of the economy has globalized the sex industry also. Prostitution is not only a consequence of industrialization but is itself industrialized. Like multinational industries, sex industries have become autonomous economic forces. Thus encouraging large (as well as small) scale organized trafficking networks operate across borders, actively recruiting girls and women, especially from villages, city streets, and transportation centres.

Economic Factors

Although migration involves risk for all types of migrating population who undertake it, however trafficking mainly involves people at the lower end of the skilled level scale. As for this group migration is more an issue of survival rather a personal or professional development. "Internal mobility is critical to the livelihoods of many people especially tribal people, socially deprived groups and people from resource-poor areas".Women and children form the largest group of this unskilled paid labour. These migrants are exposed to large uncertainties and are also forced to take risks, so are likely to get trapped more easily. Migrant labour from this category is also preferred because they lack the requisite support structrues to defend or demand their right, both during migration and at the new work sites. Their limited 'bargaining power' impairs their ability to overcome vulnerability or resist exploitation.

Feminizaton of Migration

The Action Research on Trafficking in women and children highlights that 68.6 per cent of trafficked women and children are from rural areas. As per the 1991 census, 44.8 per cent of women have moved out of their native place to neighbouring districts within their states for employment purposes. And 18.9 per cent of women have moved on to other states. This increasing trend of intra-state and inter-state migration of women in India and in Asia Pacific region had led to "feminization of migration", i.e. the population movements are dominated by women (Skeldon, 1999). This in turn is due to "feminization of poverty" in the region and world over, due to many complex factors (UN, 2000). The data of victims and survivors collected for the action research on trafficking find out those three southern states of India, namely Andhra Pradesh, Tamil Nadu and Karnataka are among the top five source areas. Some migration studies on women in India indicate a significant number of women migrate out of economic necessity. They migrate alone, not as a part of a household or because of marriage. However the relationship between increasing number of women migrants and trafficking has not been fully explored in India.

Commercialization of Recruiting Process

The recruitment industry has become highly commercialized especially in the Middle East countries. The International recruiting agencies in these countries adopt a number of malpractices and have a major role in increased irregular migration. These agencies working at source locations link up with intermediate recruiting agencies in the destination countries and charge exorbitant fees from the aspiring migrants with the promise of providing jobs in the destination countries. Intermediary agencies in the destination countries may not have any relationship with the genuine employers and their labour requirements. As a result people from source countries enter countries like Bahrain and Kuwait and find that there are no jobs for them and thus acquire the status of illegal mirgants and immediately fall into the trap of the traffickers (Blanchet, 2002).

Political Factors (Labour and Employment Laws of various Governments)

Although globalization has rendered the movement of goods and capital across the borders acceptable, the movement of people is not easily accepted. Another structural factor implicated in the rise of human trafficking is *restrictive immigration policies.* It is normal in many countries to consider trafficked women as migration criminals, i.e. as illegal migrants who should be deported from a country when police raids are conducted on brothels or clubs. Victims of trafficking are often treated as "undesirable and criminal aliens" in countries to which they are trafficked. This perspective is often reflected in national legislation in destination countries that make immigration more restrictive thus obstructing the flow of migrants seeking to enter countries legitimately. Ironically, these restrictive immigration policies tighten up border controls that often are used to harass vulnerable migrants but have little effect on the traffickers. What we are seeing in many industrialized countries, particularly in "Fortress Europe," is a mentality promoting globalization of capital, but not globalization of humane and regular migration. Countries want cheap labour, and sex industries want a new and fresh supply of exotic women for prostitution, but in most parts of the world, the possibilities for legal migration have decreased substantially. As immigration become more restrictive and discriminatory, ineffective border controls are utilized in receiving countries, traffickers become the major international players who facilitate international migration because the legitimate channels are so restrictive. This in turn creates higher risks for illegal migrants being trafficked. Traffickers would like to execute their control over the illegal migrants by taking advantage of the fear and avoidance of facing the authorities of illegal migrants to control the freedom and movement of illegal migrants. However, it is not always the case that stringent immigration rules are responsible for the growth of illegal migration and trafficking. Sometimes, the opposite situation, i.e. lax immigration laws, as in the case of India and its border situation with Nepal, may also create problems. The porous nature of the border between these countries has allowed trafficking to flourish and close cultural and historical ties make it very difficult to place restrictions.

Linkages and Social Networks in Migration

Social links in the form of friends, relatives, members of the same community living in cities or some awareness about the opportunity available in bigger cities or developed countries play a major role in promoting the process of migration. The migrant community establishes itself a network with the population residing in the source or place of origin and provides information about the opportunities available in the destination location, which then acts as an inspiration to undertake migration among the people in source locations. These networks provide the support systems necessary for the migration process. Similar networks form essential components even in the process of trafficking. However, in trafficking the agents who are responsible for trafficking feed the people with false information about the opportunities available in destination locations. They target the people belonging to deprived and socially isolated families as these people neither have access to the genuine social networks nor aware of the real situation in destination locations. In such conditions, the perception about the migration undertaken by the victim and the agent responsible for the process are entirely different. Hence in such situations, even if the journey is undertaken with the consent of the victim, the consent is not an 'informed consent'.

A dominant stream in migration is from rural to rural but in case of trafficking the dominant stream is from rural to urban centres. The low rate of rural to urban migration among women suggests unavailability of support networks for women, which the traffickers exploit to their advantage while trafficking women from rural to urban areas. Data collected for (ARTWAC) study confirms this observation as the study finds out that almost 68.6 per cent of the trafficked women and children come from rural areas.

Cross-border Migration and Trafficking

As the cross-border migration requires many documents like visa, passports, work permit, immigration documents etc.

There is more likelihood involvement of trans-border organized crime gangs and networks in smuggling and trafficking the people especially women and children across the borders.

Factors Responsible for Migration which Lead to Trafficking

Socio-cultural

Social discrimination based on gender, especially in developing and underdeveloped countries decline women and children from enjoying certain basic human rights like education, food and employment etc., thereby make them vulnerable to physical, and emotional torture and violence (UN, 2000). This creates an urge especially among women and girl children to migrate to other locations in search of better living conditions. Such people become an easy pray to the traffickers who make false promises. The field data collected during the research project on trafficking reveals that among the 561 survivors of commercial sexual exploitation interviewed, about 65 per cent of the respondents belonged to troubled and distressed families. Similarly, of the 510 trafficked child labourers interviewed, 72 per cent were from disturbed and unstable families.

Factors like breakdown of traditional family and support structures under the impact of urbanization and industrialization, are putting an extra burden of supporting and sustaining the family and children on women especially from agricultural sector in rural areas. These women carry greater risks of being trafficked as they are looking for ways and means to migrate to areas with better livelihood earning opportunities.

Exposure to media is also encouraging women and children to look for economic independence, emotional freedom and also a way out to escape the drudgery of life, which in turn encourage them to migrate to towns and bigger cities. Such people get lured by the false promises made by the traffickers.

Migrating for a job opportunity or for the purpose of marriage is customary practices in the society, especially for female population. Taking advantage of this established practice, traffickers tend to lure away their targets. According to study conducted by Asian Development Bank, 35 per cent of the women trafficked from Nepal have been given the false hopes of marriage or good jobs by the traffickers. The data collected during the Action Research on Trafficking in Women and Children also substantiate findings of the ADB. The study shows that 52.4 per cent of the survivors, around 68 per cent of the victims and 74 per cent of trafficked child labourers have stated that the lure of marriage or job opportunity is the reason for being deceived by the traffickers.

One study reveals the case of a trafficker who "married thirty Nepalese girls in one year, and sold them one by one to brothels in India and then gone to Nepal to marry again" (Shalini, 1996). A study on international migration in the context of Bangladesh and India describes this process in detail. Agents working on both sides of the border send a matchmaker, usually a female who is an original resident of a nearby village, to find recruits. A secret marriage is conducted, and they move across borders, illegally assisted by a smuggling agent. The girl is then sold to another. Even if she is not sold, instead taken to her husband's place, where she was kept in a slave like conditions and made to work in the bangle factories in exploitative conditions (Association of Community Development, 1995).

The Action Research project has reported the instances of girls from poor Muslim families of Hyderabad in Andhra Pradesh are trafficked to red-light areas of Mumbai through fake marriages to Arab Sheikhs. It has been reported that in such cases, initially the girls' parents were approached by some middlemen with money and promise to get their daughter married off to a rich Arab Sheikh. The parents are not given a chance to check the antecedents neither of the prospective groom nor the credibility of the agent. The girls are then hurriedly married to the Sheikh in a secret ceremony and taken out of their native city. Later the Sheikh abandons her after exploiting her sexually. The girl is left at the mercy of the middle men who in turn sells her off to brothels.

Terrorism, Ethnic Violence and Militancy

People from countries and states which are experiencing terrorism, ethnic violence, militancy, violation of human rights, and civil war like conditions for prolonged periods are willing to migrate to relatively safer countries and states as refugees, with a hope to save their lives and lead a peaceful life. In their anxiety to migrate to safer places, internally displaced people tend to play into the hands of the traffickers in the hope of being rescued and then obtaining the legal migrant/refugee status with the help of the safety nets provided by the host countries.

Natural Calamities and Disasters

People whose normal livelihoods get effected by massive and destructive natural disasters such as cyclones, earthquakes, floods and famines etc., would tend to migrate to safer places in search of livelihood. Very often such destabilized and displaced populations under traumatic conditions become easy targets for trafficking. Studies have reported increased trafficking of women and young girls from among the migrants of Orissa cyclones and earthquakes in Lattur in Maharashtra (Pandey *et al.*, 2002).

Influence of Migration on Trafficking

Migration not only provides traffickers with victims, it also pays a crucial role in sustaining the demand especially in sex industry. Ali (1997) reports that in areas where there are large number of migrants they create a demand for sex workers from similar linguistic and cultural backgrounds as that of migrants, leading to trafficking of women for CSE. Today the highway sex work sector services mainly floating population of truck drivers and migrants.

Prevalent Approaches adapted to Counter Trafficking

Although there are several theories to explain reasons for international and internal migration, there is no strong theoretical construction, which could deal with trafficking or smuggling within the broader context of migration and which can take into account both the process and outcome of trafficking. However most of the researchers follow one of the two most prevalent approaches to analyze the process of trafficking. First approach considers trafficking as an economic activity and places trafficking in a broader concept of business in which agents/institution 'commodity' trafficking and seek to make profit out of people's mobility. Second approach follows a legal perspective and considers trafficking as a criminal activity in which legal provisions of state and human rights have been violated. The main weakness of both the perspectives is neither of them focuses on the outcome of trafficking that is abuse, exploitation and human rights violations of the person.

Due to these ambiguities in theoretical understanding of the nexus between trafficking and migration, many initiatives undertaken at global and regional level have limited success. In many parts of the world, human trafficking is dominated by organized crime. However, trafficking is more like a cottage industry than of an organized crime, with many small-scale agents operating along the way. In such a situation tightening the control over the movement of people may encourage a move towards more organized form of smuggling as happened in the case of US-Mexico border. The effect of this would most likely to strengthen the organization of criminal networks, concentrating benefits in fewer hands making the situation more dangerous for migration.

The existing migration policies of some of the originating countries based on bans/restrictions on migration of women abroad for employment purposes and restrictive migration policies of some destination countries are failing to manage global population movement especially trafficking in persons. Rather, these policies are pushing the flow underground making innocent people more vulnerable to fall pray to criminal gangs. Lack of gender responsiveness is becoming a major limitation hampering the effectiveness of counter trafficking interventions.

Suggested Measures to Solve the Problems of Trafficking that Arise due to Migration

Understanding the interlink between migration and trafficking helps indentifying the key facets of trafficking such as vulnerable section of migrants, supply areas, routes followed and also the kind of interventions required during the transit etc. However, while working out any interventions to combat trafficking, care should be taken to protect the freedom of people to migrate. Migration very often is the only option left for many families and communities to earn a living. Migration has a positive impact in enhancing the socio-economic development of many developing countries.

One of the approaches suggested to counter the problem of trafficking is human rights based approach. Phill Marshal who advocates this approach suggests monitoring the forced labour will be more productive when compared to border monitoring, while combating trafficking. Phill Marshal advises to acknowledge, irregular migration as one of the major causes for trafficking and take necessary measures to tackle irregular migration. Another approach suggested by Phill Marshal is migration based approach, which involves regularization of labour migration, providing alternatives to migration wherever feasible, protecting the rights of migrants, strengthening return, repatriation and monitoring impact.

Besides modifying the migration policies, initiatives such as mapping of migration routes, monitoring foreigners entering the country, and maintaining records may assist in tracking the offenders especially in cases of sex tourism. Another initiative which can help in controlling trafficking is to provide vital indicators to agencies dealing with anti-trafficking to distinguish trafficked victim from a migrant.

In summary, the basic difference between migration and trafficking is the intention of the agent. In the case of trafficking it is basically exploitation. Trafficking essentially is non-consensual and unlike migration it is demand driven. Even when there is consent, it is not an informed and willing consent, but a consent taken by force, fraud or deception. Trafficking is subsumed under migration and traffickers exploit the migration processes to realize their agenda. Migration influences and sustains trafficking by providing an easy supply of people. Understanding the relationship between migration and trafficking is crucial for planning and chalking out preventive strategies to combat trafficking while not jeopardizing the people's right to movement. Hence the interventions aimed at controlling and preventing trafficking should be designed taking account of the issues such as:

- Facilitating migration wherever there is demand for labour;
- Educating people on the realities and dangers involved in irregular migration;
- Equipping the potential migrants with information regarding possible abuse and ways in which they can protect themselves from abuse and exploitation;
- Recognizing the rights of migrants irrespective of their legal status;
- Promoting increased understanding and tolerance for migrants and trafficked victims among receiving countries; and
- Assess laws and policies around sex work in terms of their impact, as well as their intention.

REFERENCES

Ali, Salma 1997; *Surveys in the areas of child and women trafficking, Dhaka*, Bangladesh National Women Lawyers Association.

Association for Community Development (ACD) 1995; *International migration: A study on causes and consequences*—Dinajpur (Bangladesh).

Blanchet Terese 2002; *Beyond boundaries: A critical look at women labour migration and the trafficking within Dhaka*, USAID

ESCAP 2003; *Combating human trafficking in Asia: A resource guide to international and regional legal instruments, political commitments and recommended practices;* New York, United Nations.

Gallagher, A. 2001, *The international legal response to human trafficking,* Techinal consultative meeting on Anti-trafficking programmes in South Asia, Kathmandu, September 11-13, 2001.

Haque, Md. Shahidul 2005; *Ambiguities, and confusion in migration-trafficking nexus: A development challenge;* Regional Conference on Revisiting the Migration-Trafficking Nexus: The South Asian Scenario, Dhaka 4-6 April 2005.

Marshal, Phill 2001, *Globalisation, migration and trafficking: Some thoughts from the Southeast Asian Region;* Occasional paper No.1 UN inter agency project on trafficking in women and children in the Mekong sub-region.

Pandey Balaji *et al.*, 2002; *Trafficking in women in Orissa: An exploratory study; Bhubanewar;* Institute for Socio-Economic Development.

Raymond, J. *et al.*, 2002, *A comparative study of women trafficked in the migration porcess,* Massachusetts, CATW International.

Skeldon, R. 1999; *Migration of women in the context of globalization in the Asian Region and Pacific Region;* Women in development discussion paper series no.2, New York UNESCAP.

Shalini, SCN and Lalitha S.A. 1996; *Women soliciting change,* New Delhi, Indian Social Institute and Joint Women's Programme.

United Nations 2000; *Integration of the human rights of women and gender perspective: Violence against women,* New York.

United Nations 2001; *Integration of the human rights of women and the gender perspectives in violence against women*—Report of the special rapporteur on violence against women: mission to Bangladesh, Nepal, and India on the issue of trafficking of women and girls; New York UNESAP.

2

Victims of Commercial Sexual Exploitation

Introduction

Victims of commercial sexual exploitation have an important role to play in combating the problem of trafficking in women and children. Being victims of trafficking, they will be in a position to narrate their experiences in first person, from the time they have been trafficked from their native place till the time they have been forced into the profession as commercial sex workers. Documentation and analysis of their narration and experiences will provide insights in terms of trends and developments of the problem of trafficking, which in turn help in devising efficient strategies to combat the problem. The NHRC-ISS research team interviewed almost 1500 victims of commercial sexual exploitation spread across around 12 states of India. The interviewees include both victims who are still being commercially exploited (referred to as victims) and those who have been rescued from commercial sexual exploitation and rehabilitated by law-enforcement agencies and NGOs (referred to as survivors). This chapter analyses the data collected through interviewing the victims of commercial sexual exploitation. The interviews were aimed at getting insights on aspects such as profile of the victims, process of trafficking, profile of the traffickers, experiences during the CSE, experience with law-enforcement and other agencies, health awareness among commercial sex workers etc.

Profile of the Victims

Age of the Victims: Around 6.4 per cent of the respondents in the category of survivors reported their age under 16 years, and 14.3 per cent were in the 16-17 age group. Almost one fifth of the survivors were minors, below 18 years of age. However in the category of victims only about 5 per cent of the respondents reported their age below 18 years. Some of the reasons for this difference in the percentage in both categories could be because, victims being still under the control of brothel owners, are scared to reveal their true age, whereas survivors, who were rescued from the clutches of brothel owners need not fear from anybody. So they can reveal their true age. Other reason could be due to emphasis of law enforcement agencies to rescue as many as child victims during their rescue operations, there is a considerable percentage of respondents among survivors belonging the age group of below 18 years.

Among the adult respondents majority belong to the age group of 22-35 followed by 18-21 age group. Even though percentage of population belongs to 22-35 age group, it has to be noted that many of the respondents of this age group have been in the trade for many years, implying that they were forced into the trade in their childhood only.

Table 2.1: Age Profile of the Survivors: State-wise

States	*Age Group*				*Total*
	0-15	16-17	18-20	21+	
Delhi	0	6	42	33	81
Bihar	0	2	1	7	10
West Bengal	14	10	17	13	54
Goa	4	16	7	3	30
Tamil Nadu	1	1	0	78	80
Karnataka	3	3	11	42	59
Andhra Pradesh	2	7	29	66	104
Maharashtra	10	31	38	7	86
Uttar Pradesh	1	3	11	31	46
Assam and Meghalaya	0	1	2	0	3
Rajasthan	1	0	3	4	8
Total	36	80	161	284	561

Table 2.2: Age Profile of Victims: State-wise

States	*Age Group*					*Total*
	0-15	*16-17*	*18-20*	*22-35*	*36-50*	
Delhi	2	1	7	68	9	87
Bihar	4	6	31	53	5	99
West Bengal	2	0	0	36	21	59
Goa	0	0	7	51	5	63
Tamil Nadu	0	1	11	60	36	108
Karnataka	3	10	10	37	4	64
Andhra Pradesh	0	0	8	82	13	103
Maharashtra	0	2	12	89	15	118
Uṭter Pradesh	4	3	10	69	4	90
Assam and Meghalaya	0	1	10	27	0	38
Rajashtan	3	2	31	64	0	100
Total	18	26	137	636	112	929
Percentage	1.9	2.8	14.7	68.5	12.1	100

Literacy Level of the Respondents: Majority of the respondents, around 65 per cent are illiterate or barely literate. Around 15 per cent studied up to primary level, 11.7 per cent studied up to middle level, 8.7 per cent could reach up to higher secondary level. Less than one per cent of the respondents completed graduation or above.

Marital status and age at the time of marriage: Of the 561 survivors interviewed about 63 per cent were unmarried and around 12.5 per cent were divorced/deserted/widowed. About 24 per cent of the married respondents have husbands, who are still living. About half of the victim respondents are unmarried and about half of the married respondents are either widowed or separated or deserted by their husbands. Majority (around 65 per cent) of respondents from both the categories mentioned that they were married when they were below 18 years of age.

Number of Children: Almost 75 per cent of survivors, and 54 per cent of victims are childless; around 12 per cent of survivors and 19.5 per cent of victims have a single child. 9.8 per cent of survivors, and 16.6 per cent of victims have two children, and rest of the respondents have more than 2 children.

This data reveal that majority of the children are living with their mothers in brothels and are thus exposed to the exploitative conditions from very early in their life. These children are prone to sexual exploitation and trafficking.

Exposure to domestic violence and sexual abuse: About 464 respondents reported that they have been exposed to domestic violence in terms of physical torture, mental harassment and sexual abuse either by various male members from in-laws family or by relatives.

Socio-economic conditions of the family prior to trafficking: About 30 to 35 per cent of the respondents could give any details of their family monthly income. 45 per cent of the respondents informed that their family income was Rs. 2000 per month or less than that. Only around 15 per cent stated their family income was more than Rs. 2000 per month, indicating that majority of the respondents comes from very poor families.

Socio-religious background: Over three-fourths of the respondents are Hindus, 15 to 16 per cent are Muslims, around 4 per cent are Christians and rest belonged to various other communities. Almost 55 to 60 per cent belong to socially deprived sections like scheduled castes. Almost 70 per cent have come from rural areas, around 20 to 25 per cent have come from urban areas, and rest of the respondents belonged to urban slum areas.

Nationality of the respondents: 94 per cent of the respondents stated their nationality as Indian, around 2 per cent are from Bangladesh, and another 3 to 4 per cent are from Nepal.

Experiences during the Commercial Sexual Practice

Income sharing in brothels: While giving details about the income earned and expenditure incurred during the time of commercial sexual practice, survivors could reveal more freely when compared to the victims. As per the data provided by the survivors, majority of survivors stated that their monthly income was around Rs. 3000. Total monthly income of a brothel worked out from the responses given by the survivors came to be Rs. 41,76,130 and average revenue generated by each survivor came to be Rs. 11,600. However, most of the money never reached the sex workers. Major share of the revenue was shared among the various stakeholders like brothel owners, agents, pimps, financiers, *goondas* and sometimes the law enforcement officials. Victims also responded in the same fashion as far as the revenue sharing of the brothels was concerned. However, victims could not give exact details of the income earned by each victim individually. Monthly income computed from whatever data provided by the victims come out to be Rs. 6076 per victim. There are sharp differences in monthly incomes of victims belonging to various states.

Expenditure and savings: Major part of the income was spent on food, clothes, cosmetics and miscellaneous household items in that order. 2.8 respondents spent their income on addictives like alcohol etc., 1.9 per cent on medicines. Around 6 per cent of the respondents mentioned that they invested their money in some property.

As far as the savings are concerned, majority of the respondents could not save any money. Around 15 per cent could save up to Rs.10,000, around, 10 to 12 per cent had savings up to Rs. 20,000. Among the survivors only 4 per cent and among victims only 9 per cent could save up to Rs. 50,000. Very few could save more than Rs. 50,000.

Among survivors almost 26 per cent of the respondents mentioned that they sent money regularly to their families. 46 per cent respondents among the victims are in the habit of sending money to their families. Rest of the respondents either chose not to answer or answered in negative.

Linkages with family: Respondents were asked questions like, whether families knew the plight of the respondents and whether their families made any efforts to rescue them. Around one-third of the respondents mentioned that their families knew that they were trafficked and around 15 per cent of the respondents were aware of their families' effort to rescue them. However majority of the respondents did not maintain any contact with their families and they also didn't know whether their families ever tried to rescue them.

When asked whether the respondents ever tried to establish contact with their families, and the reasons for their initiatives. About 50 per cent of the respondents mentioned in positive and rest answered in negative. Among the respondents who tried to establish the contact, majority of them went to meet their family members and get little respite from the exploitative situations of the brothels. Some went to deliver money to their family. However, a small percentage around 8 per cent went to procure more girls for commercial sex. Thus a small percentage of victims themselves turned into traffickers.

Among the respondents who haven't maintained any contact with their families, around 40 per cent were doubtful of societal and family acceptance. 35 per cent were scared of traffickers and brothel owners. A small percentage mentioned that they no longer remember their native place, so they have no place to go back.

First Sexual Encounter: To study the extent and level of sexual exploitation undergone by the respondents, the research team had tried to collect the data on the earliest age at which the respondent had their first encounter with sex. The disturbing fact is that almost 70 per cent of the respondents had their first encounter when they were below 18 years of age. Of these around 42 per cent happened to have the first experience when they were less than 16 years of age, thus making them the victims of child rape under Section 375 of the Indian Penal Code, which states that sexual intercourse with a child below 16 years of age, even with her consent constitutes rape.

Revealing the way in which they underwent the first sexual experience, majority of the respondents about 61 per cent mentioned that it was forced on them. In most of the cases the first assaulter is a known person to the victim, i.e. relatives, school teachers, family members in the in-laws house etc. indicating the vulnerability of the girl child in various social settings including familial, social, educational and even religious. Another disturbing fact is around 70 per cent of the respondents mentioned that sexual abuse became a regular affair after the first experience.

Age at which CSE began: Respondents were asked the age at which they were introduced to commercial sexual exploitation (CSE), as it helps in understanding the extent the problem has penetrated into the society and also helps in formulating strategies to combat the problem of trafficking. Majority of the respondents about 62 per cent belonging to survival category mentioned that they were forced into commercial sexual practice, when they were below 18 years of age. However only about 44 per cent of respondents belonging to victim category mentioned that they were in the sex trade from the age below 18 years. The difference in percentage can be attributed to the fact the survivors being relieved from the control of the brothel owners were free to reveal the true age at which they started practicing commercial sex. Around 34 per cent mentioned their age was 18-21 when commercial sex exploitation was commenced. There were instances where respondents were forced into commercial sex when they were barely six years of age indicating the demand for children in brothels.

It was noted that the age at which first sexual encounter occurred has a bearing on the age at which a victim is trafficked and has been quantitatively substantiated through simple linear regression analysis. There is a causal link between the two variables, namely age at the time of first sexual encounter and at the time of trafficking. Persons who are prone to trafficking are those who are prone to sexual abuse. These findings suggest that the policies and strategies formulated to address the problem of trafficking also have to look into the aspect of child sexual abuse.

Victims' mobility: Respondents were asked to state whether they have been relocated, or taken to other places during the period of CSE, to establish the fact that victims are often re-trafficked, or sent by brothel owners to other places for CSE. 55 per cent of the respondents belonging to victim category and about 63 per cent of survivors mentioned that they were moved to other places or brothels for reasons like client's demand, or to earn more money. Some of them have disclosed that the brothel owners have resold them to other brothels.

Clientele: Attempt was made to collect data on the type of clientele, the respondents had to entertain and the number of clients entertained daily to study the extent of exploitation the respondents were put through by the brothel owners and also to study the demand side of the CSE. Majority of the respondents mentioned that on an average around 5 to 7 clients have been entertained by the respondents. There are even cases in West Bengal, Karnataka and Delhi where some of the respondents entertained almost 40 to 45 clients per day. Similarly, some of the respondents from Tamil Nadu entertained around 25 clients on a single day.The cleint base includes men from almost all walks of life like students, labour class, businessmen and people from rich and affluent families, personnel from law-enforcement, professionals, and tourists including Indians and foreigners, people from film industry so on and so forth.

Experience with Law-enforcement

Arrests by the Police: On matters related to arrest 52.6 per cent of the victim category and 42.1 per cent from the survivor category never got arrested. Around 25.8 per cent of the victims and 57.9 per cent of the survivors were arrested by the police once or more than once.

When asked about the charges on which the respondents were arrested, all the respondents from the victim's category mentioned 'soliciting' as the reason for their arrest, whereas only 39.4 per cent from the respondents category mentioned soliciting as the reasons for their arrest. Rest of the respondents did not know the reasons for their arrest.

Respondents were also asked how they were released from the police custody. Majority (72.5 per cent) mentioned that they were bailed out by the brothel owners by paying fine in the court, 20 per cent got themselves released by bribing the police. About 7.5 per cent were released by the intervention of NGOs.

Evading the Arrest: Majority, 58.4 per cent of respondents who were never arrested, mentioned that the brothel owners received a tip off about the police raids hence the brothel owners removed them to other places before the police could conduct a raid. Around 24 per cent of respondents said that brothel owners used to hide them in specially made attics, cubicles and boxes etc. 17.7 per cent mentioned that brothel owners bribe the police to ignore the presence of the victims in brothels.

Knowledge about Laws pertaining to Trafficking and Child Sexual Abuse: Awareness about laws related to trafficking is almost negligible among the respondents. Almost 85 per cent of respondents under survivor category, and 80 per cent of respondents belonging to victim category said that they are not aware of the existence of ITPA. Similarly around 80 per cent of the survivors and 63 per cent of the victims do not know anything about laws related to child sexual abuse. Even those respondents, who have little awareness of these laws, are ignorant about various provisions dealing with prevention of trafficking and protection of rights of the victims. Around 72 per cent are of the opinion that the laws are to punish the women who are subjected to CSE. Around 20 per cent mentioned that is for stopping the women from soliciting. This lack of awareness makes these women more vulnerable and an easy prey for the traffickers.

Attitude of the Police: A little above 43 per cent mentioned that the police had behaved with care during the rescue operations. Around 28 per cent had experienced a neutral or uncaring attitude from the police. 11 per cent respondents spoke about the abusive behaviour of the police. One-fifth of the respondents chose not to answer.

Attitude of NGOs: Respondents are impressed by the caring attitude of NGOs as 57 per cent of respondents have positive experiences with NGOs. While 16 per cent said that NGOs are uncaring. Only 1 per cent felt that NGOs displayed abusive behaviour towards them. A quarter of the respondents never come in contact with NGOs.

Profile of Rescue Homes

The survivors were asked to narrate their experiences during their stay at rescue homes. The following issues have been looked into while collecting information on rescue homes.

Duration of the Stay: 24.2 per cent stayed for more than a year. 9.8 per cent stayed more than five months, and 16.9 per cent stayed for one month or less. Around 37 per cent could not provide any definite answer. The maximum period stayed by one respondent is for two years. The data indicate the loopholes and delays in the existing repatriation and rehabilitation programmes leading to long stay in the rescue homes, which are supposed to be the short stay shelters. Overstay in rescue homes may also become a cause for violation of the human rights of the victims.

Familiarity with the Inmates: A significant number of the respondents know most of the inmates in a rescue home. Cited reasons for this familiarity are—come from the same area (62.4 per cent), got familiar during their stay at rescue home (37.6 per cent), which throws light on two aspects: firstly, traffickers traffic women in masses from identified sources areas; secondly, in most cases, the victims rescued get to stay in the rescue homes for longer periods due to procedural delays in repatriation and rehabilitation.

Agencies responsible in rescuing the victims: Around 56 per cent of the respondents are rescued by the police, 38 per cent were rescued by NGOs, and rest had managed to escape on their own.

Purpose of staying in rescue homes: Only 36.2 per cent stated the purpose as rehabilitation and reformation, 12.5 per cent were interested in tracing their parents. Rest of the respondents did not know the reason for which they were lodged in rescue homes.

Frequency of rescue: 17.5 per cent of the respondents are rescued once before, 1.8 per cent were rescued twice and 6.6 per cent are rescued more than twice. 74.1 per cent are rescued for the first time. One-fourth of the respondents are rescued provisionally, i.e. they were taken to rescue homes and shown in the records as having been rehabilitated, but in reality they have been re-trafficked. These findings highlight that there are serious flaws in the exiting programmes of rescue, return and rehabilitation and human rights of the victims are violated and they have been re-victimized.

Counselling Services: Roughly around 44 per cent of the respondents could be counselled, 20.5 per cent did not get any counselling facility. Rest of the respondents could not answer the question. Respondents who availed counselling rated the quality of the services as average.

Quality of General Facilities and Infrastructure at Rescue Homes: Respondents were not at all satisfied with the quality of the food given, supply of essentials like sanitary napkins etc, behaviour of other inmates and care provided for small children. Respondents expressed an average satisfaction level over the rest of the facilities like health-care etc.

How They have been Trafficked

Factors leading to Trafficking: Forces, lure, and deceit seem to be the major factors that lead to the respondents being trafficked. Other influencing factors being domestic violence or marriage related disputes, child sexual abuse, culturally sanctioned practices and migration etc. 62.4 per cent of survivors, and 51.8 of victims have been trafficked by falling prey to deceit, force or lure of traffickers. 18 per cent of survivors, and 22 per cent of victims have been trafficked due to domestic and marriage related violence. 6.6 per cent of survivors and 5.4 per cent of victims were subjected to sexual abuse as children. 1.8 per cent among survivors and 7.3 per cent among victims cited family tradition as the factor lead to trafficking. Very negligible per cent from survivors and victims gave migration as the leading factor for being trafficked. Around 11 per cent of survivors and 13 per cent of victims cited poverty as the factor for their trafficking.

Modus Operandi of Trafficking by Traffickers: In order to assess the methods used by traffickers to trap their targeted victims, the respondents were asked, how they came to know about the traffickers and the pretexts given by the traffickers. More than half of the respondents said that the traffickers used indirect channels, i.e. the traffickers used their social networks to get in touch with victims or their family members. 17 per cent mentioned family members through whom they came in touch with traffickers and almost 37 per cent mentioned relatives and other familiar persons have brought them in touch with traffickers. Rest of the respondents got in direct contact with traffickers who belonged to the same village as that of the victims.

In direct contact, traffickers met their targeted victims at railway stations, bus stands, city markets and on board in a train. Majority of the respondents were given false hopes and promises. The following table gives the details of the *modus operandi* of the traffickers.

Table 2.3: Promises made by the Traffickers (Victims' Responses)

Nature of Promise	*Percentage*
Job Offers	68.1
Marriage	16.8
Better Living Conditions	6.2
Sightseeing/ Outing	2.9
Shelter and Security	4.6
Other Promises	1.4

Experiences during the Transit

Stay in Transit Locations: Data collected on the places or locations, in which the respondents were detained or lodged enroute their final destination indicate that traffickers use small time brothels, way side hotels or residences of traffickers as transit locations. However, majority of the respondents could not give any answer.

Sexual Abuse during Transit: Almost 70 per cent respondents under victims category mentioned they were sexually abused at first place of transit, remaining people mentioned that CSE began after reaching the brothels.

Emotional Stress during the Transit: More than half of the respondents experienced helplessness and blamed themselves for their fate. Rest of the respondents could not recall their emotional state at that time of transit.

Avoidance of Law by Traffickers: To avoid the attention and detection of law-enforcement agencies, the offenders often give the impression that they are relatives, friends of the victims by claiming close acquaintance with the victims.

Number of Offenders involved in Trafficking Operations: Although more than half of the respondents could not give any information about the number of people involved in their trafficking, whatever information collected during the interviews suggests that on an average two to three traffickers get involved in one trafficking operation.

Profile of Traffickers

Prior Acquaintance with Traffickers: An important finding of this study is that only little over 11 per cent of the respondents mentioned the traffickers were strangers to them. Around 52.5 per cent of the respondents say that traffickers were known persons but not relatives. Rest of the respondents said that family members like in-laws, parents, siblings were involved in their trafficking.

Age Profile of Traffickers: Majority of the traffickers (64.3 per cent) falls into the age group of 26-40. Around 12 per cent were of the 18-25 age group.

Gender Profile: As per the information provided by the respondents, both the sexes were equally involved in trafficking. However, the point to be noted is, respondents were only aware of the immediate procurers. They were unaware of the existence of master operators and kingpins of the overall trafficking nexus.

Awareness about Illegal Assets of the Traffickers: Almost two-thirds of the respondents were aware of the illegal assets acquired by traffickers through trafficking. 35 to 40 per cent of the respondents said that the traffickers invested in purchasing immovable properties like houses, 18 to 20 per cent of the respondents informed the traffickers purchased vehicles, Around 10 to 12 per cent mentioned that electronic gadgets were purchased. One-third of the respondents were not aware of the assets acquired by the traffickers. As the assets acquired by illegal activities can be confiscated by police, respondents may be used as witnesses in the confiscating operations.

Awareness about Arrests of Traffickers: Majority of the respondents were not aware of whether traffickers were ever got arrested. Only 8.5 per cent mentioned that traffickers were arrested, 35 per cent mentioned that traffickers were not arrested. Of those 8.5 per cent respondents who were aware of the arrests of traffickers mentioned that traffickers got arrested once. More than half of the respondents said the offenders were bailed out in courts. A small percentage mentioned that the traffickers were in jail.

Health Issues

Respondents were very hesitant to reveal the status of their health, for fear of facing social ostracism. Almost two-thirds of the respondents belonging to survivor category answered in negative. Of the one-third who mentioned about some health problems 8.3 per cent disclosed the HIV+ AIDS status. This was in contrast to the victim category where out of 921 respondents only 0.6 had revealed their HIV+ AIDS status. Around 30 to 40 per cent respondents in both the categories were suffering from STDs. Rest were suffering either from general health problems or from other reproductive health problems. Among the Confirmed HIV/AIDS respondents, 6 were from West Bengal, one from Tamil Nadu, three each from Andhra Pradesh and Karnataka and two from Maharashtra.

Almost 20 per cent of the respondents were suffering from various health problems for over five years. 33.7 per cent were suffering between one to five years, and rest were suffering for less than a year. Majority of them expressed lack of medical facilities as the reason for their prolonged illness. Majority opts for government hospitals for their treatments followed by private clinics. Some of them could avail of medical services only at medical camps organized by NGOs.

Re-trafficking

There were cases of re-trafficking among both the victims and survivors. When asked about the reasons for their re-trafficking, 35.7 per cent cited lack of livelihood options as the reason. Another 35.7 per cent cited the coercive behaviour of brothel owners and traffickers as the reason. Non-acceptance by the family and the community, debit bondage were the other reasons for rescued victims entering into the trafficking cycle. The findings suggest that the rehabilitation programmes have to be very thorough in empowering the victims both financially and emotionally, so that the rescued victims could resist the pressure tactics adopted by brothel owners and traffickers.

Rehabilitation

Effective rehabilitation goes a long way not only in controlling the problem of trafficking but also providing livelihood options to the victims of trafficking. Respondents' impressions on the availability and quality of the existing rehabilitation programmes would help in developing more effective rehabilitation programmes. Less than half of the respondents on survivor category availed counselling and training from rehabilitation centres. Of the people who received services from rehabilitation centres, more than half, i.e. around 55 per cent were not satisfied by the training provided to them. They were of the impression that the training imparted was not sufficient to provide effective livelihood options.

Respondents felt that existing rehabilitation programmes would be more effective;

- —if it included legal counselling and assistance
- —training programmes should be more job-oriented and related to users' interests
- —counsellors have to be more professional while imparting training
- —counselling should group-oriented
- —more counsellors have to be recruited.

Conclusion

Information given by almost 1500 respondents, gives valuable insight into aspects that lead to trafficking and perpetuation of commercial sexual exploitation. It also helps in understanding the status of law-enforcement, gaps and loopholes in existing laws, and procedures of rescue, repatriation and rehabilitation. The plight of the victims calls for stricter implementation of laws in order to catch the real culprits like traffickers, brothel owners and other agents involved in the trafficking chain. Victims' impressions on existing rehabilitation programmes and the functioning of rescue homes suggest that, authorities have to delve into improving the infrastructure and other facilities in existing rescue homes and there is a great dearth of services like counselling, legal assistance, vocational training etc. Rehabilitation programmes have to be designed in such a way that the programmes would empower the victims economically, emotionally and enable them to be accepted by the society. More short stay homes have to be set up in high demand and high supply zones. There is a great urgency and need for authorities, NGOs and other community based organizations to come together in order to control the menace of trafficking by devising various effective intervention measures.

3

Trafficking in Humans for Non-Sex based Exploitation

To provide a holistic and comprehensive view of the problem of trafficking in women and children, the Action Research on Trafficking in Women and Children (ARTWAC) conducted an extensive study on trafficking for non-sexual exploitation. Although majority of trafficking takes place for sex-based exploitation, trafficking in humans for non-sex based exploitation including industrial labour, domestic labour, begging, camel jockeying, organ trafficking etc. is also on the rise. Victims of non-sex based trafficking include men, women and children including boys and girls. Illiterate women, children belonging to poor and marginalized sections of the community, farmers and artisans suffering from poverty usually become the targets of trafficking. This chapter briefly explains some of the prevalent non-sex based exploitation forms for which children, women are trafficked.

To Perform in the Circus

Children especially girls are trafficked to work in circus companies. Victims are promised good salaries by the traffickers and then sold to the owners of circus companies. Interviews conducted by the research team with 13 girls rescued from a circus troupe by Nepal-based NGOs called ABC Nepal and Pravasi Napali Mitr Manch revealed the extent of exploitation faced by the girls trafficked to perform in circus troupes. The victims used to be beaten up for slightest mistakes committed during the circus shows. Girls had to face sexual abuse by men working in the circus. They were paid very low wages like Rs. 5. per day. They were under constant supervision of the owners and not allowed to leave the premises. The information gathered from the rescued girls also indicate that girls from Nepal are lured to join Indian circuses. Some parents themselves send their children to join the circus groups, as they remain unaware of the problems faced by the girls after they join the troupes.

Camel Jockeying

Camel races are very famous in the Middle-east countries. For jockeying the camels during the races, the organizers of camel races recruit small boys as young children are light in weight and therefore, do not overload the camel while racing. Boy camel jockeys are always underfed in order to control their body weight. Many boys from countries like Bangladesh and Pakistan are trafficked to Middle-east countries to be the camel jockeys. During the camel races, these young boys are tied through ropes to the backs of camels, so that they do not jump off the camel's back. However many a time, the ropes become loose and the boys are thrown off the camel backs and dragged over stones and sand. There were incidents in which the boys who fell on the ground were trampled to death by other camels on the track. In 1993, the Camel Jockey Association of the United Arab Emirates has prohibited the use of children as jockeys. However, the practice still continues. Traffickers use the Kolkata route to traffic children from Bangladesh and then the children are transported to Bangalore or Chennai, from there they are flown to Middle-east countries.

Begging

Many pious and religious people feel eager to help the beggars on the traffic crossings, at religious places and other places of worship and pilgrimage. However for traffickers and other organized criminal gangs this is one of the sources of profit making. A large number of children are trafficked for begging purposes. Children with disabilities belonging to poor families are at high risk of being trafficked for begging as it is easy for children with disabilities to gain popular sympathy. In a case study done in West Bengal, the ARTWAC research team found that small children are drugged for the purpose of begging, as sleeping children evoke more sympathy from the people, and fetch more money to the people involved in the racket. Children get trafficked for begging both within and outside country. There are media reports and other secondary data confirming that children are being trafficked to Mecca for begging during Haj. In 1997 a large number of Bangladeshi children were deported to India from Saudi Arbia, where they had been taken on the pretext of visiting Mecca. It was found out that many children in that group had broken limbs and mutilated bodies. By sending children to Mecca, the religious minded parents feel happy that their children get a chance to visit Mecca, free of charge.

Domestic Labour and Industrial Labour

There is great demand for domestic help in metropolitan cities and other urban centres. Employing children of tender age as domestic help is a common practice among rich and middle class families in India, which results in trafficking young girls for domestic services. As per general perception as a domestic help children would be in protected environment and the basic needs of the domestic servants like food, shelter and clothing will be guaranteed by the employers. However, studies conducted by the ARTWAC team reveal that the domestic servants are subjected to distressing working conditions. Most of the time they are subjected to work till late at night and seven days in a week without any holidays and rest. Case studies done in Tamil Nadu and Goa for the research purpose revealed the instances of sexual abuse of children brought as domestic help. A case study from Goa shows that agents bring children from different parts of the country to Goa and then send them as domestic help to different houses. Agents charge money from both the employers as well as the parents. These agents even maintain secrecy about the parents as well as employers. As a result parents of the children do not often know where their children are employed and hence are not in a position to be aware of the atrocities caused to their children. Districts like Salem, Virudhunager and Villupuram in Tamil Nadu are the most vulnerable areas for trafficking children for domestic labour.

Case studies conducted in Guru Bazar, in Amritsar, Punjab unearthed the exploitation done on small children trafficked from distant villages in West Bengal. Guru Bazar in Amritsar is famous for jewellery shops. The jewellery owners employ small children trafficked from West Bengal for very low wages and torture them to work for long hours, without any rest. According to the child victims rescued from these 'sweatshop labour' establishments, the victims are subjected to physical as well as mental exploitation by the employers. The traffickers promise the parents of the victims that, they would be paid handsome wages. But in reality the children are put to work in most unhygienic and difficult conditions and paid paltry wages.

Adoption

Adoption is another major factor for which small children are trafficked. In developed countries due to low fertility rates and low birth rates, there is great demand for adoption of small children. Some people take advantage of the situation and traffic small children for selling them to foreigners for high prices for adoption. Some tribal communities in Andhra Pradesh (particularly Lambada community) are known sources for adoptions within India. Tribals living in districts like Rangareddy, Nalgonda, Medak and Mehaboobnagar of Andhra Pradesh are prone to sell their children for adoption. Similarly, Salem district in Tamil Nadu is also known as a major source area of trafficking children for adoption purposes. Gender discrimination, and poverty are some of the major factors encouraging the parents to sell their children to agents of adoption rackets. It is generally observed that in most of these adoptions girl children are given for adoption rather than male children. Giving the girl children away in adoption has become a social habit among the tribal communities like the Lambada community in Andhra Pradesh. Traffickers tend to cash on this habit by brainwashing the parents with ideas like 'by sacrificing one girl child' the rest of the family can better their economic conditions or their girl child will be better off if given in adoption rather than live in abject poverty etc. The poor parents fall prey to such reasoning and get ready to sacrifice their girl children.

The *modus operandi* in this adoption racket is that, the agents employed by the adoption organizations go to villages and procure children from poor parents by paying meagre amounts. They sell those children to institutions and agencies involved in arranging children for adoption. These agencies in turn sell those children for hefty prices to foreigners. There are instances where the agents have even paid to the husbands of pregnant women to sell their still to be born children. Sometime agents kidnap newly born children from government hospitals, nursing homes and even primary health centres with the help of some nurses, ward boys etc. In 2001 *'The Hindustan Times'* a prominent national daily newspaper has reported about an adoption agency called Precious Moments Adoption Centre, located in Hyderabad in Andhra Pradesh, which was involved in trafficking children for adoption in a major way (*The Hindustan Times*, 2001). Police, found many fake relinquishment deeds during the raids conducted on the premises of this institution.

The Supreme Court of India in the case of *Laxmikant Pandey* vs. *Union of India* (WP Crl. No. 171/1982), looking into the complaints against some of the social organizations engaged in coordinating the adoption of Indian children by foreign parents mentioned that it is desirable that a Central Adoptions Resource Agency (CARA) be set up by the Government of India with regional branches in various states. The CARA would then act as a clearing house of information and forward the applications of foreigners to one of the government recognized social or child welfare agencies in the country. The Court also opined that demanding large sums of money for giving a child in adoption is almost akin to trafficking in children.

Following the directives of the Supreme Court, the Ministry of Social Justice and Empowerment set up the CARA, which regulates and monitors inter-country and intra-country adoptions. In 1995, the Ministry revised the guidelines for adoption of Indian children to regulate the inter-country adoptions. Various state governments have also issued orders to regulate adoptions in their respective states. The Andhra Pradesh Government has issued an order prohibiting the biological parents from relinquishing their children to orphanages citing poverty as the reason.

For Organ Trade

Over the past few decades, on the one hand medical technology has made tremendous progress by which organ transplantation has become a fairly common therapeutic procedure, which can be carried out in many hospitals and clinics throughout the world. On the other hand, due to changes in lifestyles, a very large population in the world are suffering from serious diseases, whose remedy lies only in organ transplantation. On a rough estimate there are about 50,000 people on the waiting list for various organ replacements in the United States of America only. However, rules for organ procurement are very stringent in many countries. Most countries require living donors to be family members or organs must be removed from cadavers, usually accident victims. The rules are very strict and stringent for removing the body organs from living people as removing body organs, for money is unethical and illegal in many countries. There is a large gap between demand and supply of the organs in the world market. With the result India and China have become international centres mainly for kidney transplantation.

Although Government of India enacted an Act titled "Transplantation of Human Organs Act" in 1994 prohibiting the trade in human organs, due to certain loopholes in the law, the Act was not successful in stopping the organ trafficking in

India. A study carried out by Sanjay Kundu, an IPS officer in India, explains the depth of the problem, the nexus among qualified doctors, police officials, legal and judicial officials and the traffickers, and how the traffickers target their potential victims etc. The traffickers target mostly people like farmers, local artisans, agricultural labour, who are struggling to provide food for their families and people suffering from debt bondage etc., and promise them good money for donating one of the kidneys. Then these donors are brought to the medical centres where the organ transplantation operations will be conducted. The donors are categorized based on their blood groups. Thereafter the lawyers make fake and false affidavits on behalf of the donors as well as the recipients. The doctors conduct necessary diagnostic tests on donors and then they will be operated for removing the kidney. The doctors are paid a fees around Rs. 75,000 to Rs.1,25,000 per operation. The donors are given a paltry amount of Rs. 15,000 to Rs.20,000 as a reward for donating a kidney. Most of the times, middlemen try to take their share from the amount given to the donors. On an average the recipients are charged around Rs. 8 lakhs for an organ transplant operation. Some amount of money is spent in bribing the officials in concerned departments (Sanjay Kundu, 2004).

The study mentions that, allurement for money is the main reason for unrelated donors to come forward to donate their kidneys. Most of the people who are willing to donate a kidney live in dire poverty. Hence, whatever money is promised by the middlemen is a windfall. Even after donating the kidney for payment, the donors still cannot overcome their poverty firstly because the amount paid to them is meagre, when compared to the hefty amounts collected from the recipients; secondly, in many cases the health of the donors deteriorates after the operation. In some cases the donors died on the operation table itself. In this process of kidney transplantation the potential donor is the one who is exploited and abused physically as well as psychologically (Sanjay Kundu, 2004). According to another study, of all the kidney transplants done in India only 30 per cent are from relatives whereas 64 per cent are from unrelated "donors" and 6 per cent come from donors classified as 'brain dead' (Sanjay Kumar, 2001). There is a need to create awareness among the potential donors about the consequences of selling of kidneys, because awareness among the potential donors might discourage them from trading their health by selling kidneys.

Besides kidney trafficking there are media reports on trafficking in other body organs like cornea of the eye. In 2001, a news service agency reported a suspected case in Andhra Pradesh in which an young orphan girl was blinded by an adoption agency for removing the cornea of her eyes (IANS, 2001).

It is very difficult to get reliable data on trafficking in humans for organ trade as in other cases of trafficking in humans. Authorization committees set up to safeguard illegal kidney transplantation have failed to be effective. Even law enforcement officials lack necessary sensitivity, and professional skills to handle the cases of organ trafficking. Organ trafficking is a very complex issue and requires a multi-pronged approach to combat and control the problem. There is an urgent need for a strong political and societal will and proper enforcement of existing legal and constitutional provisions in order to curb the problem.

REFERENCES

India Abroad News Service (IANS), 2001, *Adoption Body Suspects Organ Sale Racket In Andhra Pradesh,* May 1.

Kumar Sanjay (2001), *Despite Ban, Organs still sold in India,* Reuters Health March 9, 2001.

Kundu Sanjay (2004), *Human Trafficking in India,* SVP National Police Academy, Hyderabad.

The Hindustan Times, 2001, Child trafficking racket busted AP tightens laws, 22 April.

4

Trafficking and Law Enforcement

Trafficking in human beings, especially women, girls and boys is a matter of serious national as well as international concern as it involves not only gross violation of human rights of trafficked victims but also because organized crime gangs are doing multimillion dollar business by forcefully putting the trafficked victims through commercial exploitation including sexual abuse and exploitation. Good legal-framework at national and international level and efficient and effective law enforcement by all the countries are important for controlling and preventing the menace.

Legal Framework at International Level

International organizations have worked out several measures in the form of declarations, conventions and resolutions prohibiting trafficking in human beings, especially in women and children. These international instruments help in devising suitable laws and acts by the member states to combat the problem of trafficking. Upon ratification of a particular international convention or resolution the member states are obligated to suitably amend the existing laws or frame new laws to implement the treaty. Till the time suitable laws are not enacted by member states, the courts in member states working within the purview and scope of the Constitutions of their country, can give judgments based on the provisions of international law.

Some of the Important International Laws related to Trafficking are:

- International Convention for the Suppression of Trafficking of the Women and Children, 1921.
  The treaty prohibits the enticing or leading away of women or girl for immoral purposes, to be carried out in another country.
- Slavery Convention, 1926.
  States, Parties are enjoined to discourage all forms of forced labour. Slavery means control over another person, without full informed consent, for the purpose of exploitation.
- Universal Declaration of Human Rights, 1948.
  Article 4 of the Declaration prohibits all forms of slavery and the slave trade. Article 13 recognises the right of persons to freedom of movement and residence and Article 15 recognises the right to nationality.
- Convention for the Suppression of Trafficking in Persons for Exploitation, Prostitution and others, 1949.
  This convention is a compilation of four previous conventions (conventions of 1904, 1910, 1921 and 1933). This convention made procurement, enticement etc., for purposes of prostitution punishable irrespective of the age of the person involved and his/her consent to the same (Article 1). Brothel keeping was also denounced to be illegal, and punishable (Article 2). The convention provided for repatriation (Article 19) and rehabilitation (Article 20). However, the 1949 Convention is limited to trafficking for prostitution and other related activities.
- Supplementary Convention on the Abolition of Slavery, Slave Trade and Institutions and Practices of Slavery, 1956 (Slavery Convention).
  Condemns various slavery like practices including debt bondage and forced marriage. States Parties undertook to establish suitable minimum ages of marriage and registration of marriages.
- Abolition of Forced Labour Convention, ILO, 1957.
  Under this Convention, States Parties undertook abolition of any form of forced or compulsory labour

as a means of political coercion, economic development, labour discipline, or racial, social, national or religious discrimination.

- International Covenant on Civil and Political Rights, 1966.
  Forced labour and slavery are prohibited by Article 8 of the ICPR. Article 24 outlines the rights of children.
- Convention on the Elimination of all forms of Discrimination Against Women, 1979 (CEDAW).
  Article 6 of CEDAW requires States Parties to take all appropriate measures, including legislation, to suppress all froms of trafficking in women.
- Tourism Bill of Rights and the Tourist Code 1985.
  Adopted by the WTO, the code enjoins that the State should preclude any possibility of the use of tourism to exploit others for purpose of prostitution.
- Convention on the Rights of Child, 1989.
  Article 11 requires States Parties to take measures to combat the illicit transfer and non-return of children abroad. Under Articles 34 and 35, States Parties must take appropriate national, bilateral and multilateral steps to protect the child from all forms of sexual abuse as also to prevent the abduction, sale of or trafficking in children.
- Optional Protocol to CEDAW, 1999
  Enables individuals or group who have exhausted national remedies to directly approach the Committee under the Protocol.
- UN Protocol to prevent, suppress and punish Trafficking in persons, especially Women and Children, 2000.
  This protocol is an important milestone in efforts to control the problem of trafficking in women and children because,

— This Protocol establishes the first common international definition of "trafficking in persons" it shall mean the recruitment, transportation, transfer, harbouring or receipt of persons, by means of threat or use of force or other forms of coercion, of abduction, of fraud, of deception, of the abuse of power or of a position of vulnerability or of the giving or receiving of payments or benefits to achieve the consent of a person having control over another person, for the purpose of exploitation. Exploitation shall include, at a minimum, the exploitation of the prostitution of others or other forms of sexual exploitation, forced labour or services, slavery or practices similar to slavery, servitude or the removal of organs.

—It is intended to prevent and combat such crime and facilitate international co-operation against it. The protocol also highlights the problem associated with trafficking in persons that often leads to inhuman, degrading and dangerous exploitation of trafficked persons. As is the case with the Parent United Nations Convention against Transnational Organized Crime, 2000, the Protocol is expected to standardize terminology, laws and practices of countries in this area of the law.

Some of the key provisions of this Protocol are:

—While the United Nations Convention against Transnational Organized Crime, 2000, provides for basic measures to prevent and combat transnational organized crime, its Protocols provide for specific measures to deal with specific crimes. As such, the Protocols should be interpreted together with the Convention. The provisions of the Convention apply *mutatis mutandis* to each Protocol.

—The Protocol applies to the prevention, investigation and prosecution of trafficking offences, as well as to the protection of the trafficked persons.

—The key definition, "trafficking in persons", is intended to include a range of cases where human beings are exploited by organized criminal groups, particularly where there is an element of duress involved and a transnational aspect, such as the movement of people across the borders. According to the definition, the consent of the victim is irrelevant where illicit means are established, although criminal law defences are preserved.

The need for an appropriate balance between crime-control measures and measures to support or protect victims of trafficking arises in two primary places in the Protocol: provisions expressly providing for protection and support; and provisions dealing with the return of persons to their countries of origin.

—The Protocol contains a series of general protection and support measures for the victims. These include a list of social support benefits such as counseling, housing, education, medical and psychological assistance and an opportunity for victims to obtain legal status allowing them to remain in the country of the receiving State Party, either temporarily or permanently.

Legal Framework at Regional Level

At the regional level also there have been several initiatives by the governments of South Asia and Asia-Pacific regions.

- SAARC Convention on Preventing and Combating Trafficking in Women and Children for Prostitution, 2002.

  The objective of this convention is to promote cooperation amongst member states to effectively deal with various aspects of prevention, interdiction and suppression of trafficking in women and children; repatriation and rehabilitation of the victims of trafficking and preventing the use of women and children in international prostitution networks, particularly where the member countries of SAARC (Bangladesh, Bhutan, India, Maldives, Nepal, Pakistan, and Sri Lanka) are the countries of origin, transit and destination. The convention is legally binding on its signatory parties. It is the first regional anti-trafficking treaty from the Asian continent.

On December 2005 the SAARC convention came into force as all the member countries have ratified the convention.

Legal Framework at National Level

India has a fairly wide framework of laws to combat the problem of trafficking in human beings especially women and children.

- Article 23 of the Constitution of India
  Guarantees right against exploitation, prohibits trafficking in human beings and forced labour, and makes their practice punishable under the law.
- Article 24 of the Constitution of India
  Prohibits employment of children below 14 years of age in factories, mines or other hazardous employment.
- Indian Penal Code, 1860
  There are 25 provisions relevant to trafficking, some of the significant provisions are:
  Section 366A—Procurement of a minor girl (below age of 18 years) from one part of the country to another is punishable.
  Section 366B—Importation of a girl below 21 years is punishable.
  Section 374—Provides punishment for compelling any person to labour against his/her will.
- Immoral Traffic (Prevention) Act (ITPA), 1956 (renamed as such after amending the Suppression of Immoral Traffic in Women and Girls Act, 1956)
  This special legislation deals with trafficking. The Act defines the terms "child", "prostitution", "brothel", "corrective institutions", "protective home", "public place", "special police officer", and "trafficking officer". The objective of the Act is to inhibit/abolish traffic in women and girls for the purpose of prostitution as an organized means of living. Offences specified under this Act are:

- punishment for keeping a brothel or allowing the premises to be used as a brothel (S.3).
- punishment for living on the earnings of prostitution (S.4).
- procuring, inducing or taking persons for the sake of prostitution (S.5).
- detaining a person in premises where prostitution is carried on (S.6).
- prostitution in or the vicinity of public places (S.7).
- seducing or soliciting for the purpose of prostitution (S.8).
- seduction of a person in custody (S.9).

The law confers wide powers on the concerned authorities in matters of rescue and rehabilitation of victims and survivors and provides for stringent action against the exploiters including closure of brothels, surveillance, externment, as well as aggravated punishment when the offences are committed on children.

- Child Labour (Prohibition and Regulation) Act, 1986
  Prohibits employment of children in specific occupations set forth in the part A of the schedule of the Act. The Act lays down conditions of work for children. As per the Act, no child should work for more than three hours he/she had an interval of rest at least for one hour.
- The Child Marriage Restraint Act, 1929.
  Defines the terms "child marriage", "child", "contracting parties", "minors", etc. It sets the legal age of marriage for girls as 18 years and for boys as 21 years. The new amended Act empowers the court to issue injunctions prohibiting child marriage.
- The Information Technology Act, 2000
  Extends throughout India and also has extra-territorial jurisdiction. Section 67 penalises the publication or transmission of any material in electronic form, which is lascivious, or appeals to prurient interests, or if its

effect is such as to tend to deprive and corrupt persons who are likely having regard to all circumstances to read, see or hear the matter contained or embodied therein.

- Juvenile Justice (Care and Protection of Children) Act, 2000

  Enacted in consonance with the convention on the rights of the child (CRC). Focus of the Act is to provide proper care, protection and treatment by catering to the child's development needs and by adopting child-friendly approach in the adjudication and disposition of matters in the best interest of children and for their ultimate rehabilitation through various institutions established under the Act.

  The Act is in the form of a Code and incorporates in itself not only punitive and rehabilitative provisions but also spells out the procedure to be followed in detail.

  The Act is relevant to children who are vulnerable and are therefore likely to be trafficked.

Some of the States in India like Andhra Pradesh, Goa and Karnataka have also enacted certain laws to control and prevent certain prevalent culturally sanctioned practices such as Devdasi System, [Karnataka Devdasi (Prohibition of Dedication) Act, 1982 and Andhra Pradesh Devdasi (Prohibiting Dedication) Act, 1989] and to prevent exploitation of children for sex tourism purposes as in the case of Goa (Goa Children's Act, 2003).

Limitations of the Existing Legal Framework

The commitment of International Organizations, and National and State Governments can easily be gauzed by the wide framework of laws enacted by them. However, there are certain gaps in this legal framework, which pose problems in effective implementation of these laws, and enable the traffickers and other agencies involved in trafficking to escape punishment. Some of the major gaps in the existing legal framework are:

Lack of protection to victims during prosecution for the acts performed by the victims under coercion.

Lack of proper measures for victim assistance, victim care, reintegration and repatriation.

Lack of conceptual clarity between various processes like migration and trafficking, trafficking and prostitution.

Status of Law Enforcement

Status of law enforcement in controlling and preventing trafficking in women and children for commercial sexual exploitation can be measured by analyzing the crimes reported under ITPA, Indian Penal Code etc. Parameters such as number of crimes reported in a year under ITPA, sex of the person arrested, age of the persons arrested, number of cases charge sheeted, conviction rate of the crime reported etc., give a clear indication on the status of law enforcement and also the attitude of law enforcement personnel while dealing the cases of trafficking.

Number of Crimes Reported under ITPA

In India very few crimes are recorded related to non-sex based trafficking and exploitation. Most of the crimes recorded are related sexual exploitation as envisaged under ITPA. The data collected by National Crime Records Bureau between the years 1997 and 2001 show that there was steady increase in the all India reporting of crimes under ITPA except for the year 2001, when there was slight dip in reported cases compared to the previous year.

Regional patterns reveal that a high number of cases are reported in the State of Tamil Nadu. The adjoining States Andhra Pradesh and Karnataka have a relatively low number of cases reported.

However the field survey conducted during the action research on trafficking reveals that among the women and children trafficked for exploitation a large percentage of victims come from States like Andhra Pradesh, Karnataka and Tamil Nadu, indicating that a large number of cases go unreported or unregistered. Similar is the case with West Bangal. Though the number of crimes reported under ITPA are very low, the field survey conducted in the red-light areas in cities like Mumbai, Delhi and Goa reveals that a large number of trafficked victims belong to West Bengal.

Table 4.1: Number of Crimes Registered under ITPA in India

States	*1997*	*1998*	*1999*	*2000*	*2001*	*Total*	*Average*
Andhra Pradesh	613	507	737	482	1332	3671	734
Arunachal Pradesh	0	0	1	0	0	1	0
Assam	20	34	5	17	6	82	16
Bihar	21	37	38	9	29	134	27
Delhi	117	75	78	94	95	459	92
Goa	134	30	28	28	28	248	50
Gujarat	5	8	40	47	61	161	32
Haryana	7	4	14	13	21	59	12
Himachal Pradesh	1	1	0	1	1	4	1
Jammu and Kashmir	2	1	4	2	7	16	3
Karnataka	1645	1403	1225	1308	1356	6937	1387
Kerala	41	27	62	92	132	354	71
Madhya Pradesh	16	16	33	23	15	103	21
Maharashtra	1653	444	390	160	223	2870	574
Manipur	0	0	0	0	4	4	1
Meghalaya	1	0	0	0	0	1	1
Mizoram	1	0	0	2	2	5	1
Nagaland	0	0	0	1	1	2	0
Orissa	11	11	22	17	24	75	17
Pondicherry	42	29	50	48	39	208	17
Punjab	3	5	14	26	32	80	16
Rajasthan	41	47	85	110	68	351	70
Tamil Nadu	3863	5937	6462	6950	5232	28444	5689
Uttar Pradesh	57	31	24	30	26	168	34
West Bengal	28	43	39	49	31	190	38
Grand Total	8322	8690	9351	9509	8765	44637	8927

Source: Crime in India, National Crime Report Bureau, 1997-2001.

Pattern of Registration of Cases under Various Sections of ITPA

In ITPA Section 3 to Section 9 deal with various offences related to trafficking like,

- Punishment for keeping a brothel or allowing the premises to be used as a brothel (S.3).
- Punishment for living on the earnings of prostitution (S.4).
- Procuring, inducing or taking persons for the sake of prostitution (S.5).
- Detaining a person in premises where prostitution is carried on (S.6).
- Prostitution in or the vicinity of public places (S.7).
- Seducing or soliciting for the purpose of prostitution (S.8).
- Seduction of a person in custody (S.9).

Data pertaining to the pattern of registering cases under various sections of ITPA are not available for most of the states in India except in Tamil Nadu. Data on Tamil Nadu give a clear picture of the way ITPA is invoked in several cases and it gives a clear indication on the trends in registering cases throughout India.

Table 4.2: Details of Cases Reported under ITPA in Tamil Nadu in 2002

Section of ITPA	*Reported*	*Under Investigation*	*Pending Trial*	*Convicted*
Section-3	74	3	44	27
Section-4	247	8	91	148
Section-5	6	—	6	—
Section-6	5	—	1	4
Section-7	34	5	6	23
Section-8	2778	61	167	2550
Total	3144	77	315	2752

Source: Data Received from the Government of Tamil Nadu.

Analysis of the data obtained from Tamil Nadu reveals that very large number of cases are registered under Section 8, i.e. penalty for seducing or soliciting for the purpose of prostitution. The study also reveals that there are two distinct approaches adopted by law-enforcement agencies while dealing with offences related to ITPA. One approach treats the female as a soliciting prostitute and charges are levelled against her mainly under Section 8 of ITPA and sometimes, other add-on sections. The other approach considers females as victims and concentrates on registering cases against the exploiters, traffickers, pimps and brothel owners.

Arrests under ITPA—The Gender Perspective

Arresting suspected persons is an important aspect of law-enforcement. Analysis of the arrests made under ITPA suggests strong gender discrimination by the law-enforcement agencies. Out of the total 65,602 persons arrested under ITPA, during the period between 1997-2001, only 8452 persons arrested were males, whereas 57,150 persons arrested were females. The percentage of females arrested to the total number of arrests was highest at 90 per cent in 1998, and lowest at 80 per cent in 2001. There is a steady decrease in the percentage of females arrested to the total number of arrests made since 1998, even then the difference in the number of arrests made between males and females is alarming.

Table 4.3: All India Pattern of Arrests under ITPA (Segregated by Sex)

Year	*Males Arrested*	*Females Arrested*	*Total Arrested*	*% of Females to Total Arrested*
1997	1302	10069	11371	89
1998	1260	11605	12865	90
1999	1570	13195	14765	89
2000	1779	12073	13852	87
2001	2541	10208	12749	80
Total	8452	57150	65602	87

Compiled from the Data Crime in India by NCRB, for 1997-2001.

Age of the Arrested Persons

Assessing the age of the arrested persons is very difficult, as in most of the cases the persons themselves are not aware of their exact age. Very often the brothel owners try to deliberately give wrong age of the persons arrested from their brothels, in order to avoid punishment for keeping the minors in their custody. Studies show that there is lot of discrepancy between the recorded data and ground reality.

There were several instances where the girls' age was shown as above 18 years. The field surveys conducted indicate that, most of the brothel owners and other stakeholders are well aware of the fact that holding a minor in forced confinement can entail severe punishment under the law. So they try to cover up the crime by stating the age of the victim above 18 years. As the law-enforcement agencies are casual towards the persons rescued, they treat the statements made by the brothel owners as final as far as the age of the victims is concerned. As a result minor girls get bailed out, and are pushed back into the profession. Assessing the age of the arrested girl is very crucial to combat trafficking and to stop commercial sexual exploitation of children.

Conviction Rate in ITPA Cases

Conviction rate is a good indicator of the foolproof method of the investigation, and prosecution processes.

There is a great variation in the conviction rates not only among the various states of India, but also within the state from one year to another during the five-year study period. The average conviction rate for five years is as high as 99.1 in Tamil Nadu followed by Pondicherry (96.2) and Karnataka (90.7), but status like Haryana with 9.1, Orissa (10.8), Assam (16.5) have very low conviction rates, followed by Kerala (33.4) and Delhi (48). Data are not available for all the years under study, for many states like Gujarat, Himachal Pradesh, Manipur, Mizoram and even Punjab.

Table 4.4: All India Conviction Rate (in percentage) of ITPA Cases (1997-2001)

States	*1997*	*1998*	*1999*	*2000*	*2001*	*Average*
Andhra Pradesh	72.74	71.23	67.1	44.3	82	67.5
Assam	0	0	12.5	30	40	16.5
Bihar	73.08	50	31.3	7.7	16.7	35.8
Delhi	40.48	30.14	38	37.7	93.6	48
Goa	84.75	43.21	77.1	85.7	97	77.6
Gujarat	20	—	0	0	77.8	19.6
Haryana	0	0	20	14.3	11.1	9.1
Himacal Pradesh	—	0	—	33.3	—	6.7
Jammu and Kashmir	—	—	—	50	0	10
Karnataka	90.76	92.43	92.7	87.2	90.2	90.7
Kerala	43.48	21.05	31	43.2	28.2	33.4
Madhya Pradesh	50.09	75	0	70	53.1	51.4
Maharashtra	86.54	89.66	77	7.8	62.5	64.7
Manipur	—	—	—	—	100	20
Mizoram	100	—	—	—	—	40
Nagaland	—	—	—	—	100	20
Orissa	0	0	11.1	20	23.1	10.8
Pondicherry	91.49	91.67	100	97.9	100	96.2
Punjab	20	—	—	20	50	55.8
Rajasthan	52.11	56.14	41	63	66.7	55.8
Sikkim	—	—	—	—	—	—
Tamil Nadu	98.7	98.83	99.2	99.4	99.6	99.1
Uttar Pradesh	57.65	66.67	60	73.8	88.6	69.3
West Bengal	76.47	88.89	85	80	0	66.1

Source: Crime in India Crime Records Bureau, 1997-2002.

Another interesting conclusion can be drawn from the data is, there is a steady decline in conviction rates in some states like Bihar from 1997 to 2000. However in 2001 in Delhi the conviction rate suddenly jumped to 93.6.

All India conviction rate stood at 51.1 per cent in the year 2001, indicating that only 50 per cent cases have resulted in conviction. One of the reason for this low conviction is delay in trial proceeding, as all pending cases are treated as non-convicted, the statistics do not match with the charge-sheeted cases for the corresponding years.

Pattern of Conviction under Various Sections of ITPA

Study of the data for the period 1997-2002 highlights the pattern of conviction under various sections of ITPA. In Goa during the study period 100 per cent convictions were made under section 8 indicating that all females arrested under section 8 were convicted. Similar is the case with Tamil Nadu and Kerala. This high rate of conviction under section 8 corresponds to the high rate of registration of cases under section 8.

However, in some states like Rajasthan there are more convictions under section 5 compared to section 8. During the study period of 1997-2002 a total of 12 cases were convicted under section 8 in comparison to 37 cases convicted under section 5 and related sections. It is interesting to note that there are more women convicted under section 5 indicating that in Rajasthani women are increasingly involved in trafficking, running the brothels and acting as pimps etc.

Crimes Registered under the Indian Penal Code (IPC)

There is a special law (ITPA) enacted by the Government to deal with the problem of trafficking in women and children. However, certain Sections, namely 336A (procuring of minor girls under 18), 366B (importation of girls under 21 years from foreign country), 367 (kidnapping for slavery, unnatural lust, etc.), 372 (selling minors under 18 years for prostitution), 373 (buying minors under 18 years for prostitution), 376 (rape), 377 (unnatural offences), etc. of substantive law, i.e. Indian Penal Code also have direct relevance to trafficking in women and children. Invoking sections of substantive law along with ITPA facilitate in awarding of more stringent punishment to the culprits, thereby control the crime.

The All India data collected show that more number of cases are reported under Section 366A, i.e. procuring of minor girls.

Field surveys reveal that law enforcement agencies generally do not invoke the relevant IPC sections along with

ITPA, resulting in violation of human rights of the victims and at the same time giving a chance to the culprit to escape with lesser or no punishment.

Arrests under Criminal Procedure Code, Local and Special Laws

Arresting the persons under wrong laws leads to not only human rights violation but also decreases the efficiency of law enforcement in tackling the problem of trafficking in women and children. Research carried out on these issues highlights the misuse of other laws in many states. It has been observed that in many states action has been taken against females on charges of indecent exposure, public nuisance etc., and under several other laws other than ITPA. For example, in Delhi 'sex workers' were being booked under Section 92/93 of the Delhi Police Act, in Assam it has been reported that Section 109 of Cr.P.C. is initiated against women for soliciting. It has also observed that Section 145(b) of the Indian Railways Act being invoked in some states to deal with trafficked victims.

Limitations to Effective Law Enforcement

For successful implementation of laws, sensitivity, sincerity and awareness and knowledge about various laws and their implications is highly important among all the ranks of law enforcement agencies besides having good infrastructure, scientific and technological facilities, co-operation of the civil society and NGOs and other voluntary organizations.

An extensive study was carried out by the research team of trafficking in women and children project to study and understand the perceptions, attitudes prevalent among the police personnel on the problem of trafficking as it has direct bearing on law-enforcement. Around 850 police personnel belonging to supervisory ranks and investigating ranks were interviewed across the country as a part of the research programme. Some important findings of the exercise are:

Lack of Training and Orientation

About 56 police personnel received some training on matters related to women and children. Even among those 56 personnel, majority of them belong to supervisory ranks, indicating that the grassroots officials who are actually involved in the process of investigation and prosecution have not been adequately trained to handle the issues related to trafficking.

Low Priority Given to Cases of Trafficking

At present the police attach very low priority to the cases of trafficking as well as commercial sexual exploitation of women and children. From the responses it is very clear that police personnel are not sensitive to the violations of human rights of women and children in brothels and in places where women and children are repeatedly exposed to sexual abuse.

Wrong Perception that 'Trafficked Women and Children are Part of the Anti-social Set Up'

Most of the police personnel are of erroneous view that women and children caught from brothels are part of the anti-social set up, therefore to be arrested and placed behind bars. Very few police personnel use intelligence networks and adopt strategies to catch traffickers, pimps and brothel owners etc. There is an imperative need to inculcate human rights perspective in police personnel to deal with the problem of trafficking.

Gender Discrimination in Booking the Culprits under ITPA

Overwhelmingly a large number of persons arrested are females and very few males are arrested under the Act. A large number of females arrested are charge-sheeted and convicted. This speaks of not only lack of sensitivity among the officers but also ignorance of the various provisions of law.

Lacunae in Investigation and Prosecution Processes

It has emerged from the responses given by the police officials that, women arrested during the raids are first arrested and then FIRs are registered against them, and then investigation commences. In such a scenario, the tendency of the investigating officer is to document and marshal the evidence rather than a thorough investigation. of the case. Very often arrested women were not given sufficient time to state their views.

Even the prosecution is conducted in a hurry for quick disposal of the case. Investigating and prosecuting officers often ignore the fact that women remain under threat, duress, coercion or compulsion by the brothel owners or other such exploiters. It the women are given sufficient time may speak thc truth to prove their innocence and expose the real culprits.

Bail

Obtaining bail of the arrested persons is very easy. Almost in 80 per cent of the cases, bail is granted to the arrested persons, majority of them are bailed out by the brothel keepers and pimps. This results in debt bondage on the part of the victims, leading to further exploitation by the traffickers.

Traffickers and clientele are seldom booked. This often happens due to nexus between the police and culprits.

Limitations in Effective Law Enforcement due to Lacunae in ITPA

From the viewpoint of law enforcement officials interviewed, there are certain gaps in ITPA, which hinder effective implementation of the law.

- ITPA is lenient towards the perpetrators.
- Fails to link rehabilitation with rescue and law enforcement, lacks mandatory requirement of women witness for conducting rescue and interview.

Strategies for Effective Law Enforcement

Following measures can help the police in effective implementation of the law:

1. Police stations the core units of policing have to be strengthened. There should be improvement of infrastructural facilities to enable the police to function properly and to help victims after rescue operations. Police stations should also be provided with adequate human resources. Police capabilities should further enriched through training programmes and discussions.
2. There is an utmost need to build up institutional partnership among police, concerned departments of the Government and NGOs for purposes of prevention, rescue and rehabilitation. Panchayati Raj Institutions can play an effective role in generating awareness of the menace among the community and keeping surveillance over the exploiters. It may be mentioned that Tamil Nadu (Department of Social Defence) has developed a good model in this direction.
3. Intelligence collection and intelligence sharing has to improve. At present there is very little intelligence sharing between police agencies in different states in India on traffickers and their links and operatives. There is no institutional mechanism, except some *ad hoc* initiatives by some individual officers. It is necessary to have institutional network for collection and dissemination intelligence and follow-up action among the police agencies.
4. There is need for recruiting adequate number of women police officers for each police station. Section 13(13) ITPA provides that the special police officers (SPO) notified by the State Government shall be assisted by an adequate number of subordinate police officers, including women officers. Whenever women police officers of the rank of Inspector or above are available they should be notified.

5. Under Section 13(4) of ITPA, the Government of India can notify anti-trafficking police officers (ATPO) with jurisdictions throughout India. Such officers can be appointed for investigating offences under ITPA or under any law dealing with sexual exploitation committed in more than one state. The GOI has now appointed officers (refer notification No. 2-27/2001-CP dated 28th August, 2001 of Department of Women and Child Development, Ministry of Human Resource Development) of and above the rank of Inspector of Police in CBI as Trafficking Police Officers with jurisdiction throughout the country to investigate offences under ITPA.
6. According to Section 18(2) of ITPA the Court convicting a person of any offence under Section 3 ITPA (keeping a brothel etc.) and Section 7 of ITPA [for misuse of public place for Commercial Sexual Exploitation (CSE)] may pass order of closure of brothels and eviction of the offenders. Therefore, in the event of conviction under Sections 3 and 7 of ITPA the police/prosecutor should immediately move the Court for closure/eviction under Section 18 of ITPA.

5

Trafficking and Missing Persons

'Missing Persons' generally denotes the people who had run away from their respective homes on their own will. Various factors may contribute to their decision to run away from their homes including family tensions, torture at home, work/community pressure, fear of getting caught in the case of people involved in unlawful deeds etc. In the case of children, the reasons could be lack of attention and care from parents/elders, domestic violence, failure in their studies/work, exposure to adult life at a very young and impressionable age or involvement of criminals, i.e. kidnapping/abduction for ransom etc. Whatever may be the reason, in most of the cases the society and law enforcement agencies put the blame and responsibility on persons gone missing. This being the prevalent attitude in the society and among the law enforcement agencies, there is a lack of priority and sensitivity to investigate thoroughly into the cases of missing persons.

However, it has been observed many a time that women and children rescued during raids in brothels or sweat shops or such similar places, have been reported missing elsewhere in the country, indicating that there is a link between missing persons and trafficking. Although women and children might have left the house on their own will in lure of good jobs, bright future etc., but in reality they might have been trafficked. Parents/guardians unaware of this fact tend to lodge a complaint with the police that their wards are missing. While trafficking is a serious crime, 'missing persons' is not viewed as a crime. The seriousness of the issue gets diluted by registering the case under 'missing persons' category. An effort was made to study the seriousness of the link between 'missing persons' and trafficking during the action research on trafficking in women and children.

Investigation in cases of 'Missing Persons'

In the present day scenario, no FIR is registered by the police against the complaints related to missing persons. Instead, an entry is made in the General Station Diary (GD) or in some cases a zero FIR is registered. Zero FIR means, no crime number is assigned. The follow up is same for both GD entry and Zero FIR. The Station House Officer (SHO) forwards the information regarding the missing persons to the Superintendent of Police/ Deputy Commissioner of Police, who in turn forwards it to the Office of Chief of Police. At the field level, the local police officials publicize the particulars of the missing persons in the media.

The messages that reaches the Police Headquarters in the States are normally lodged with the Missing Person Bureau, which is a wing of CID (Crime Investigation Department) of the State Police. They in turn send the message to the Missing Persons Wing in NCRB (National Crime Records Bureau) in New Delhi. NCRB coordinates in transmitting the information to different states and acts as a documentation centre of crimes reported in the country. NCRB has no role to play in investigation, monitoring or recovery of the missing persons. However, it will update its records if informed by the State Police after tracing the missing persons by the State Police.

Different States in India follow different procedures to deal with the cases of missing persons. For example, in Mumbai city, the information is relayed through a 'police notice' along with other information pertaining to vehicles stolen, vehicles recovered, appeal for identification of dead bodies etc. More often efforts to trace down the missing persons stop at this stage.

Interactions and interviews carried out with some of the victims of commercial sexual exploitation as a part of the action research project on trafficking in women and children have revealed a strong linkage between missing persons and trafficking. A fourteen year old girl belonging to a village in Raichur district, Karnataka was reported missing by her parents. In reality, the girl was trafficked by a man who was living in her neighbourhood and who took her to Mumbai on the pretext of securing her a job as domestic help. She accompanied him to Mumbai in April 2003. After reaching Mumbai he sold her to a brothel, where she was held for 20 days. After rescuing her from the brothel, police sent her to the special rehabilitation centre at Deonar in Mumbai. Due to sincere efforts of the police and the NGOs like Saathi (An NGO operating in the Karnataka State), she was returned to her parents in July 2003.

In another case study, a 15-year old girl was reported missing in the police station of her native village in Pondicherry State on 3rd May, 1998 by her parents stating that she was missing from home since 25th April, 1998. The case did not proceed any further after conducting the initial formalities and the girl remained missing. However, police acted on the basis of a letter received on 5th July, 1998 by the parents of the girl, describing her plight in a brothel and requesting to rescue her from that place. Police arrested two persons involved in running a brothel, where the girl was held captive. The two accused were prosecuted and given a sentence of seven years imprisonment and fine by the Additional Sessions Judge, Pondicherry.

In India a large number of people, especially women and children are reportedly missing every year. As per the data compiled by collecting from the state police agencies, almost 24,000 adult women and around 46,500 children were reported missing in the year 2001 alone. Around one-fourth (6181 of adult women and 10,589 of children) of these missing persons remained missing till date. Analysis of the data collected from various states and union territories for the period starting from 1996-2001 shows that a very high number of cases of missing persons are reported from States like Andhra Pradesh, Karnataka, Madhya Pradesh, Maharashtra, Orissa and Tamil Nadu in comparison to States like Arunachal Pradesh, Goa, Haryana, Himachal Pradesh, Uttaranchal etc. where the number is low. This difference could possibly be due to lack of awareness among the people, or due to stigma attached to the issue of missing persons, or due to apathy of law enforcement agencies in registering the cases. Details of the data compiled are given separately under various categories like number of adult females reported missing, total number of adult females who remained missing total number of children reported missing, total number of children remained missing, percentage of female adults remained missing to the total number of adult females reported missing and percentage of children remain missing to the total number of children reported missing.

Table 5.1: Total Number of Adult Females Reported Missing

State/Union Territory	*1996*	*1997*	*1998*	*1999*	*2000*	*2001*	*Total for 6 years*	*Yearly average*	*2001 over 1996**
Andman and Nicobar Islands	13	19	10	25	28	37	132	22	185%(+)
Andhra Pradesh	698	656	724	778	850	921	4,627	771	32%(+)
Arunachal Pradesh	12	16	14	27	21	42	132	22	150% (+)
Assam	297	289	317	385	442	459	2189	365	55%(+)
Chandigarh	43	53	68	51	52	56	323	54	30%(+)
Chattisgarh	115	94	107	106	119	95	636	106	17%(-)
Delhi	1948	2016	1920	2141	2114	2116	12255	2043	8%(+)
Goa	308	303	274	280	295	279	1739	290	9%(-)
Gujarat	622	773	900	1040	1151	1104	5590	932	77%(+)
Haryana	78	76	101	105	129	143	632	105	83%(+)
Himachal Pradesh	203	157	178	212	227	218	1195	199	7% (+)
Karnataka	1682	1693	1724	1572	1630	1766	10067	1678	5% (+)
Kerala	883	911	924	774	823	848	5163	861	4% (+)
Madhya Pradesh	2451	2750	2982	3192	3443	2881	17699	2950	17% (+)
Maharashtra	7466	7793	7578	8410	8590	8781	48618	8103	18% (+)
Meghalaya	4	3	2	2	3	2	16	3	50% (-)
Nagaland	0	1	0	0	2	2	5	1	100% (+)
Orissa	241	168	250	275	300	300	1534	255	24% (+)
Pondicherry	0	0	0	0	3	12	15	2.5	1200%(+)
Rajasthan	676	1579	713	688	798	836	5290	882	24% (+)
Tamil Nadu	2143	1874	1996	2112	2222	2218	12565	2094	3% (+)
Tripura	61	56	49	51	67	53	337	56	13% (+)
Uttaranchal	113	104	124	155	163	174	833	139	54% (+)
Uttar Pradesh	250	264	405	432	316	498	2165	361	99% (+)
West Bengal	187	182	192	198	161	193	1113	186	3% (+)
Total	*20494*	*21830*	*21552*	*23011*	*23949*	*24034*	*134870*	*22480*	*17% (+)*

* Shows difference (+) increase; (-) decrease.

Source: Data received from the State Police Agencies.

Table 5.2: Total Number of Children Reported Missing in India

State/Union Territory	*1996*	*1997*	*1998*	*1999*	*2000*	*2001*	*Total for 6 years*	*Yearly average*	*2001 over 1996**
Andman and Nicobar Islands	47	42	85	76	83	95	428	71	102% (+)
Andhra Pradesh	1642	2048	1936	2054	2011	2353	12044	2007	43% (+)
Arunachal Pradesh	36	26	23	86	95	112	378	63	211% (+)
Assam	576	585	612	850	1030	1055	4708	785	83% (+)
Chandigarh	24	27	27	33	34	32	177	30	33% (+)
Chattisgarh	156	175	137	183	170	165	986	164	6% (+)
Delhi	6193	6525	6474	5793	6223	6151	37359	6227	1% (-)
Goa	215	245	220	195	237	202	1314	219	6% (-)
Gujarat	1333	1413	1673	1948	1737	1639	9743	1624	23% (+)
Haryana	188	166	225	283	325	318	1505	251	69% (+)
Himachal Pradesh	181	157	153	145	142	154	932	155	15% (-)
Karnataka	3943	3861	3574	3533	3530	3523	21964	3660	11% (-)
Kerala	762	884	795	616	629	554	4240	707	27% (-)
Madhya Pradesh	4280	4739	4823	5378	5354	4914	29488	4915	15% (+)
Maharashtra	14470	13988	12797	14045	13875	14108	83283	13881	3% (-)
Manipur	0	0	0	0	0	3	3	0.5	—
Meghalaya	14	10	15	13	19	15	86	14	7% (+)
Nagaland	4	3	5	5	4	8	29	5	100% (+)
Orissa	572	445	379	503	360	696	2955	493	22% (+)
Pondicherry	7	0	0	1	2	35	45	7.5	400% (+)
Rajasthan	1894	1972	1918	1966	2001	2032	11783	1964	7% (+)
Tamil Nadu	2511	4553	4596	4943	5606	5498	27707	4618	119% (+)
Tripura	39	37	33	44	78	37	268	45	5%% (-)
Uttaranchal	313	339	321	286	305	281	1845	308	10% (-)
Uttar Pradesh	1595	1694	1791	1942	1612	1988	10622	1770	25% (+)
West Bengal	415	679	624	453	405	379	2955	493	9% (+)
Total	*41410*	*44613*	*43236*	*45374*	*45867*	*46347*	*266847*	*44476*	12% (+)

* Shows difference (+) increase; (-) decrease.
Source: Data received from the State Police Agencies.

The fact is that missing persons is not recognized as a crime under any special or substantive laws of the country. Hence searching for and locating the missing persons does not figure in the priority list of the law enforcement agencies. It is handled in a casual and *ad hoc* manner. As searching for missing persons comes last in the priority of law enforcement, in some cases even after getting information about missing persons, there will be a great time lag in disseminating the

Table 5.3: Total Number of Children Remain Missing

State/Union Territory	*1996*	*1997*	*1998*	*1999*	*2000*	*2001*	*Total for 6 years*	*Yearly ave-rage*	*2001 over 1996**
Andman and Nicobar Islands	—	2	1	4	7	11	24	4	1000% (+)
Andhra Pradesh	251	353	277	352	325	446	2004	334	78% (+)
Arunachal Pradesh	6	2	2	20	58	59	147	25	883% (+)
Assam	206	214	272	402	489	517	2100	350	151% (+)
Chandigarh	9	9	13	12	9	14	66	11	56% (+)
Chattisgarh	24	5	30	32	31	44	166	28	83% (+)
Delhi	3837	4258	4722	4377	3848	2666	23708	3951	31% (+)
Goa	54	41	31	36	47	39	248	41	28% (+)
Gujarat	133	135	202	213	223	239	1145	191	80% (+)
Haryana	64	77	107	126	120	155	649	108	142% (+)
Himachal Pradesh	39	52	48	43	33	53	268	47	36% (+)
Karnataka	411	428	433	439	483	479	2673	446	17% (+)
Kerala	193	160	251	136	153	163	1056	176	16% (-)
Madhya Pradesh	1092	776	800	597	995	857	5117	853	22% (-)
Maharashtra	2340	2214	2470	2365	2327	2435	14151	2359	4% (+)
Manipur	0	0	0	0	0	1	1	0.16	—
Meghalaya	2	—	—	—	4	1	7	1	50% (-)
Orissa	419	373	301	417	280	541	2331	389	29% (+)
Pondicherry	0	0	0	0	0	2	2	0.33	—
Rajasthan	154	200	187	202	216	278	1237	206	81% (+)
Tamil Nadu	186	331	776	728	464	547	3032	505	194% (+)
Tripura	2	0	2	12	35	8	59	10	300% (+)
Uttaranchal	59	33	32	26	31	45	226	38	24% (-)
Uttar Pradesh	665	518	668	669	549	775	3844	641	17% (+)
West Bengal	260	413	374	285	216	214	1762	294	18% (-)
Total	*1046*	*10594*	*11999*	*11493*	*10943*	*10589*	*66024*	*11008*	*2% (+)*

* Shows difference (+) increase; (-) decrease.
Source: Data received from the State Police Agencies.

same information to other police stations, districts and states. This delay defeats the purpose and makes recovery of missing persons more difficult. There is a probability that missing persons might be trafficked, and hence the problem has to be given due attention. Law enforcement agencies have to work out more efficient documenting and monitoring mechanisms to deal with cases of missing persons. Vigilance and surveillance systems by police and social activists have to be strengthened by eastablishing partnership with each other. As of now there is no involvement of any other government agency in locating the missing persons. However it is learnt that Ministry of Social Justice, Government of India is considering to develop a National Monitoring System by linking up all concerned government agencies. A national centre for missing and exploited children can be set up to function across the country for forging linkages between government and Non-Governmental agencies and thus ensuring a coordinated and integrated fieldwork in recovering the missing children.

Table 5.4: Percentage of Adult Females remain Missing to the Total Number Reported Missing

State/Union Territory	*1996*	*1997*	*1998*	*1999*	*2000*	*2001*
Andman and Nicobar Islands	8	11	10	16	25	14
Andhra Pradesh	21	21	19	22	18	21
Arunachal Pradesh	8	19	29	15	38	40
Assam	39	35	37	38	47	40
Chandigarh	23	51	44	37	48	54
Chattisgarh	34	20	15	15	20	36
Delhi	74	78	84	81	60	58
Goa	23	22	23	16	21	17
Gujarat	11	15	14	13	14	19
Haryana	37	49	60	37	50	62
Himachal Pradesh	35	34	44	34	34	31
Karnataka	12	11	15	14	16	18
Kerala	24	25	24	27	24	25
Madhya Pradesh	8	14	23	7	24	28
Maharashtra	19	19	21	17	20	21
Meghalaya	50	33	50	50	33	50
Orissa	78	81	85	83	87	78
Pondicherry	0	0	0	0	33	33
Rajasthan	13	6	14	14	15	15
Tamil Nadu	2	12	11	10	3	9
Tripura	2	2	2	14	25	11
Uttaranchal	21	28	16	20	17	16
Uttar Pradesh	37	45	39	32	48	41
West Bengal	76	63	65	72	65	73

Source: Data Received from the State Police Agencies.

Table 5.5: Percentage of Children Remain Missing to the Total Number Reported Missing

State/Union Territory	*1996*	*1997*	*1998*	*1999*	*2000*	*2001*
Andman and Nicobar Islands	2	5	1	5	8	12
Andhra Pradesh	15	51	18	19	19	22
Arunachal Pradesh	17	8	9	23	61	53
Assam	36	37	44	47	47	49
Chandigarh	38	33	48	36	26	44
Chattisgarh	15	3	22	17	18	27
Delhi	62	65	73	76	62	43
Goa	25	17	14	18	20	19
Gujarat	10	10	12	11	13	1
Haryana	34	46	48	45	37	49
Himachal Pradesh	22	33	31	30	23	34
Karnataka	10	11	12	12	14	14
Kerala	25	18	32	22	24	29
Madhya Pradesh	26	16	17	11	19	17
Maharashtra	16	16	19	17	17	17
Manipur	0	0	0	0	0	33
Meghalaya	14	10	7	8	21	7
Orissa	73	84	79	83	78	78
Pondicherry	0	0	0	0	0	6
Rajasthan	8	10	10	10	11	14
Tamil Nadu	7	7	17	15	8	10
Tripura	5	0	6	27	45	22
Uttaranchal	19	10	10	9	10	16
Uttar Pradesh	42	31	37	34	34	39
West Bengal	63	6	60	63	53	56

Source: Data received from the State Police Agencies.

Presently realizing the need for locating the missing persons especially children and to ensure that rights of the child are not abused by exploiters, some National NGOs like National Centre for Missing Children (NCMC), Children India Foundation, and Young at Risk (YAR), and international NGOs like Child Quest International, U.S.A. based National Centre for Missing and Exploited Children (NCMEC) and Child Fund of America have developed dedicated websites, which provide information on the missing children, by providing photographs, profiles and other vital clues required to identify and locate the missing children.

6

Culturally Sanctioned Practices and Trafficking

Introduction

In India there are certain culturally sanctioned practices enabling trafficking and commercial sexual exploitation. One of the prominent features of these practices is that a girl from a family is dedicated to a deity or an object of worship or to a temple. Devadasi System is one of such culturally sanctioned practices highly prevalent in India, even today. The term *Devadasi* is a Sanskrit word denoting *Deva*—the God, and *dasi*—female slave, which literally means 'female slave of the God'. The institution of dedicating young girls to temples or deities of worship happens to be a pan-Indian phenomenon. However it came to be known by different names in different parts of the country owing to the variety of cultures and traditions prevailing in different parts of the country. In Goa, the girls who are dedicated to temples are called as 'Bhavin', in West Coast they are called as 'Kudikar' in Andhra Pradesh, they are known as 'bogam' or 'jogin', in Tamil Nadu as 'murali', 'jagateen', in Maharashtra as are 'dhini', in Karnataka as 'jogati' or 'basavi', in Orissa as 'ganika', as 'nati', in Assam and so on.

Genesis of the Practice

Although there is no substantial evidence of the origin of culturally sanctioned practices in India, historical and literary records show that in South India, Devadasi System began to flourish during Pallava and Chola dynasties from the sixth to thirteenth century A.D. Devdasis were a special and venerated group of women attendants, some of whom like the Vestal Virgins of Rome, were dedicated to the temple at birth or very young. They were required to participate in almost all daily rituals and occasional ceremonies. It was a matter of prestige for temples to employ devdasis in good number. Devdasis used to enjoy the ritual sanctity and social eminence. But over a period of time the system was abused and degenerated to the extent that the devdasis have become the victims of commercial sexual exploitation.

Social scientists, who studied the origin of Devadasi System, cite the belief that mother Goddess would ensure the fertility of soil and bless the community, if girls from some families are voluntarily dedicated to the mother goddess as the reason for the origin of Devadasi System. Another theory suggests a prevalent belief among the people of earlier communities that the gods would be pleased and would reward the devotees if girls were offered to the deity. As a result many devotees with serious health problems or some serious family and financial problems would promise to offer their girls to the deity, if their problems are taken care of, by the deity. In the course of time the priests started demanding for virgin girls in the guise of divine desire to satisfy their sexual desires (Singh, 1997: 29).

Though the Devdasi system was practiced by almost all major Brahmanical temples, particularly the Shivaite temples in South India, in some regions it had attained its maximum growth, e.g. Chingleput, North and South Arcot, Tanjavur, and Tiruchirapalli districts of modern Tamil Nadu; Krishna, Guntur and Nellore districts of Andhra Pradesh and Dharwar and Kolar districts in Karnataka. The population of Devadasis in these regions had attained such a number that they emerged as a separate sub-caste, with their own traditions, code of conduct, etiquette etc. They started having their own panchayats, whose decisions were binding on all members.

The study conducted by the ISS on trafficking in women and children reports on the culturally sanctioned sexual exploitations observed among the Dommara community in

Chilakaluripet in Krishna district of Andhra Pradesh. The people belonging to Dommara community are mostly artists, dancers and entertainers. They earn their living by touring various towns and give performances in those towns during festivals and other functions. The women and girls of Dommara community also work as prostitutes and concubines. The girls of the Dommara community are well looked after, once they attain puberty. The parents look for rich customers and then initiate the girls into the profession.

Instances of devadasi system can also be observed in Western India (Maharasthra, Rajastan), Central India (Madhya Pradesh) and Eastern India (Orissa), with slight modifications. Although it had not spread into northern India, North India there are certain castes as Tawaif, Ghandarb and Patur, who are dancers, singers and victims of CSE.

In the olden times, in Maharashtra, women who failed to have children used to promise the God Khandoba at Jejuri in Pune district that they would sacrifice their first born daughter to God Khandoba, if the god would gift them with more children. If their wish would come true, the mother used to offer the first-born girl child to God Khandoba by tying a necklace of seven cowries around the little girl's neck. Once the girl reaches the marriageable age, she would be formally married to the God. Such girls were not permitted to marry any other man and they came to known as 'muralis'. Usually such girls earned their living through prostitution and the society never considered this as a sin as the girls belong to God Khandoba. However, it is interesting to note that the people belonging to upper castes, who promise to God Khandoba to offer girls, would never sacrifice their own daughters to the God. Instead they would buy girls from lower caste families for a small sum and offer those girls to Khandoba to keep their promise.

Even today this is practiced in Maharashtra. Some of the families belonging to lower castes such as Kunbis, Mahars and Mangs make their daughters as muralis. According to a survey conducted by Samyukta Mahila Vedike, a Bangalore-based voluntary organization, 98 per cent of households with devadasi background belong to scheduled castes and are engaged in prostitution (Shankar 1994: 50).

According to some estimates, there are about 2.5 lakh women and girls dedicated to various deities like Yellamma, Hanuman and Khandoba, in the Maharashtra-Karnataka border area. The backward areas of Belgaum district such as Saundati, Kokatnur and Yellamman Gudda are more prone to this practice, and act as main supply areas for urban brothels. A case study of the ISS's research on trafficking in women and children authenticates this observation, where girls belonging to scheduled castes are often taken by some of their relatives or known people to big cities like Mumbai, with a promise to get jobs for the girls. Upon reaching the big cities, these girls are forced to become devadasis and then initiated into prostitution.

Degeneration of Culturally Sanctioned Practices Leading to Trafficking

Over the period all the culturally sanctioned practices, which originated as religious practices saw gradual decline. Patronage from royal, priestly and upper classes for their evil and sensual desires is one of the reasons for the degeneration of these practices. The fact remains true even today as many research studies on the subject reveal that many women belonging to Scheduled Castes and Tribes are encouraged by upper castes to undergo initiation ceremony, and accept the devadasi way of life in order to gain access to desirable women of lower castes to appease their extra marital sexual needs. Later on these women are forced to take up the profession of prostitution in their native town or in nearby cities.

Some of the Reasons for the Continuity of these Culturally Sanctioned Practices

Abject poverty: Peasant and agricultural labourers who depend on the land to earn a living are able to get full labour only for three months in a year. In cases of natural calamities like drought, floods and famine earning a living for those three months also becomes very difficult and sometimes even impossible. Under such circumstances they opt to become a devadasi to earn a living (Trivedi, 1976: 84-85).

The Action Research Team of the ISS has observed a new way of inducing girls into the devadasi system in Goa. Due to strict legal actions against devadasi practice in Karnataka, there was short supply of girls from Karnataka to Goa (which gets girls from States like Andhra Pradesh, and Karnataka) resulting a shift in supply areas and gave rise to socially ratified exploitative practices in new areas, till now unknown to have such practices.

Katem Baina, is a slum area situated adjacent to Baina Beach Red-light Area (BRLA). The residents of Katem Baina are mostly of Kannada origin. The brothel keepers of BRLA keep a watch on the families living in the slum especially families with girl children. The brothel owners would offer financial help to these families in times of financial crisis caused due to illness or death of an earning member etc. Later on the brothel keepers pressurize the families to return the loan with interest. As the poor families are unable to pay back the money they will advise the families to induce their girls into devdasi system and then trade them to the brothels. The brothel keepers even support the expenses incurred for the initiation ceremony. As devdasi system is a culturally sanctioned practice, the parents of the girls tend to agree without a feeling of guilt.

Besides sanction from the community and religion, due to absence of a law against Devdasi System in Goa; absence of livelihood options; absence of penal action against the perpetrators of CSE due to poor law enforcement, the evil practice is thriving in Goa.

Sanction from Religion and Society: It has been noticed that in comparison to other commercial prostitutes who are non-devdasis, prostitutes coming from devdasi community find it relatively safe to operate. Their status as culturally sanctioned practitioners prevents police and the law courts from arresting and punishing them. As a result initiation of girls as devadasis has become a paying proposition. Further, those who are already practicing the commercial prostitution buy this licence to get immunity, thus resulting in continuity and flourishing of the devadasi practice (Tarachand, 1991: 129-130).

Acceptance from the Community: As against other victims trafficked for commercial exploitation, girls and women who enter into the profession do not suffer from societal taboos and stigmas and they need not face social alienation. Commercial prostitutes belonging to the devadasi community are accepted back in the family and community, when they grow old or become sick and unable to continue the profession. Where as this may not be the case with prostitutes belonging to non-devadasi community. In fact devadasis enjoy better social status than other women of their community.

Process of induction into Commercial Prostitution

Senior devadasis who retire from active prostitution become brothel owners and they regularly visit their native villages with the purpose of introducing young girls into the profession. After selecting the required number of girls the procurers make advance payments to the families to initiate the girl into devadasihood at the earliest possible opportunity. The amount paid as advance will be adjusted against the earnings of the girls. Later on the procurers make arrangements to bring the grils to the cities by bribing police, travel agents and other concerned authorities.

Initiatives by the Government

In 1990, the Government of Maharashtra appointed a study group for the rehabilitation of victims of trafficking and commercial sexual exploitation. Based on the recommendations given by the study group, the Government of Maharashtra has started a pension scheme under which a monthly pension of Rs. 300 is given to davadasis over 40 years of age. Other schemes initiated by the Government include:

- Financial assistance of Rs. 10,000 for the marriage of unmarried davadasis, or for the marriage of the daughter of a devadasi.
- Construction of hostels to provide vocational training and education in several districts of Maharashtra.
- Assistance of Rs. 10,000 per year for NGOs working towards eradicating the devadasi system from the society.
- Seed capital of Rs. 35,000 for davadasis to set up a business connected with agriculture, transport, rural development, cottage and small-scale industries etc.

Karnataka Government also has initiated schemes such as:

- Financial assistance of Rs.10,000 for the couples in which the bride is a devadasi.
- Creation of a special cell in the Government for the eradication of devadasi system and other culturally sanctioned practices.

Madhaya Pradesh Government has launched 'Jawali' a scheme in partnership with voluntary organizations in an attempt to eliminate commercial sexual exploitation from the states, especially amongst the Bedia community. The focus of the scheme is children belonging to certain scheduled castes and tribes in which trafficking and commercial sexual exploitation is an accepted norm.

Law Enacted by States to Prohibit Culturally Sanctioned Practices such as Devadasi System

Karnataka

Even during pre-independence period, the then Mysore State had taken steps to prohibit the devadasi system. The Karnataka State Government has passed the Karnataka Devadasi (Prohibition of Dedication) Act, 1982, which declares that, the very act of dedicating girls (with or without the consent of the dedicated women) is illegal.

Andhra Pradesh

Similarly, the Andhra Pradesh Devadasi (Prohibition of Dedication) Act, 1989 declares that whosoever performs, promotes, abets, or takes part in a dedication ceremony is liable to punishment with three years imprisonment and fine.

Goa

The Goa Children's Act, 2003 provides for stong action against making children available for commercial sexual exploitation including posing obscenely, selling, or abetting sale of children even under the guise of adoption, or dedication of a girl child as a devadasi.

Despite constitutional provisions and legislation enacted by the Government banning some of these culturally sanctioned practices like *devadasi* and *jogin* systems, there has been no encouraging improvement in the situation.

REFERENCES

Singh, N.K. 1997. *Devadasis—Divine Prostitution,* New Delhi, APH Publishing Company.

Shankar, Jogan; 1994. *Devadasi Cult: A Sociological Analysis,* New Delhi, Ashish Publishing House.

Tarachand, K.C. 1991, *Devdasi Custom: Rural Social Structure and Flesh Markets;* New Delhi, Reliance Publishing House.

Trivedi, H.R. 1976. *Scheduled Caste Women : Studies in Exploitation,* New Delhi, Concept Publishing Company.

7

Combating Strategies

Introduction

The Action Research on Trafficking in Women and Children (ARTWC) has sought to demystify the problem of trafficking and analyse the factors and forces responsible for its continuation and perpetuation. During the research work, various issues that deserve immediate attention of all concerned were identified and analysed. In the light of the findings of the research work done some recommendations have been made for effectively combating and containing the problems of trafficking. For the convenience of readers this chapter has divided into two parts. Part one comprises general recommendations concerning prevention of trafficking; protection of victims and survivors; improvements in law enforcement. Part two comprises of changes proposed in ITPA.

PART-I

General Recommendations

Developing a Human Rights Perspective: To deal with the problem of trafficking effectively, prevalent, paternalistic 'law and order' perspective and moralistic welfare perspective have to be substituted by human rights' perspective, as trafficking involves primarily violation of human rights like, right to dignity and individuality, right to development and progress. Human rights approach is holistic. All policies, programmes and projects aimed to help the trafficked victims/survivors have to be based upon the human rights perspective. National Human Rights Commission and various State Human Rights Commissions should help in evolving strategies to bring about the paradigm shift.

Awareness Generation: Research has shown that, there are many myths and misconceptions as far as the definition, scope, causes of trafficking are concerned. There is an urgent need to create awareness not only among all the law enforcement agencies, judiciary but also all other agencies who either directly or indirectly have a role in dealing with the problem such as immigration authorities, NGOs, agencies involved in tourism etc. Awareness has to be generated among the personnel working in these agencies on issues like migration trafficking, smuggling and the correlationship of these phenomena etc.

Setting up of National Nodal Agency: Issues related to trafficking in women and children cut across many government departments, agencies. But so far the response from governmental agencies is segmented and often uni-dimensional. A nodal agency has to be set up by integrating anti-trafficking activities of Central and State governments, especially involving the DWCD (Department of Women and Child Development), Department of Labour, Social Justice, Health, Home, Tourism, Railways, Information and Broadcasting, Law and Justice, and agencies like NACO (National AIDS Control Organization) and the CBI (Central Bureau of Investigation). An MoU among these agencies on similar lines as that of MoU of Thailand has to be worked out for effective co-ordination among these agencies. Thailand government has established three types of MoU, namely:

1. MoUs among various related government agencies;
2. MoUs among various NGOs working on anti-trafficking issues; and
3. MoUs between government departments and NGOs in order to combat the problem of trafficking.

The national nodal agency can be set up by the DWCD, under the aegis of NHRC (National Human Rights

Commission). Many of the State Governments at the instance of NHRC have already earmarked two nodal officers in each state. Integrating them into the proposed national nodal agency could institutionalize the functioning of these nodal officers from all States. The National agency can function as the coordinator of all anti-trafficking activities. The national nodal agency also integrates the national network of NGOs. A concerned endeavour is called for to deal with the problem effectively.

Partnership of Government and Non-government Organizations

During the research it was observed that there is paucity of police personnel, especially female staff, and also resources for speedy disposal of repatriation cases and rehabilitation etc. So in order to effectively combat the problem of trafficking and to involve community in preventing the trafficking in women and children, government agencies can collaborate with NGOs in certain activities like setting up rescue homes, counseling and rehabilitation centres etc. The Andhra Pradesh model of co-management of rescue homes and co-ordination committees at state and district level is a good example to be replicated in other states. And also involving NGOs in repatriation process, as done in Tamil Nadu is a good practice. Notifying NGOs as stated under Section 13(3) of ITPA [Immoral Taffic (Prevention) Act] would strengthen the GO-NGO partnership. At present many States have not taken any initiative in this direction. The research findings indicate that it would be better if NGOs are notified at district level or at regional level so that their services are co-opted into law enforcement activities conducted locally.

National Network of NGOs

There are many NGOs working on various aspects of anti-trafficking all over the country. Some of the NGOs have setup networks of NGOs within the States, and across borders. For example, Sanlaap and SLARTC (Socio-Legal Aid Research and

Training Centre) from India, BNWLA (Bangladesh National Women Lawyers Association) from Bangladesh and Maiti from Nepal have set up a trans-border network. Similarly there are NGO networks like ATSEC (Action Against Trafficking and Sexual Exploitation of Children), and NASCET, which have established effective links. However majority of NGOs work in isolation and very often their activities overlap. Hence there is a need to integrate and co-ordinate the activities of all NGOs.

Bilateral Trans-border Co-operation

The jurisdiction limitations hinder the law enforcement and other concerned agencies from taking effective action to combat trafficking. This has become a serious impediment to trans-border anti-trafficking activities and programs. The SAARC convention envisages the setting up of a taskforce for dealing with trans-border trafficking. Since the Convention has now been ratified by all the member countries, taskforce can be set up. To start with informal networks including government officials and NGOs from both countries could be institutionalized so that they can carryout anti-trafficking activities effectively. Already some ad hoc taskforces or cross-border committees have been set up on the initiatives of local government or law enforcement agencies manning the border are in operation in many places along the border. SEVA—an NGO in Gorakhpur district in Uttar Pradesh lying on Indo-Nepal border has set up human rights awareness cells along the border.

Given the seriousness of the trans-border trafficking Ministry of Home Affairs has organized interface between law enforcement officials, NGOs etc. on various places on Indo-Napal border. In the year 2002, two meetings were organized by MHA for Indian officials and for appropriate authorities from Nepal on trans-border trafficking issues. Similar meetings were held with Bangladesh also.

Some other initiatives that can be taken are:

- Developing victim/witness protection protocols,

- Setting up of child help lines in the countries concerned so that trans-border issues of missing and trafficked children can be effectively attended to.

Setting up a Resource Centre on Anti-trafficking

One of the important findings of the ARTWAC is that, the information and knowledge pertaining to trafficking and related issues is scant and scarce. Although a plethora of conferences, seminars and workshops are being organized by a number of agencies. The information is not consolidated and not made easily available for decision-making. So to document and disseminate information in a more systematic way on a regular basis, there is an urgent need for setting up a national level resource centre, with assigned authority to collect, collate document and disseminate information. This could be set up in DWCD, or in NHRC or by an NGO dedicated to the cause. Similar resource centres could be set up at state level and all the state resource centres will be interlinked with national level resource centres and also with each other. Some of the activities taken up by these resource centres could be :

- Preparing databases of traffickers, exploiters at state, national and if possible at regional level.
- Preparing databases on best practices, models and important judgments of the courts.
- Hosting a web portal on trafficking, which can provide information on missing persons, intelligence and alert notices on suspected traffickers and other related information on trafficking.

Prevention of Trafficking

Vulnerability Mapping of Source and Demand Areas

For controlling and combating problem of trafficking, mapping of source and demand areas and conducting micro level studies is very essential. Because effective strategies can be devised only after understanding various factors that contribute to trafficking thoroughly. District officials with the help of NGOs working in the field are appropriate agencies to carry out mapping and micro level studies. Mapping has to be done not only from the point of law and order perspective but keeping all the parameters and dimensions in view. Since PRIs (Panchayati Raj Institution) have a major role to play in preventing trafficking in their respective panchayats, their services have to be utilized effectively. The initiatives of Tamil Nadu Government in involving PRIs could serve as model. In Tamil Nadu the village watchdog committees headed by the village panchayat president were constituted by the Tamil Nadu Government. These committees have members from NGOs and self help groups, who are active in that area. These committees help the concerned State Government departments in rehabilitating the victims, in mapping the vulnerable areas etc. The situation in Northeastern region of India demands special attention in and mapping of the vulnerable areas of demand source of this region.

Addressing the Vulnerabilities

Trafficking causes an exodus like situation for women and children from the economically and socially oppressed sections of the society and from areas affected by natural/man-made calamities. Lack of livelihood options, prevailing cultural practices, excessive poverty are driving the families from socially oppressed and economically weaker sections of the society to convert the girls child which is otherwise considered as a liability into an asset by selling her or abetting in trafficking her. These poor families thus get trapped by the lure created by traffickers and allow their girls and women to be trafficked. So strategies designed to prevent trafficking have to address these issues by:

- Designing development programmes specifically addressing the social and economic empowerment of vulnerable sections through education, public awareness campaigns and community involvement.

- By educating the adolescents, who are more prone to be trafficked about the sexuality, rights of women etc.
- Develop community values, which inculcate respect for women and girl child, and thereby discourage exploitation of women and children.
- Community policing initiatives are essential in preventing trafficking. As community is involved, the community can act as watchdog and keep track of potential traffickers, potential victims and help concerned agencies to take timely action. It also facilitates the police in getting the witnesses for rescue operations, and reuniting the rescued victims with their families, etc.
- Discourage communities in which CSE is a culturally sanctioned practice by providing alternative livelihood options.

Family, community, local government institutions such as PRIs, community based organizations, grassroots NGOs and even corporate houses all have a major role to play in preventing the trafficking in women and children.

Combating Sex Tourism

Government agencies including immigration authorities, corporates, hoteliers, travel and tour operators and other stakeholders have to be involved and encouraged to devise tourism promotion strategies aimed at controlling sex tourism and respecting the rights of women and children. Other State Government should also form legislation to combat sex tourism on the lines similar to Goa Children's Act, 2003.

Addressing Culturally Sanctioned Practices

In India there are still several culturally sanctioned practices which encourage trafficking in women and children and CSE. There is an urgent need for more social legislations like Devadasi (Prohibition of Dedication) Act, 1982 of Karnataka and Goa Children Act, 2003. Programmes to rehabilitate women and girls who have been trafficked and exploited needs to be given special attention. For effective intervention, initiatives taken by Delhi High Court, which had a positive influence on rehabilitation of girls from Bedia community in Rajasthan have to be replicated by other state governments.

Intervention to prevent Trans-border Trafficking

In Sonouli, a small village on the Indo-Nepal border an NGO called Manav Seva Sansthan "SEVA" in partnership with the police works for protecting the suspected trafficked victims. The volunteers of the NGO maintain a network of informers and also keep a vigil on the movements of people across the border. In case of suspicion or doubt, the volunteers intervene and invite the suspected trafficked victims to the centre and inform them about their rights. As a result of these interventions this NGO-police partnership in Sonouli could prevent and protect many innocent potential victims from falling prey to the traffickers. SEVA has also networked with its counterpart NGO called Maiti in Nepal and ensured that potential victims are not subjected to any further attempts of trafficking. More such initiatives from NGOs should be encouraged.

Protection of Victims and Survivors

Handbook of Dos and Don'ts and Setting up Minimum Standards for Rescue and Post Rescue Activities

The research brought out violation of the victims rights by Government and Non-Government agencies during and after rescue operations. In order to ensure that the human rights of the victims are protected a number of steps have to be taken:

- Police officials working in the field have to be provided with guidelines on dos and don'ts that are to be followed before, during and after rescue operations, to bring accountability to the police.

- Certain minimum standards have to be developed for care and protection of the victims during the rescue and post-rescue efforts.
- Since it is an important issuse affecting a larger community not only with in india, but across countries, regional protocols have to be developed.

Segregation of Victims and Exploiters

The research findings indicate that very often victims and exploiters are rounded up by the police (sometimes by NGOs also) and taken to the police station. They are kept together in police station while registering FIR and in the course of investigation and interview. As a result victims remain under constant threat from the exploiters, hence unable to reveal true facts to the investigating officers. There is a need to separate victims from the exploiters not only to protect the rights of the victims but also to elicit truth out from victims, which will help in prosecuting and punishing the exploiters and thereby controlling the problem of trafficking.

Legal Representation

The need for legal representation of rape victims, pointed out by the Supreme Court of India in the case of *Delhi Domestic Working Women's Forum* vs. *Union of India* [1995(1) SCC 14], becomes applicable to CSE workers also, as very often they are victims of rape. The services of the Free Legal Aid Authority can be extended to CSE workers also.

Rehabilitative Mechanisms

Rehabilitative Mechanisms have to be Holistic: The research surveys revealed that there is an acute shortage of medical and health care facilities including counselling for traumatized trafficked victims, shortage of CWCs (Child Welfare Committees), and shortage of human, and infrastructural resources in existing rescue homes etc. There is an urgent need to upgrade and improve:

- Medical care and attention of the rescued persons. Concerned health departments have to be sensitized to give attention to the health care of the rescued victims on a priority basis as it helps in investigation processes.
- Psychological counselling, by appointing trained professionals at every police station by networking with welfare departments and other agencies like CSWB (Central Social Welfare Board). Police departments can also set up family counselling centres in police stations. All the professionals appointed for providing trauma counselling have to be sensitized enough to deal with the trafficked victims. Training programmes organized by a Delhi-based NGO called Saarthak can be replicated.
- Communication protocols between rescue homes and police departments. There were instances of human rights violations during the rescue operations, due to inadequate communication between rescue homes and the police, as the former was unprepared to receive and accommodate large contingents of victims with short or no notice.
- CWCs, which are competent bodies to take care of the trafficked victims especially children. CWCs have to be linked with child help lines to provide speedier assistance. The research observed cases where due to lack of these facilities rescued children were produced before the magistrate and were denied the privileges due to them under the Juvenile Justice Act.

Persons requiring rehabilitation from CSE can broadly be categorized into three groups. The first group comprises newly trafficked women and children, who have to be rescued as early as possible and have to rehebilitated on a priority basis. Second group comprises those, who have been subjected to sexual exploitation for many years and now been condemned by the brothel owners. The people in this category usually live in utter poverty and disease due to lack of livelihood options. The third category includes middle-aged women, who continue to live in brothels due to lack of alternative income generating options. The rehabilitative strategies for each group should be differently devised by keeping the best interests of the victims based on the informed consent of victims/survivors.

Rehabilitation programmes have to be designed keeping the following points in consideration:

- Rehabilitation programmes have to be sustainable
- Micro credit and other facilities have to be made available to the victims
- Livelihood options have to based on marketable skills and knowledge
- Legal requirements of victims/survivors
- Rehabilitation programmes have to be made accessible to 'yet to be rescued' victims also
- Provide help lines etc., to victims
- Should include monitoring mechanisms by local administration to check re-trafficking of the rehabilitated people.

Protecting the Anonymity of Rescued Person: The provisions of 228A IPC and 22 Juvenile Justice Act have to be strictly adhered and any violation of these provisions have to be dealt with seriousness.

Law Enforcement Improvement Strategies

Increasing the Staff in Law Enforcement Agencies

The study revealed severe shortage of police personnel especially women police, as well as infrastructural resources to deal with the problem of trafficking. There is an urgent need for increasing the police staff at field level and for giving adequate importance and attention to the problem of infrastructural deficiencies.

Registration of Cases

Registering the cases of trafficking is first step towards prosecuting criminials involved in trafficking. Hence strict instructions have to be given to field staff of the law enforcement agencies to register all the cases of trafficking. Presently most often the cases are either under reported or non-reported. The community has to be sensitized to report the cases of trafficking to the police.

Proper use of Section 8 of ITPA

ARTWAC study found that the ITPA has not been implemented properly. Several sections, which deal with traffickers and other exploiters, are rarely utilized, whereas section 8 of the ITPA, wherein victims can be arrested, prosecuted and even convicted on the charge of soliciting, has been highly misused against the victims. The legal concept of *mens rea* has to be investigated and the person should not be chargesheeted or convicted if *mens rea* is lacking. A person who is made to solicit under force, duress, coercion, and threat cannot be charged with the offence of soliciting. There is no *mens rea*. If the investigation is perfunctory, the court can call for further investigation. This calls for greater sensitivity and accountability among all segments of the criminal justice system.

Justice Delivery

The research observed delays in justice delivery due to:

- Lack of any yardsticks in awarding sentences
- Delays in awarding compensation due to victim even after convicting the offenders
- Convictions not followed by closure of brothel or other such externment proceedings.

The redressal of victim grievances requires effective implementation of the law. The judicial pronouncements delivered by Delhi High Court and the Supreme Court of India has to be put to practice.

Human Rights Perspective in Law Enforcements: It was proven by the judicial interventions like that of Delhi High

Court, that it is possible to shift focus from punishing the victims to punishing the exploiters. To adopt the human rights approach in law enforcement, certain modifications have to be brought in the current practices of law enforcement like:

- Declaring trafficking offences as 'grave offences' or 'special report' crimes, which are to be supervised by the officer of the rank of SP/DCP and above.
- Fixing the accountability of the officers concerned for acts of commission and omission.
- Police and prosecution officials have to be sensitized.
- Activities and initiatives that uphold the right of women and children have to be publicly commended.
- Circulars and directives by the government and police chiefs have to be sent to concerned derpartments on these practices.
- Personnel belonging to district police, railway police, special outfits like CBI and CID have to be trained on a priority basis as they have an important role in controlling trafficking in women and children.

Conjunction of Juvenile Justice Act, Indian Penal Code and other Laws with ITPA: The lagislations which are currently in implementation, especially ITPA, Juvenile Justice Act have a lot of strength and scope for dealing with the offenders and providing justice to all victims. These existing laws can be used in conjunction with each other for example:

- Invoking Juvenile Justice Act if the victim appears to be of under 18 years age and is in need of care and protection under Juvenile Justice Act.
- Invoking Section 376 under IPC in cases where the victim is below 16 years of age and has been subjected to sexual assault.
- Invoking section 18 of the ITPA to close brothels and evict offenders.

This will help in condign punishment of the offenders.

Preventng Misuse of Local and Special Laws: There were instances where Section 110 of Mumbai Police Act, Section 95 of Delhi Police Act, and Section 145 of the Railways Act have been used against the victims. State police chiefs, and government should carry out social audits to find out the action taken by concerned police officials under these sections and to ensure that human rights of victims have been protected. NHRC may provide guidelines for compliance and respective State Human Rights Commissions could supervise that they have been followed.

Extending Investigations beyond Brothels: It is encouraging to notice that, there is an emerging trend of punishing the brothel owners and exploiters. However, investigations have to go beyond brothels, which are the most obvious sites of crime to reach the source of trafficking and to expose trafficking routes, crime syndicates and gangs involved etc. This calls for multi-disciplinary and in-depth approach. And efforts also have to be made to unearth illegal assets of the traffickers and to confiscate and forfeit these assets.

Organized Crime Approach: Trafficking is an established organized crime. Therefore, special provisions of the law should be brought in wherever appropriate. Many state governments have already enacted special laws to deal with various other organized crimes. Trafficking has to be brought under the ambit of such special laws.

National Database and Data Surveillance

For effective monitoring of trafficking cases, a national database on trafficking cases has to be developed. The database should have provisions to provide on various parameters like:

- Cases registered under various sections of ITPA, related sections of IPC and local laws as well as under the preventive sections of the Cr.P.C. (Criminal Procedure Code).
- Details of the cases registered, charge-sheeted, and convicted etc., total figures as well as break up of figures based on sex and age group of the offenders.
- Details on the number of rescued persons including sex and age-wise break up of rescued persons.
- Details of the person's repatriated/rehabilitated.

Surveillance of such data will help in effective monitoring of trafficking cases and also facilitate checking and controlling the human rights violations in the course of law enforcement. National Crime Records Bureau (NCRB)'s annual publication "Crime in India" should also reflect cases on trafficking in women and children as per the above mentioned details.

Setting up a National System of Intelligence Dissemination on Traffickers and Exploiters: At present there is no national criminal intelligence dissemination mechanism to share information among the affected countries and various states within the country. Some of the NGOs working on issues related to trafficking do have large databases, which can be used effectively by the police. However there is a need to set up a national criminal intelligence organization to collect, collate all connected data and then disseminate it to all concerned agencies. The initiative has to be taken by an appropriate law enforcement agency. Recently Delhi High Court acting on a public petition directed the CBI to start a cell in the criminal records of abductors and kidnappers. Similarly, DWCD authorized the CBI to investigate cases under the ITPA. Using these developments as catalysts, a national database on traffickers can be started by the CBI. The national system of nodal officers can be linked to this database at CBI.

Central Anti-trafficking Establishment

So far trafficking is not considered as a federal crime. As a result while dealing with trafficking cases restrictions of jurisdiction pose problems in investigative processes. Although as per Section 13(4) of the ITPA, the DWCD has notified all officers of the rank of Inspector and above of the CBI as the Trafficking Police Officers (CTPO). However for want of jurisdiction under Section 5/6 of the DSPE Act, CBI cannot *suo motu* take up crimes of trafficking for investigation, even if they have international ramifications. At the same time, the state police agencies do not have the wherewithal to carry out such inter-state/international investigations. Therefore, there is an urgent need to set up a national task force, duly empowered to take up the investigation of such crimes. It is important to note that the Supreme Court appreciated the CBI's role as nodal agency in *Gaurav Jain* vs. *Union of India* (1998 4 SCC 270), where the Supreme Court held that "the ground realities should be tapped with meaningful action imperatives, apart from the administrative action which aims at arresting the immoral traffic of women under the ITP Act through interstate or Interpol arrangements and the nodal agency like the CBI is charged to investigate and prevent such crimes." As the CBI has been notified by the DWCD, it would be preferable to have the CTPO establishement working under the Director of CBI. The CBI should be given contiguous powers of investigations in all the states at par with the Narcotics Control Bureau, which can take up any case of the NDPS Act in any state. The discretion of taking over the cases should be left to the Director of the CBI who will take decisions keeping in view the multi-state and international ramifications of the cases concerned. This calls for setting up of a special cell in the CBI. The CTPO officials need to be specially trained to deal with trafficking offences. The suggested national nodal agency and the national rapporteur should co-ordinate with the anti-trafficking establishment to function in sync and to avoid duplication of efforts.

Age Verification

To prevent and control the serious anomalies in establishing the age of the victim, the presumption of age at first sight should be drawn in favour of the victim/survivor. The interview of the survivor needs to be carried out by trained persons, who can help the survivors in determining the exact age. In all borderline cases police have to consult a CWC representative to determine the age of the victim.

Victim Assistance Programmes

While certain changes are under consideration in laws related to trafficking to incorporate specific provisions on the subject, even within the existing legislation, there is scope for extending assistance to victims such as:

- Section 327 of Cr.P.C. provides for an in-camera trial for rape and related offences;
- Section 357 of the Cr.P.C. provides compensation for the victim. These provisions should be invoked in appropriate cases to ensure victim's rights.

Setting up a Criminal Injuries Compensation Board: The Supreme Court has advised setting up a criminal injuries compensation board in *Delhi Domestic Women Workers' Forum* vs. *Union of India* case. Since most of the trafficked victims are without any financial support after being rescued, it is essential that they should be provided with resources to sustain themselves. The compensation to be imposed on the accused under Section 357 of the Cr.P.C. can come into effect only after the conviction of the accused. Board should be set up with adequate funds to provide for post-rescue assistance without waiting for the closure of the judicial trial. The Tamil Nadu Government has already set up a Social Defence Fund for giving financial assistance to the rescued victims. Andhra Pradesh Government has a scheme of financial help for all victims immediately after rescue. These models can be considered by other states also.

Video Conferencing

Very often it has been noticed that the trial judges are severely handicapped in disposing of the cases and awarding sentences to the accused due to:

- The reluctance of the trafficked victims to make statements in the court in the presence of the accused;
- The victims who have been rehabilitated in far off places cannot come as often necessary to the court at the time of trial. There are instances of girls rescued from Delhi brothels being rehabilitated in their native places in Bangladesh. In such situations the Delhi High Court's order on video conferencing if implemented properly can speed up the trial processes and also avoid repeated appearances of the victims in courts.

Nationality of Trafficked Victims

Nationality of the trafficked victims is a serious issue to be dealt with immediately. As far as trafficked victims from Nepal are concerned nationality has not been a problem so far. However, victims from Bangladesh are often convicted on the charges of illegal immigration under Section 14 of the Foreigners' Act. But in reality they had been lured by deceit, or coercion. So how can they be considered as illegal immigrants? There is a need to define the status of these victims to avoid prosecuting these victims for violating the provisions of the Passport Act or Foreigner's Act, till such time as they are required to stay in the country for purposes of the trial. Ministry of External Affairs, Ministry of Law and Justice and Ministry of Home Affairs have to pay attention to this issue.

Setting up District-level Monitoring Committees

To check trafficking at district or village level itself, it is advisable to set up district level monitoring committees comprising, members belonging to PRIs, NGOs and other professionals working in the field. The Tamil Nadu model where the monitoring committees have been formed even at village level can be followed.

Appointing Special Police Officers under the Juvenile Justice Act and the ITPA: As per the Juvenile Justice Act, 2000, special police officers are to be posted at all police stations and special cells to be constituted at the district level. Similarly, the ITPA authorizes District Magistrates to confer upon any retired police officer or military officer (not below the rank of inspector or commissioned officer respectively) all or any of the powers under the ITPA. ITPA also empowers the District Magistrates to identify competent personnel, especially women, train them and utilize their services in dealing with trafficking. However, most of the states in India have not taken any initiatives to appoint these special police officers. State government should implement these provisions without any further delay.

Strengthening the Prosecution System

Prosecution forms a major part in the justice delivery process. However there has been no attempt to keep the prosecutors updated with latest trends and developments in the justice delivery process. The prosecution system suffers from:

- Acute shortage of information resources including law books and copies of relevant judgments delivered by the Supreme Court and various High Courts.
- Lack of training programmes for the prosecutors except in few states.

The prosecution system can be strengthened by:

- Providing training to orient and sensitize prosecutors on human rights approach and by following the SLARTC, Kolkata experiment. Private lawyers can be encouraged to carryout prosecution work for the trafficked victims.

Coordinating Law Enforcement on Missing Persons

National Bureau of Missing Persons at NCRB, New Delhi has to be reorganized as a coordinating agency by linking it up with missing persons bureaus at state level and with other helplines.

The issue of missing person has to be given priority in law enforcement. All concerned agencies like MHA (Ministry of Home Affairs), Ministry of Social Justice and Empowerment, DWCD, Ministry of Information and Broadcasting, Department of Education, and other agencies like CBI, RPF, state police, GRP, NCRB as well as children's networks and other voluntary agencies have to come together to form suitable strategies to control and trace the missing persons especially, children and preventing the missing persons being trafficked.

Increasing the Involvement of DWCD in Monitoring

The ITPA comes under the purview of the DWCD. However, DWCD is not even a party to the several fora, where crimes related to trafficking are discussed. DWCD has to be actively involved in not only monitoring but also in developing working partnerships between law enforcement agencies, welfare and development departments and NGOs.

PART II

Background

The Immoral Traffic (Prevention) Act, 1956 was initially known as the Suppression of Immoral Traffic Act, 1956. In 1950 the Government of India ratified an International Convention of Immoral Traffic in Persons and the Exploitation of the Prostitution of Others. Under Article 23 of the Convention, trafficking in human beings is prohibited and contravention of the prohibition is an offence punishable by law. Under Article 35 such a law has to be passed by the Parliament as soon as may be after the commencement of the Constitution.

The Suppression of Immoral Traffic in Women and Girls' Bill having been passed by both houses of Parliament received the assent of President on 30th December, 1956. It came on the Statute Book as the Suppression of Immoral Traffic in Women and Girls Act, 1956 (104 of 1956). By section 3 of the Suppression of Immoral Traffic in Women and Girls (Amendment) Act, 1986 (44 of 1986) the nomenclature of the Act has been changed with effect from 26th January, 1987. Now it stands as THE IMMORAL TRAFFIC (PREVETION) ACT, 1956 (104 of 1956).

Reviewing the effectiveness of ITPA and suggesting further amendments was one of the objectives of the Action Research. For this purpose, the study team has conducted a series of activities like:

- Interviewing many police officials.
- Organizing focused group discussion of judicial officers under the aegis of NHRC.

- Organization of several training programmes of judicial officers in various parts of the country.
- Held group discussions with lawyers who are specifically working on ITPA.
- Review of literature on the subject.
- Studied the critical articles and comments written by eminent jurists.
- Review of the two draft legislations prepared by National Law School of India, Bangalore and the report prepared by the Lawyers' Collective in 2003.

Suggested Changes in the ITPA

The following changes and amendments in ITPA are considered necessary for effectively combating the problem of trafficking.

1. It would be appropriate if the existing law is replaced by a comprehensive law that covers all forms of trafficking. The emphasis of the proposed legislation should be on the process of trafficking, instead of the purpose of trafficking. Commercial Sexual Exploitation (CSE), will include brothel-based and non-brothel-based exploitation, paedophilia, pornography, cyber pornography, sex tourism, and sexual exploitation under the façade of massage parlours, beauty parlours, beer bars, and escort services etc. The other category includes other types of exploitation including camel jockeying, begging, forced delinquency, organ transplant by force, deceit, coercion or lure, false marriages, false adoptions as well as trafficking for labour in the field of industry, entertainment, domestic environment or any other exploitative situation.

2. There is a need to provide a legal definition to the term 'Trafficking'. This is missing from the existing Act. For defining trafficking some of the salient ingredients have to be kept in mind.

- Consent is immaterial for any person who is under 18 years of age.
- The definition should lay emphasis on exploitation, which could be physical, sexual or emotional.

- It should be all encompassing to include violation of human rights and dignity and should include even customary activities that are exploitative.
- It is also necessary to redefine brothel in view of the fact that commercial sexual exploitation of women and children has moved out of traditional brothels to places like beauty parlours, massage parlours, beer bars etc., all such places have to be brought under the ambit of the law.

Definition of the Child

The term 'child' should be redefined as in the Juvenile Justice Act, 2000 to include all persons who have not attained 18 years of age. The ITPA should be amended to provide for separate treatment (care and attention) of child victims and child offenders in tune with the Juvenile Justice Act, 2000.

Sections 2(f) ITPA

This section of the ITPA provides definitions for 'prostitution' and 'prostitute'. The definition should be amended to include both males and females.

Sections 3, 4, 5, 6 and 9

Provides punishment for keeping a brothel (Section 3), living on the earnings of prostitution (Section 4), procuring or inducing a person for the sake of prostitution (Section 5), detaining of persons in premises for carrying out prostitution (Section 6), seduction of person in custody (Section 9).

These sections should be made triable by sessions judge, with a minimum punishment of five years (wherever it is not provided for). The fine amount should be increased to a minimum of Rs. 25,000.

Section 4 ITPA

This section dealing with punishment for living on the earnings from prostitution should have a provision to ensure the welfare of the children of the person subjected to CSE, so that they are not victimized due to the fact that they are looked after by the mother from her earnings in the brothel.

Section 5 of the ITPA

Deals with procuring, inducing and taking persons for the sake of prostitution. This section should be more exhaustive, explicit and comprehensive. It should cover all types of trafficking and all types of associates, accomplices, financers, transporters, facilitators, promoters and exploiters within the ambit of the law. Section 5.1(b) of the ITPA talks about the intent of the person. This should be replaced with 'intent or knowledge', so that all these exploiters are brought to book.

Section 7

Provides punishment for the two categories of persons:

(a) Any person who carried on prostitution, and
(b) The person with whom such prostitution is carried on. The second category is applicable to the 'customers' or 'clientele'. As trafficking cannot be prevented unless deterrent action is taken against those who 'demand' such services, stringent punishment should be given to the 'customers'.

Section 8

Deals with seducing or soliciting for the purpose of prostitution. Very often trafficked victims are arrested and convicted on the charge of soliciting. There should be a provision, which explicitly states that a person under 18 years of age will not be liable to conviction at all under this section. The Immoral Traffic (Prevention) Amendment Bill, 2006 now before the President omits this section.

Notification of the Special Police Officer

Section 13(1) and Section 13(4) of the ITPA deal with special police officers and trafficking police officers. There should be a provision that such officers should be specially trained in women's and children's rights, human rights and the principles of Victimology. There should be mandatory training for SPOs before they are put on the job.

Section 15(4) of the ITPA

It authorizes the SPO to remove all persons found in brothels and other places where CSE is carried out. There should be a provision added to this section that, the police officer should ensure during such operation that, the rights of the persons being removed, including those of their children or wards, if any are protected against any violation whatsoever. After removal, the police officers should ensure that the rescued persons and their children/wards if any are given appropriate security and shelters, so that their rights are properly protected.

Section 15(5A)

This provides for the mandatory medical examination of the rescued persons for the purpose of determination of age, or detection of any injuries caused during sexual exploitation, and the presence of any STDs. Since the person has a right to decide whether he/she should be subjected to a HIV/AIDS test, which has been upheld by the Supreme Court ruling, so it is necessary to introduce appropriate changes in this section. Further a provision should be added section 15(5A) making it incumbent upon all doctor(s) to carry out tests without any loss of time and hand over all the reports to the investigating officer within a specified time frame.

Section 17(3)

Deals with the custody of rescued persons, lays down "a magistrate by making inquiry into a case under sub-section (2) pass order that deem proper for the safe custody of the persons". The following words should be added to this section 'a recognized rehabilitative institution.'

The Sunset Clause

There should be a 'sunset' clause—that the period of stay in the safe custody and other homes should be for a minimum period to be decided by the magistrate concerned. The magistrate should review the decision at regular intervals.

Section 17(5)

To make the involvement of the community mandatory in after care activities. This section says that a Magistrate may summon a panel of five persons. In this provision, the word 'may' be substituted by 'shall'.

Section 18

This has five sub-sections. A sixth sub-section may be added bringing in a provision for attachment/confiscation/seizure/sale of all the assets of the traffickers and other exploiters, movable or immovable, wherever they are, if acquired through any criminal act defined in the ITPA.

Section 19

This section is related to application by a person seeking permission for being kept in a protective home. This should be amended to authorize NGOs, or an advocate or any person working for the cause of victims of exploitation to file such an application.

Section 21

Authorizes the state government to set up protective homes. Besides establishing the corrective institutions, the state governments should recognize the 'appropriate agencies' to do the needful.

Extraterritorial Legislation

In accordance with the provisions of the UN Traficking Protocol as well as the Optional Protocol to the Convention on the Rights of Child (CRC), there is a need for extraterritorial legislation. An offence under this Act should have universal jurisdiction. A crime by anybody in India should be made triable in the country he/she belongs to. Similarly, any crime under this law, if committed by an Indian national anywhere in the world will be deemed to be an offence under this law and should be tried by any court in India (which is otherwise authorized to try an offence under this Act).

Counsellors

There is a need for legal provisions for providing one or two counsellors to assist the victim during legal proceedings. If the victim cannot afford to bear the expenses and no agency comes forward to help her, the court can order the district administration to bear the cost in this regard. Similarly the procedures for ensuring proper care and reception for the victims, especially in post-rescue situations need to be brought into the law.

Provisions for the Handicapped

There should be a specific provision in the law for offences against women and children who are handicapped. They should not only provide stringent punishment for the violators, but should shift the onus of defence onto the accused.

Guidelines

The law should mandate that the government brings out specific guidelines regarding tourism, hoteliering and other similar businesses, as well cyber sex, so as to ensure that women and children are not subjected to CSE and sex tourism.

Suggestions accepted in the Immoral Traffic (Prevention) Amendment Bill, 2006

The following suggestions are already incorporated in the latest Immoral Traffic (Prevention) Amendment Bill, 2006, which is before the President for his assent.

Section of 5(I) of the principal Act, relating to the punishment for sexual offences committed on a child says "Provided that if the person in respect of whom an offence committed under this section, is a child, the punishment provided under this sub-section shall extend to rigorous imprisonment for a term of not less than seven years but may extend to life."

New sections have been inserted under section 13A relating to Constitution of Central Authority and 13B relating to Constitution of State Authority.

13A(1) The Central Government may constitute an Authority for the purposes of effectively preventing and combating the offences of trafficking in persons.

(2) The members of the Authority shall be appointed by the Central Government and shall be of such number and chosen in such a manner as may be prescribed.

(3) The Chairperson of the Authority shall be one of the members appointed under sub-section (2) to be nominated by the Central Government.

(4) The term of office of the members of the Authority, the manner of filling vacancies among and the procedure to be followed in the discharge of their functions by the members shall be such as may be prescribed.

13B(1) The state government may constitute an Authority for the purposes of effectively preventing and combating the offences of trafficking in persons.

(2) The members of the Authority shall be appointed by the state government and shall be of such number and chosen in such a manner as may be prescribed.

(3) The Chairperson of the Authority shall be one of the members appointed under sub-section (2) to be nominated by the state government.

(4) The term of office of the members of the Authority, the manner of filling vacancies among and the procedure to be followed in the discharge of their functions by the members shall be such as may be prescribed.

Sections 8 and Section 20 of the Principal Act have been omitted.

8

Trafficking in Women and Children
Global Patterns

Trafficking of women and children into the sex trade and sweatshop labour is a burgeoning form of organized crime. This has developed in the recent years as the *"ominous flip side to globalization"*. The International Organization on Migration (IOM) estimates that global trafficking industry generates up to US$ 8 billion each year from what may be described as *"trade in misery"*. It has become one of the leading criminal enterprises of the early 21st century, affecting every country around the globe. It is estimated that between 600,000 and 800,000 people are trafficked across borders each year. And if trafficking within countries is included in world figures, official US estimates are that 2 to 4 million people are traffickied annually.[1] International Labour Office (ILO) estimates that there are some 12.3 million victims of forced labour at any given time. Of these victims, 80 per cent are thought to be women and 50 per cent are thought to be under 18 years of age.

Though trafficking affects virtually every country in the world, but normally the flow of trafficking is from less developed countries to developed and industrialized nations or towards neighbouring countries with marginally higher standards of living. Since trafficking is an underground criminal enterprise, there are no hard data and precise statistics on the extent of the problem and all estimates, by and large, are unreliable. The largest number of victims trafficked internationally are from South and South East Asia. The former Soviet Union has also become a new larger source for trafficking for prostitution and sex industry. Many people are also trafficked to Eastern Europe. Other source regions include Latin America, Caribbean and Africa. Most of the victims are sent to Asia, Middle East, Western Europe and North America. They end up in large cities, tourist resorts, or near military bases where the demand is highest.

Causes of Rise in Trafficking

Both demand and supply factors relentlessly drive the trafficking industry. Some key push factors are inadequate employment opportunities, lack of social safety net, globalization, feminization of poverty, rise in sex tourism etc. The globalization of the world economy has increased the movement of people across borders, legally or illegally, from poorer to wealthier countries. International organized crime has taken advantage of this free flow of people and services to further extend its own reach and operations. Other contributory factors include:

(a) Poor status of women in many societies—Many societies favour sons and look upon women as an economic burden.

(b) Chaos and dislocation caused by the collapse of communism in former Soviet Union and Eastern Europe as well as wars in former Yugoslavia. With the weakening of law enforcement systems in post-communist societies, criminal organizations have grown and involved themselves in the business of international trafficking.

(c) Large profit and low risk nature of operations encourage the operators—Many law-enforcement agencies and governments seek to downplay the nature and magnitude of the problem. In many countries there is a nexus between the police, other governmental agencies and traffickers. Many countries have also no specific laws to deal with trafficking in women and children.

(d) Due to priority given to checking illegal migration in many countries, trafficking is looked upon as a problem of illegal immigration. The victims are treated as criminals and often detained and punished.

Today many criminal organizations are closely involved in trafficking in women and children. International trafficking trade is highly organized, involving sophisticated international network of procurers, document-forgers, escorts, corrupt officials etc. Chinese, Asian, Central American, Russian and other former Soviet Union gangs are among the major traffickers of people. Russian gangs increasingly interact with local networks to provide transportation, safe houses, local contact and documentation. According to Global Survival Network, an NGO group, Russian traffickers can obtain false documentation in order to enable a minor to travel to destination countries to work as a prostitute from corrupt officials in the Ministry of Foreign Affairs for approximately $ 800[2].

The International Organization of Migration (IOM) reports that Russian organized crime groups control European Prostitution Industries such as those in Poland and Germany. One major Russian criminal syndicate *Mogilevich* owns nightclubs in Prague, Riga, and Kiev and are engaged in trafficking in women and children for forced prostitution in these clubs.

Regional Trends

But largest number of victims are trafficked from South-East Asia and South Asia. Thailand, Cambodia, Philippines, India have become popular destinations for the sex tourists including paedophiles from western countries, Japan and Australia. Japan is considered to be one of the largest markets for Asian women trafficked for sex[3]. Japanese organized crime syndicate *Yakuja* is now involved in a big way in trafficking in women. Local brokers approach women in their home countries and offer well paid jobs in legitimate professions abroad. Once in

Japan they are sent to their actual employers who have purchased rights from source-country brokers. Victims come mainly from Philippines and Thailand. Cross border trafficking is prevalent in the Mekong region of Thailand, Burma, Laos, Cambodia, Vietnam and Southern Yunan province of China. According to various NGO sources thousands of foreign women and children have been sold into the Thai sex industry since 1990 with most coming from Burma, Southeast China, Laos, Vietnam. Victims from South-East Asia are also sent to Western Europe, United States, Australia and Middle East.

In South Asia, Bangladesh and Nepal are the main source countries and India and Pakistan are the two important destination countries. Thousands of Nepalese girls are trafficked to India each year and sold for prostitution. Research on the trafficking of Nepalese women and girls into India points to around 5000 to 7000 Nepalese girls are yearly trafficked to India. They find entry in different brothels of the country. In the booklet *"Rape for Profit"*, Human Rights Watch, Asia, describes how the girls are tricked with promises of employment, prospects of false marriage etc. by pimps and traffickers.

Indo-Nepal border is a long and porous one with only 14 entry point along the entire stretch. This facilitates extensive illegal cross border movements. Under the 1950 Treaty with India there is no immigration control for Nepalese travelling or migrating to India so no records are maintained. A study done by the Asian Development Bank lists the districts through, which this movement takes place and identifies the major border regions used by traffickers between Nepal and India.

Similarly, thousands of women and children from Bangladesh are trafficked to India and Pakistan each year. Bangladesh has a 4156 km border with India. India has 20 official checkpoints maintained by the Border Security Force (BSF). The entire porous border is thinly guarded and BSF personnel dispersed over a long zigzag riverine area have not been effective in controlling illegal trans-border migration sustained by a well-organized bribe system. Once trafficked women enter India they are kept in West Bengal and Orissa. After being *"sorted and graded"* they are sold to pimps and sent to Kolkata, Delhi, Mumbai or Agra. Studies by Bangladesh National Women Lawyers Association (BNWLA) 1998 and Asian Development Bank (ADB) 2002[4] have listed the details of the trafficking groups in this area. The report of Asian Development Bank 2002 quotes SANLAAP[5] an NGO of Kolkata that of 10,000 women found in Kolkata brothels 70 per cent were from Bangladesh.

Debt Bondage

Women are often in debt bondage because money is withheld from the victims as payback for the purchase price. Bales, refers to these as *"contract slavery[6]"* which is extremely lucrative. Most of the victims get little money for sustenance and live on the tips received from the customers. This emotional and physical manipulation ensures complete domination of the traffickers over the victims. Rescued trafficked women also fear reprisals by the traffickers to whom they are indebted[7]. According to Amnesty International, Afghan women are sold to prostitution in Pakistan.

Australia has also become a prime source of sex tourists in Asia. The Philippines, Thailand, South Korea, Sri Lanka and Hong Kong are some of the important destinations for organized sex tours. International criminal organizations trafficked hundreds of Thai women to Australia for prostitution. However, Australia is now developing tougher laws including longer jail terms to stop the trafficking of Asian women to Australia[8].

Modus Operandi of the Traffickers

Modus operandi of the traffickers include promise for suitable employment, fake marriages and at times forcible kidnapping and abduction. The traffickers target people from refuge camps, girls from large and broken families and lure them with promise of better life abroad. Very often on arrival at the destination countries, travel documents are confiscated and victims are forced into prostitution and other similar labour exploitation where they are forced to work for unsustainably long hours. Women are very often controlled through rape, violence and threats of harming members of the family.

Situation in India

In India the most quoted figures showing the magnitude of prostitution are from Central Social Board Survey of India's six metropolitan cities in 1990. According to this study the total number of prostitutes in all the cities put together comes to between 70,000 to 100,000. But according to the 1992 estimates of *Association of the Rescue of Fallen Women,* there are 8 million prostitutes in India and another 7.5 million call girls.

An important feature of the trafficking network is an efficient coordination in what appears to be a fragmented process. The actors in trafficking network collaborate and protect one another. Persons who operate in the recruiting end often do not know the people or their activity in the receiving end. Each actor concentrates on his or her responsibility in a chain of activities involving recruitment, passage and placement in work places. Another principle of management in sex work is mobility. Women are rotated among different brothels at fixed periods. This has twin objectives. One is to disorient the women and second to prevent them from establishing long lasting contact with clients and seek their help.

Europe

The former Soviet Union and Central and Eastern Europe have replaced Asia as the main source of women trafficked to Western Europe. The victims come from Russia, Ukraine and other East European countries. Following the collapse of the old Soviet Union, trafficking in this region has become a serious problem as many criminal organizations have gravitated to this lucrative business. Russian crime groups have started taking over sex industry in a number of west European countries, and they are also active in parts of the United States[9]. Western European countries are also destination points for the victims from other parts of the world including Africa (Ghana, Nigeria, Morocco), Latin America (Brazil, Colombia and Dominican Republic) and South-East Asia (Philippine and Thailand)[10].

U.S.A.

As many as 17500 people are trafficked to the United States each year according to the recent Department of State estimates[11]. About half of the victims are forced to domestic servitude and sweatshop labour and the rest are forced into prostitution and sex industry. Women trafficked to United States mostly end up in larger cities in New York, Florida, North Carolina, Hawaii[12]. It is reported that Russian crime groups are actively involved in trafficking and controlling the sex industry in the United States. USA is also the major destination country for young children kidnapped and trafficked for adoption by couples unwilling to wait for a child to be adopted through legitimate procedures and agencies. The largest source country is Mexico. American men along with Europeans and Australians countries puts the largest groups of sex tourists in Central America (Costa Rica, Honduras), South East Asia (Philippines, Thailand) and South Asia (India, Sri Lanka). There are many companies who specialize in sex tours.

US Anti-Trafficking Legislation

On March 11, 1998, President Clinton issued directive establishing US Government-wide anti-trafficking strategies of prevention, protection and support of victims and prosecution of the traffickers. The strategy has both domestic as well as international components. On the domestic side, a Workers' Exploitation Task Force under the Department of Justice and Civil Rights was set up for investigating and prosecuting cases of exploitation and trafficking. In addition the Department of Justice reviewed existing US criminal laws and their enforcement to see if they adequately deal with the crime of trafficking. The US also passed the Victims of Trafficking and Violence Protection Act of 2000 along with miscellaneous anti-terrorist provisions (PL 106-386). Some of its key provisions are:

1. It directed the Secretary of State to provide an Annual Report listing countries that do and do not comply with minimum standards for the elimination of trafficking;
2. Called for measures to enhance economic opportunities for the trafficked victims as a method to deter trafficking and to increase public awareness, particularly among the potential victims of the dangers of trafficking and the protection available to the victims.
3. Amended the code to make funds derived from the sale of assets seized from and the traffickers available for victims assistance programme under this Act.

The State Department in its annual report on trafficking *"Trafficking in Persons"* June 2006, as mandated by P.L. 106-386 has focused on 158 countries. Thus a problem, which so long remained invisible, has been brought in the open. It reviews recent trends in trafficking and rates countries according to whether they meet minimum standards of anti-trafficking commitment and policies. In the report, countries are ranked in four groups. Countries not included are either not seen as having a significant trafficking problem as source, transit, or destination countries (meaning more than 100 cases per year) or there is insufficient information about their role.

Tier 1, is made up of countries deemed by the State Department to have a serious trafficking problem, but fully complying with the Act's minimum standards for the elimination of trafficking. Twenty-six countries are included.

Tier 2, as in past years, includes the largest number of countreis, 79 in 2006 (up from 77 in 2005), whose governments the State Department views as not fully complying with those standards but which are seen as making "significant efforts to bring themselves into compliance."

Tier 2 Watch list[13] was first added as a category in the 2004 report. In 2006, it is made up of 32 countries that are on the border between Tier 2 and Tier 3 (up from 27 in 2005). All except seven are new to the list from 2005. Fifteen were moved down from Tier 2. Seven were moved up from Tier 3.

In Tier 3 are those countries whose governments the State Department deems as not fully complying with those standards and not making significant efforts to do so. This group includes a total of 12 countries (down from 14 in 2005), but also includes six new countries—Belize, Iran, Laos, Syria, Uzbekistan and Zimbabwe. These countries are subject to possible US sanctions after October 1, 2006, if they have not improved their performance by them. Moved up from Tier 3 were eight countries—Bolivia, Combodia, Ecuador, Jamaica, Kuwait, Qatar, Togo and the United Arab Emirates. Ecuador was moved to Tier 2, the rest were placed on the Tier 2 Watch List. A number of these countries are on the list for their failure to address forced labour among foreign migrant workers.

NOTES

1. CRS Report for Congress, *Trafficking in Person: The U.S. and International Response*, July 7, 2006.
2. CRS Report for Congress, *Trafficking in Person: The U.S. and International Response*, July 7, 2006.
3. The Coalition against Trafficking in Women (CATW), *Trafficking in Women and Prostitution in Asia*, (http://www.catwinternational.org/). The CATW is an international NGO.
4. Combating Trafficking of Women and Children in South Asia—Synthesis paper for Bangladesh, Nepal, India.
5. Sanlaap—Child Prostitution in Calcutta—A situational analysis (1998).
6. Bales, Kevin, 1999, *Disposable People: New Slavery in the Global Economy*, California: University of California Press.
7. Raymond, Jancie *et al.*, 2002. *A Comparative Study of Women Trafficked in the Migration Process*. New York: CATW International.
8. Maria Moscaritolo, "Australia takes aim at Asian sex slave trade," *Reuters*, May 26, 1998.
9. World Congress Against Commercial Sexual Exploitation of Children, Regional Profiles.

10. CRS Report for Congress, *Trafficking in Person: The U.S. and International Response,* July 7, 2006.
11. U.S. Department of State. *Trafficking in Persons Report, 2005,* June 3, 2005.
12. U.S. Department of State Bureau of Consular Affairs, Nov./Dec. 1997.
13. The Tier 2 Watch List of countries include Algeria, Argentina, Armenia, Bahrain, Bolivia, Brazil, Cambodia, Central African Republic, China, Cyprus, Djibouti, Egypt, Equatorial Guinea, India, Indonesia, Israel, Jamaica, Kenya, Kuwait, Libya, Macao, Malaysia, Mauritania, Mexico, Oman, Peru, Qatar, Russia, South Africa, Taiwan, Togo and the United Arab Emirates.

9

Trafficking and International Response

Trafficking in persons is a global phenomenon of large-scale proportions. Incidents of trafficking have been reported in all regions of the world, and, while the number of persons trafficked each year is impossible to determine, estimates range from hundreds of thousands to millions of victims worldwide. The magnitude of the problem can well be understood by the revenues the global trafficking industry generates in a year. According to the estimates of International Labour Organization, trafficking in women and children generates revenue up to US $8 billion per year. Trafficking cuts across all nations, state and regional borders. Trafficking in persons as a global phenomenon has drawn attention of all the countries of the world. Since late 1990s various countries and international organizations have taken note of this human rights violation, and efforts are underway in domestic, regional, and international fora to address the problem and define appropriate state responses. This chapter discusses in bref the response of international organizations to the problem of trafficking.

U.S. RESPONSE

The Department of State of the United States of America began monitoring trafficking in persons in 1994. Since then the U.S. has initiated many international anti-trafficking and development programmes to assist countries to combat this ever-growing phenomenon including disseminating information on the dangers of trafficking, strengthening the capacity of women's and anti-trafficking organizations to protect those groups from abuse and violence, and outreach and economic opportunity programmes for those at the risk of being trafficked. The U.S. has assisted countries to enact anti-trafficking legislation, and train law enforcement, judicial officers, and prosecutors.

U.S. Department of State officials developed a rigorous methodology to compile the three lists of countries. For each country, this determination depended upon whether or not it is "a country of origin, transit, or destination for a significant number of victims" of trafficking.

As a second step, countries that have a "significant number" of victims were then placed into one of the report's three tiers based upon these countries governments' efforts to combat trafficking. In accordance with the Act, P.L. 106-386 countries whose governments fully comply with the Act's minimum standards for the elimination of trafficking were placed in tier 1 countries whose governments do not fully comply with those standards were then placed, in tier 2 if they are making "significant efforts to bring themselves into compliance" with the standards, or in tier 3 if they are not. Each tier encompasses a wide range of countries.

Minimum standards for the elimination of trafficking defined in the Act P.L. 106-386 are:

- The Government should prohibit trafficking and punish acts of trafficking.
- The Government should prescribe punishment commensurate with that for grave crimes, such as forcible sexual assault, for the knowing commission of trafficking in some of its most reprehensible forms (trafficking for sexual purposes, trafficking involving rape or kidnapping, or trafficking that causes a death).
- For knowing commission of any act of trafficking, the Government should prescribe punishment that is sufficiently stringent to deter, and that adequately reflects the offence's heinous nature.
- The Government should make serious and sustained efforts to eliminate trafficking.

The seven criteria set out by the Act as indicators of serious and sustained efforts of Governments to eliminate trafficking are:

- Whether the Government vigorously investigates and prosecutes acts of trafficking within its territory.
- Whether the Government protects victims of trafficking, encourages victims' assistance in investigation and prosecution, provides victims with legal alternatives to their removal to countries where they would face retribution or hardship, and ensures that victims are not inappropriately penalized solely for unlawful acts as a direct result of being trafficked.
- Whether the Government has adopted measures, such as public education, to prevent trafficking.
- Whether the Government cooperates with other governments in investigating and prosecuting trafficking.
- Whether the Government extradites persons charged with trafficking as it does with other serious crimes.
- Whether the Government monitors immigration and emigration patterns for evidence of trafficking, and whether law enforcement agencies respond appropriately.
- Whether the Government vigorously investigates and prosecutes public officials who participate in trafficking, and takes all appropriate measures against such officials who condone trafficking.

According to the Act, beginning with the 2003 report, countries on the Tier 3 list will be subjected to certain sanctions, principally termination of non-humanitarian, non-trade-related assistance. Such countries would also face U.S. opposition to assistance (except for humanitarian, trade-related, and certain development-related assistance) from international financial institutions, specifically the International Monetary Fund and multilateral development banks such as the World Bank. Certain of the sanctions may be waived under certain circumstances, including upon a national interest determination by the President.

However, there is lot of criticism regarding the ranking of the countries. For instance Russia sharply condemned for placing her in the worst offenders list. Greece and Turkey claim that the U.S. has not taken into consideration many of the initiatives started by those countries. Human Rights Watch is of the opinion that certain countries were given too much credit, according to the Human Rights Watch both the countries Japan and Pakistan should be in Tier 3.

The United States is also working with the European Union, the Group of eight, the United Nations and the Organization for Security and Cooperation in Europe (OSCE). Currently the United States is supporting around 110 programmes in 50 countries to combat trafficking.

RESPONSE BY VARIOUS INTERNATIONAL ORGANIZATIONS

International Labour Organization (ILO)

ILO is committed to eradicate child trafficking through its "Forced Labour Convention", which confirms child trafficking as practice similar to slavery and calls for countries to take immediate steps to secure the prohibition and elimination of the worst forms of child labour. Since 1992 guided by the United Nations' Convention on the Rights of the Child and ILO Convention 182. A special programme titled "International Programme for the Elimination of Child Labour (IPEC)" has been undertaken by ILO. IPEC aims to eliminate trafficking of children by addressing its root causes.

UNICEF

UNICEF's response on trafficking in children focuses on four areas, namely raising awareness, providing economic support to families, improving access to and quality education and advocacy for the rights of the child.

Standards devised by the CRC are the main guidelines for all the policies devised by UNICEF. UNICEF is working for elimination of child labour in India by giving support to the Government and NGOs working on child rights issues. UNICEF is active in organizing regional workshops as a measure to address the problem of child prostitution and trafficking. It is coordinating with the National Human Rights Commission in formulating a policy on child trafficking.

The UN Office on Drugs and Crime (UNODC)

This UN Office which is responsible for crime prevention, criminal justice and criminal law reforms pays special attention to combating organized transnational crime, illicit trafficking in human beings.

To combat the threats that have come along with the benefits of globalization, the United Nations Office on Drugs and Crime has assembled teams of specialists working on the provision of assistance to countries in countering a series of identified global threats. Termed, 'Global Programmes', these are designed as focused entities striving to implement high quality technical assistance in their respective areas. Such programmes also have a strong normantive element, drawing lessons from both their own and others' experiences, disseminating this information as "best practice" to users across the world.

The focus of these global programmes is to mirror the current policy agenda of Member States, expressed in United Nations Conventions and Protocols. Thus, the global programmes are dedicated to the implementation of the Drugs Control Convention of 1988, the Convention against Transnational Organized Crime, the protocol against trafficking in persons, the anti-money-laundering provisions in Drugs and Crime Conventions.

The Global Programme Against Trafficking in Human Beings (GPAT) launched in 1999 in collaboration with the United Nations Inter-Regional Crime and Justice Research Institute (UNIRCJRI) assists the member states in their efforts to combat trafficking in human beings. It highlights the involvement of organized criminal groups in human trafficking and promotes the development of effective ways of cracking down on the perpetrators.

The Programme aims to:

- Advise on drafting and revising relevant legislation.
- Provide advice and assistance on establishing and strengthening anti-trafficking offices and units.
- Train law enforcement officers, prosecutors and judges.
- Strengthen victim and witness support.
- Promote awareness raising.

The Programme's key components are assessment and technical cooperation. The activities include analyzing the trafficking situation and involvement of organized crime groups, strengthening criminal justice responses, improving cooperation among law enforcement agencies and other relevant institutions, and improving protection and support systems for victims and witnesses. The Programme promotes a comprehensive and multi-disciplinary approach in preventing and combating human trafficking. Within this context, the Programme focuses on the criminal justice component of trafficking, including victim support and witness protection, complementing the work of other entities of the UN system.

Assessment

The assessment component includes data collection on various trafficking routes and the methods used by organized criminal groups in trafficking. Countries involved in the Programme are selected from Asia, Europe, Africa and Latin America and are assessed according to:

- Trafficking routes and forms of exploitation of trafficked people.
- Cooperation among law enforcement, prosecution and judiciary.

- Government efforts to respond, including recent legislative refroms.

Technical Cooperation

Technical cooperation projects have been initiated in Asia, Central and Eastern Europe, Latin America and West Africa. Specific intervention measures are being introduced that are designed to strengthen the capacity to combat different forms of trafficking at the national and international levels. These measures will assist countries of origin, transit and destination to develop joint strategies and practical programmes.

The Office of the High Commissioner for Human Rights (OHCHR)

Since 1998, the OHCHR has been very keen on combating the problem of trafficking in human beings in general and trafficking in women and children in particular. The High Commissioner has given high priority to the issue of trafficking and taken concrete steps such as allocation of additional human and financial resources to tackle the problem. The OHCHR adopted a two-pronged approach to address the issue. Fristly, the Office continues to enhance the quality of its support to the relevant mechanisms dealing with trafficking and related exploitation. Secondly, it has developed an anti-trafficking programme. The Programmes of OHCHR are based on two fundamental principles, namely: human rights must be at the core of any creditable anti-trafficking strategy and such strategies must be developed and implemented from the perspective of those who need most to have their rights protected and promoted.

Appointment of Special Rapporteurs

In 2004 at its sixtieth session, the Commission on Human Rights adopted a decision 2004/110, by which it decided to appoint, for a three-year period, a Special Rapporteur on trafficking in persons, especially women and children to focus on the human rights aspects of the victims of trafficking in persons. The Commission invited the Special Rapporteur to submit annual reports to the Commission together with recommendations on measures required to uphold and protect the human rights of the victims.

In 1990, due to increased international awareness of the commercial sexual exploitation and sale of children, the United Nations Commission on Human Rights created the mandate of the Special Rapporteur on the sale of children, child prostitution and child pornography. The mandate-holder is required to investigate the exploitation of children around the world and to submit reports on the findings to the General Assembly and the Commission on Human Rights, making recommendations for the protection of the rights of the children concerned. These recommendations are targeted primarily at Governments, other United Nations bodies and non-governmental organizations.

To strengthen the efforts of its different offices, the OHCHR has developed a system of intra-office coordination on the issue of trafficking and thus enhanced the links between the various mechanisms and among officials working on those mechanisms.

United Nations Development Fund for Women (UNIFEM)

UNIFEM's core agenda is to promote women's human rights, political participation and economic security. Since 1991 UNIFEM is addressing the issue of trafficking in women and children. Trafficking was identified as a special area of concern at UNIFEM's First Ministerial-Level Regional Biennial Review of the Beijing PFA in South Asia in 1996. Since then UNIFEM's regional anti-trafficking programmes are focusing on the following areas:

- Increasing political and community support at different levels in high-risk (both source and destination) areas,
- Increasing the use of reliable data and research findings in advocacy, protective and prosecution work,

- Improving monitoring and lobbying for implementation of conventions and laws etc.,
- Bringing together different alliances and networks, and
- Enhancing the understanding and focus on trafficking.

United Nations Economic and Social Commission for Asia and Pacific (UNESCAP)

UNESCAP has brought out a detailed resource guide titled "Combating Human Trafficking in Asia: A Resource Guide to International and Regional Legal Instruments, Political Comments and Recommendations". The publication provides a comprehensive framework for using legal and other instruments in combating human trafficking, especially women and children. The resource guide suggests a multifaceted response to tackle trafficking, which is multi-dimensional.

UNAIDS

UNAIDS—A global programme of United Nations on HIV/AIDS has recognized trafficked persons as a group, which is highly vulnerable to HIV/AIDS as they are often subjected to multitude of physical and psychological health problems. Trafficked women especially are vulnerable to various reproductive and other gender specific problems as they have little or no access to reproductive health care. Therefore, UNAIDS has an integrated anti-trafficking programme called Reach—beyond Borders—a consolidated UNDP special initiative for South and North East Asia covering 13 countries of the region: Afghanistan, Bangladesh, Bhutan, China, DPR Korea, India, Iran, Maldives, Mongolia, Nepal, Pakistan, the Republic of Korea and Sri Lanka in an effort to control the spread of the disease in this region.

United States Agency for International Development (USAID)

The USAID provides economic and humanitarian assistance in more than 100 countries. USAID has taken up trafficking in persons as an important area of concern and prepares the annual report on trafficking in persons required by the legislation—Trafficking Victims Protection Act, 2000 of the U.S.A.

In South Asia, USAID has a special programme called South Asian Regional Initiative—Women's and Children's Equity Programme (SARIQ) to combat the problem of trafficking in women and children.

In India, the USAID/India anti-trafficking programme is implemented in collaboration with UNIFEM. USAID provides grant support to the policy planning process within government agencies to implement the National Plan of Action, capacity building for NGOs, rehabilitation of children of sex workers through education, piloting of community based actions and advocacy.

Asia Foundation

The Asia Foundation is a non-profit, non-governmental organization committed to the development of a peaceful, prosperous, just, and open Asia-Pacific region. The Foundation supports programmes in Asia that help improved governance and law, economic reform and development, women's empowerment, and international relations. The Asia Foundation is actively engaged in the fight against human trafficking in Asia for more than a decade. In addition to targeted programmes at a regional level, the Foundation supports policy-makers, counter-trafficking practitioners, and vulnerable communities to plan and execute local, national, bilateral, and regional initiatives to combat human trafficking in eleven source, transit, and destination countries throughout Asia including Combodia, East Timor, Indonesia, Laos, the Philippines, Thailand, Vietnam, Bangladesh, Nepal, Japan, and Mongolia.

The Foundation's counter-trafficking programmes centre on the achievement of four major strategic objectives:

1. Preventing human trafficking and exploitation;

2. Improving and institutionalizing systems for effective law enforcement and prosecution;
3. Enhancing services and protection for survivors of human trafficking; and
4. Developing and strengthening cross-border and regional coordination.

Plan International

Plan International is an NGO working for children on the guidelines provided by convention on Rights of Child (CRC). Plan works in 12 Asian countries, under the following issues like:

- *Building Relationships*: Creating a worldwide community working to improve children's lives.
- *Livelihood*: Working out ways for families to improve their income.
- *Habitat*: Improving living conditions to provide a safe environment for all.
- *Education*: All children, young people and adults deserve access to learning and life skills that enable them to realize their potential.
- *Health*: Everyone has the right to grow up healthy.

Child trafficking is perceived as a grave concern by Plan and to increase awareness on this issue, Plan works with local NGOs organizes community meetings, and conducts sessions for school children to educate—how trafficking takes place.

UN Interagency Initiative on Trafficking in Nepal

The United Nations System (UNS) comprising of UNDP, UNICEF, UNFPA, ILO, UNIFEM, OHCHR, UNHSTF and NORAD in collaboration with the Ministry of Women, Children and Social Welfare (MWCSW), of His Majesty's Government of Nepal has started a joint innovative programme called "Beyond Trafficking—A joint initiative in the millennium against trafficking in Girls and Women (JIT)" to reduce the incidence of trafficking in women and children. The programme was launched in 2000. JIT is operational at district, national and cross-border levels. The focus of JIT to prevent trafficking by addressing the conditions that allow trafficking to occur such as gender discrimination and inequalities etc. It focuses on highlighting the violations of rights of women and children in order to galvanize both public and state commitment to address the problem.

Population Council

The Population Council is an international research organization working on issues like biomedical, population and social policy, reproductive health, family planning and HIV/AIDS. The Population Council conducts research in more than 70 countries in collaboration with national and state governments, institutions and non-governmental organisations.

The Population Council is working on trafficking in women and girls as one of its responses to the HIV/AIDS epidemic in South and East Asia. The topics of research include:

- Preventing trafficking in women and children
- Providing care and support for trafficked victims
- Facilitating community mobilization among the victims of CSE (Commercial Sexual Exploitation) to encourage the use of condoms and building skills of alternative income generation etc.

10

Tourism and Trafficking

Introduction

For the last few years India is witnessing a tourism boom. A study conducted by the Centre for Monitoring Indian Economy (CMIE) shows that the number of tourists visiting India is steadily growing up. Foreign exchange earnings from inbound tourists has gone up from US$2443 million (1999-2000) to US$2717 million (2000-2001). According to one estimate, by 2020, 40 million tourists are expected to visit India, constituting 4 per cent of world's tourism traffic.

Tourism has both positive as well as negative impacts on Indian society. Tourism helps development, brings foreign exchange and facilitates cultural exchange and integration. At the same time tourism provides anonymity and opportunity for various illegal acts. When the tourist is in a foreign land, the anonymity obtained relieves him from many social and legal constraints that he faces in his own country. A Japanese proverb quotes "a traveller knows no shame, away from home he becomes less moral." Anonymity enjoyed by the tourists coupled with the desire for leisure and fun, and the poverty and unemployment of the local people has contributed to the growth of what has come to be called as sex tourism. Not all tourists are sex tourists, but some of them definitely are. There is growing evidence that over the last few years increasing numbers of sex offenders go to the less developed countries, as a result of increase in vigilance and action in their own countries.

Some of the Reasons for Growing Sex Tourism

Consumerist behaviour based on the purchasing power: Research conducted on the psychology and behaviour of some of the Western and Japanese men reveal that these people enjoy playing the colonial lord and master. For them the attraction of sex tourism is the master and servant relationship they can experience between the man and the woman. Very often the German men who visit Thailand as sex tourists command the Thai girls to clean their cottages, feed them through out the day and serve them as slaves. Sex often plays a secondary role (Mies, 1993).

Suppressed Feelings and Frustrations: Men in developed countries are unable to develop healthy, egalitarian, and loving relationships with women who are equally educated and economically independent. As a result, they are on the look out for women from underdeveloped countries, who are economically, and politically weaker and who are dependent on them and whom they can control and command.

Socialization of Male Violence against Women: Which results in men viewing prostitution as a matter of choice but not as exploitation. And also male gender constructs which uphold men sexual bravado and exploits, as indication of their masculine identity.

Anonymity and Privacy: Anonymity and privacy enjoyed by foreign tourists encourage them to indulge in these acts in destination countries as they believe that they will not be held responsible for their behaviour in a new country. And also they are free from the social and moral constraints of their home countries.

Mistaken Notions about Sexually Transmitted Diseases and HIV/AIDS: There are many misconceptions among foreign tourists that children are less likely to have contracted sexually transmitted diseases, hence it is safe to have sex with children and another prevalent misconception is that HIV/AIDs can be cured by having sex with virgin girls.

Government's Apathy: Governments of many developing countries turn a blind eye to the growing menace of sex tourism as it promotes tourism industry and also the economy of the country.

Some of the Destination Countries in Asia

Thailand

Thailand is one of the major destination countries for sex tourism in Asia. Majority of sex workers in Thailand come from poor, rural families of the country's north and northeast regions. Child prostitution is a problem, which the Thai Government is aware of and there are severe penalties for anyone caught having sex with someone under the legal age limit. Thailand has a booming sex industry, which draws tens of thousands of sex tourists to the country each year. Sex in Thailand is "Big Business" and although "Prostitution is illegal", the laws are rarely enforced.

According to the Thailand Government Public Health Department, there are approximately 75,000 prostitutes in Thailand (Bangkok Post, 1995). However, several well-informed non-governmental organization (NGO) groups estimate that the number of prostitutes at any given time is close to 2 million. This figure represents 9 per cent of female adult population and 3.15 per cent of total population. The figures would go up to many millions, if they include the owners, managers, pimps and other employees of the sex establishments, the related entertainment industry and some segments of the tourism industry, the number of workers earning a living directly or indirectly from prostitution.

Philippines

Catch-Wise (Consortium Against Trafficking of Children and Women in Sexual Exploitation) an organization working on anti-child trafficking reports that Philippines is not only considered fourth among the nine nations with 60,000 to 100,000 children in prostitution, but also identified as source transit and destination country for internationally trafficked persons (Mosqueda Jr. 2005).

Cambodia

There is growing interest in Cambodia as a vacation destination. But Cambodia also is a destination for thousands of men from around the world seeking sex with children. As other developing countries such as Thailand make progress in reducing sex tourism, opportunistic men simply travel to poorer, less-developed neighbouring countries. One-third of all sex workers in the country are estimated to be children, mostly ages 12 to 17, but some even younger (Niron *et al.* 2001).

In a recent survey in conjunction with Cambodia's Tourism Ministry and its National Council for Children, World Vision found that 45 per cent of Cambodian travel agents said they had seen tour guides supply children to foreign visitors. More than 70 per cent of children surveyed around Angkor Wat and nearby towns said that tourists had approached them for sex.

Sri Lanka

Although well-known that commercial sexual exploitation of children (CSEQ) exists in Sri Lanka, its extent, the number of victims and offenders are relatively unknown. Reported figures of the number of child sex workers vary from around 10,000 to over 30,000.

Sexual abuse and exploitation of children is a phenomenon that only recently has emerged to the surface in Sri Lanka. Most of them boys in the 7 to 16 age group. Although young girls do work as prostitutes, prostitution of girls is not an organized trade as that of boys. In a society where strong patriarchal values keep women and girls under control, and men and boys have greater freedom of movement, it is perhaps inevitable that prostitution of boys is the faster developing trade in the sex industry.

Prostitution is illegal in Sri Lanka and has not become as developed an employment source as it is in Thailand or Philippines. Female prostitutes operate undercover with a network of exploitative agents, pimps, and taxi drivers who take a significant share of their earnings. The big hotels in

Colombo and other cities have sophisticated systems of providing their clients with these services.

India

In India, the child sex tourism has assumed serious dimensions. Goa, a small state on the west coast of India, Kerala and Puri in Orissa state have become hot spots for sex tourism. According to a study conducted by DARSHAN—an NGO group, Kerala Women's Commission received numerous complaints from women tourists about sex tourism in Kovalam (one of the famous beach resorts in Kerala). The NGO group also rescued 11 girls belonging to Lambada—a tribal community from Karnataka. Brothels in Kovalam also arrange for package tours to tourist destinations for their customers. DARSHAN's study also reports that there are instances where hoteliers in tourist places like Quillion, Alleppy, Ernakulam in Kerala promote sex tourism. In places like Alleppy, tourists come and stay in houseboats and sex tourism in houseboats has become a new and thriving concept in Kerala.

A study conducted by two Mumbai-based NGOs viz. Save Our Sisters (SOS) and VEDH reveals that there are about one-lakh bar girls in Greater Mumbai alone. Most of the girls come from Bangladesh, Nepal, as well as different cities of India. Though many of the girls initially join the bars as dancers or waiters in the bar, many of them become victims of sexual exploitation—fallout of globalization and tourism promotion.

A study titled "Tourism related sexual exploitation of children in the Eastern coast of India" carried by Equations, a Bangalore-based NGO explains that most of the children are trafficked from places nearer to the tourist locations. Often these children accompany tourists on their visits to nearby states. For instance children from Puri, a tourist destination in Orissa is often taken to Hyderabad by tourists.

Paedophilia and Child Pornography

Paedophilia and child pornography are inter-linked and thriving because of the involvement of highly organized criminal networks (Desai, 2001). At the outset both these nefarious activities may appear to be different. However, closer observation reveals that paedophiles and child pornographers follow a well-established *modus operandi* in their activities. The research conducted on paedophilia and child pornography highlights some of the pretexts adopted by the criminals to trap their victims.

Running an Orphanage

In a well-publicized case in Tamil Nadu, a Swami of a religious sect was carrying on the racket of paedophilia under the disguise of running an orphanage built within a huge campus. The Swamiji used to regularly abuse and exploit the residents of his orphanage. The criminal activities of the Swamiji were brought to light by the police who raided the premises based on a complaint lodged by a child who somehow managed to escape from the orphanage.

Good Samaritan

Most of the foreign nationals who were involved in paedophilia and child pornography, project themselves as 'good Samaritan', coming from a developed country to help the poor children in the developing countries. As a means to prey upon their victims, these foreign nationals set up an orphanage in some of the tourist cities, and carry out their activities under the cover of orphanage. In one of such cases Mr. Hill Heum, a Dutch national had come to visit India and set up an orphanage called 'Little Home' in Poonjeri a small village nearer to Mahabalipuram—a tourist place famous for its south Indian temple architecture, in Kanchipuram district in Tamil Nadu. There were altogether 42 children (19 girls and 23 boys) in his orphanage aged between 10-20 years. Heum used to sexually abuse the inmates of the orphanage after sedating them by administering drugs. His crimes were exposed when a child from his orphanage had managed to escape and lodged a complaint with the Tamil Nadu police. The investigation revealed that his wife was a partner in his crimes and they were successful in carrying out these activities for about eight years. Apart from sexually abusing the children himself Heum entertained many foreign nationals at the orphanage by allowing them to sexually abuse the children.

Another racket of sex tourism under the guise of providing shelther to young homeless boys and girls was brought to light by the efforts of Ms. Sheila Barse, a Mumbai-based social worker and Lawyer. Mr. Freddy Peats was a foreign national operating in Goa since 1980 without arousing any suspicion. He was respected by everybody in the locality he was living as he was providing shelter to its orphans. However police discovered during the investigation of his premises more than 2000 photographs of nude children, some of the photographs were taken while the children were engaged in sexual acts. The investigations also revealed the involvement of paedophiles from Australia, Sweden, France and Germany. Mr. Peats was convicted and sentenced to long-term imprisonment. Mr. Peats used to keep his victims under control not only by coercion but also by deceit. He used to brainwash the children to accept sexual activities as normal.

Films and Documentaries

Another common pretext by which the paedophiles and child pornographers pray upon their victims is producing films and documentaries. Foreign tourists posing as the producers of documentary films frequent the destination locations, they get befriended with street children and children coming from poor families by offering them chocolates, toys and gifts. The strategies followed by these people came to light when the Mumbai police arrested a Swiss couple involved in the child pornography racket. When police raided the hotel in which the couple was staying on the information given by FACSE—a Mumbai based NGO working against the sexual exploitation of children, the police caught the husband red-handed and his wife while recording the whole process in a camera. The laptops confiscated from the hotel room revealed that the couple regularly visit India and other Asian countries with the intention of making pcornographic films, which they used to circulate in the market.

Unearthing of such child sexual exploitation cases revealed that:

- The peadophiles procure children with the help of beach boys, or former victims of child sex tourism.
- Most of the children come from poor families living in and around beach areas, children belonging to migrant labour etc.
- Children are engaged in sexual activities in the name of playing games, or by disguising it as method of education and awareness generation. As a result victims for a long time are unable to understand the real motives of the paedophiles, hence not able to share and disclose the agony caused to them.

India is fast replacing countries in South-East Asia as the destination for sex tourists, particularly paedophiles. Unlike Sri Lanka and Thailand the problem has not been seriously looked and openly discussed in India. The very fact that the child sex abusers getting caught and punished by the system is very low encourages the paedophiles to exploit children in India.

Child Sexual Exploitation in the form of Adoption

With changing social values and shortage of children there is a growing demand for adoption of children in developed countries. However due to racial reasons, they would not like to adopt children of Afro-American origin. So couples and sometimes single individuals who are interested in adopting children would look towards India, because, Indian children with their wheatish/pale skin resemble children of South European origin. This has created a great demand for infants from India. Because of prevalent gender bias, girl babies from poor families become easy targets for this adoption racket.

A Nalgonda-based voluntary agency called Gramya Resource Centre for women in Andhra Pradesh has unearthed a major adoption racket when the agency was contacted to rescue two baby girls in the Nalgonda district. Due to the efforts of this agency, it could be learnt that girls from Lambada tribe living in Telangana district of Andhra Pradesh, such as Ranga Reddy, Mehboob Nagar, Medak and Nalgonda are often bought by fake adoption agencies and then sold off to traffickers for commercial sexual exploitation. Such instances have also been reported from other districts like Krishna, Guntur, Kurnool, Chittoor, Vishakhapatnam, Nellore, Nizamabad, Hyderabad, and Khammam of Andhra Pradesh.

Initiatives taken by United Nations and International Organizations:

Initiative of the United Nations

The United Nations Declaration on the Rights of the Child (1989) asserts that the child shall be protected against exploitation and shall not be subject to trafficking in any form. Article 34 speaks of bilateral and multilateral measures to prevent:

- Inducement or coercion of a child to engage in any unlawful sexual activity.
- Exploitative use of children for prostitution, unlawful sexual practices and pornographic purposes.

The optional Protocol for the Convention on the Rights of the Child (CRC) contains further provisions to be incorporated in domestic and international laws and multilateral agreements to cover the crime of sex tourism.

Article 1

States Parties shall prohibit the sale of children, child prostitution and child pornography as provided for by the present Protocol.

Article 2

For the purposes of thc present Protocol:

(a) Sale of children means any act or transaction whereby

a child is transferred by any person or group of persons to another for remuneration or any other consideration;

(b) Child prostitution means the use of a child in sexual activities for remuneration or any other form of consideration;

(c) Child pornography means any representation, by whatever means, of a child engaged in real or simulated explicit sexual activities or any representation of the sexual parts of a child for primarily sexual purposes.

Article 3

1. Each State Party shall ensure that, as a minimum, the following acts and activities are fully covered under its criminal or penal law, whether such offences are committed domestically or transnationally or on an individual or organized basis:

(a) In the context of sale of children as defined in Article 2.

(i) Offering, delivering or accepting, by whatever means, a child for the purpose of:

(a) Sexual exploitation of the child;
(b) Transfer of organs of the child for profit;
(c) Engagement of the child in forced labour;

(ii) Improperly inducing consent, as an intermediary, for the adoption of a child in violation of applicable international legal instruments on adoption;

(b) Offering, obtaining, procuring or providing a child for child prostitution, as defined in Article 2;

(c) Producing, distributing, disseminating, importing, exporting, offering, selling or possessing for the above purposes child pornography as defined in Article 2.

2. Subject to the provisions of the national law of a State Party, the same shall apply to an attempt to commit any of the

said acts and to complicity or participation in any of the said acts.

3. Each State Party shall make such offences punishable by appropriate penalties that take into account their grave nature.

4. Subject to the provisions of its national law, each State Party shall take measures, where appropriate, to establish the liability of legal persons for offences established in paragraph 1 of the present article. Subject to the legal principles of the State Party, such liability of legal persons may be criminal, civil or administrative.

Country Initiatives

Various countries have taken steps to counter the menace of child sex exploitation, child pornography and child sex tourism.

Thailand

In Thailand, besides prosecuting the child sex offenders, the government also punishes hotel owners, tour operators and other such agencies involved in child sex tourism, by blacklisting, licence revocation etc. In Thailand now it is mandatory for the guests to register visitors who are minors.

Brazil

Brazilian government asked the hotels to actively discourage sexual exploitation of children in the hotel premises. As an incentive hotels who observe this restriction will get an extra star in their quality rating. Brazilian government cautions the visiting tourists by distributing brochures describing the penalties to be awarded to tourists who indulge in sexual exploitation of the minors.

Countries like France, Germany, Belgium, the Netherlands and Italy have introduced a luggage tag condemning sex tourism. The Ministry of Foreign Affairs in the Netherlands has included a warning in their travel brochures.

"Goa Children's Act, 2003" addresses several issues related to child sexual exploitation in an integrated manner. Some of the salient features of the Act are:

- The term "trafficking" has been given a legal definition for the first time.
- Sexual assault has also been given a wider definition to incorporate in itself every type of sexual exploitation. Punishment also has been enhanced.
- Responsibility for ensuring safety of children in hotel premises is placed on the hotel management. Unrelated adults cannot take children to hotel rooms.
- Stringent measures have been provided to regulate children's access to pornographic materials in the electronic media and on the Internet.

The Act also provides for the setting up of Victims Assistance Units, including social workers to help children in trauma and the setting up of children's courts, to try all offences against children.

Preventive Measures

As India has become a major source, destination and transit point for trafficking and sex tourism, there is an urgent need to take measures to check and control the growing menace of child sex tourism in India. Some of the suggested measures could be:

Extraterritorial legislation to be passed by the Central Government to try any citizen of India who travels within or outside the country with an intention to have sex with the children; or engages in sex with children; or knowingly enters into arrangements which result in sex with women and children.

Strong messages against sex tourism to be displayed at strategic places publicizing legal and penal provision and cautioning potential sex tourists.

Mandatory reporting by technicians, studio owners and agents who take on film processing works on sexually explicit pornographic and audiovisual materials that come to their notice.

As Child Pornography is a technically advanced crime, set up trained and equipped police units to combat internet-based child pornography.

Central and State Governments should establish monitoring mechanisms with the cooperation of all stake-holders like hoteliers, tour operators, local authorities etc. to ensure children's safety.

A comprehensive policy for dealing with the problem must be worked out with provisions for rehabilitation programmes for the victims.

Sensitization of all the stakeholders regarding the negative and detrimental aspects of sex tourism.

REFERENCES

Desai, N. 2001, *See the evil: Tourism related paedophilia in Goa, Mumbai,* Vikas Adhyayan Kendra.

ECPAT Australia. *ECPAT Development Manual.* Melbourne, Australia, 1994, p. 37.

Lin Lean Lim and Nana Oishi. 1996: *International labour migration of Asian Women: Distinctive characteristics and policy concerns,* Geneva, ILO, 1996.

Lin Lean Lim, 1998: *The Sex Sector: The Economic and Social Bases of Prostitution in Southeast Asia,* Geneva, ILO.

Mies, Maria, 1993. White man's dilemma: His search for what he has destroyed in Mies, Maria and Shiva Vandana (eds.), *Ecofeminism,* London, Zed Books, 1993.

Mosqueda, M.W. Jr. 2005: Philippines is 4th in Trafficking of Children; *Online News Desk,* ECPAT; 12 February 2005 (http://www.mb.com.ph/prov2005021128464.html.)

Niron, N.R. *et al.,* 2001: *Children work Adults play Child Sex tourism—The problem in Cambodia;* World Vision Institute.

Office of the Commissioner of Human Rights 2000: Optional Protocol to the Convention on the Rights of the Child on the sale of children, child prostitution and child pornography adopted and opened for signature, ratification and accession by General Assembly Resolution A/RES/54/263 of 25 May 2000.

Two million Thai Prostitutes? Editorial, *Bangkok Post,* 8 February, 1995.

11

Legalization of Prostitution
Myths and Realities

It is learnt that the Government of India is debating over the issue of legalization and decriminalization of prostitution. Some feminine groups as well as human rights activists are aggressively campaigning for legalization of prostitution. Advocates of legalization hold the view that prostitution should be given the status of industry and sex work must be considered as similar to any other work. Prostitutes must be considered as legitimate sex workers. Conferences were held in Kolkata in 1997, 1998 again in 2001 demanding legalization. Many NGO groups lent their support to this demand. *Sangram,* a voluntary organization in Maharashtra working around the prostitutes champions the cause of prostitutes and glorifies the freedom supposed to be inherent in prostitution. Dr. Syeeda Hameed, former Member of National Commission for Women, feels that, *"the shame that surrounds the sex workers and illegality which brands them makes it difficult for them to seek any redress. It is necessary that they should not be treated as criminals and given rights and dignity that they deserve."*[1]

International Experience

Prostitution has been legalized in countries like Australia, Germany, New Zealand and the Netherlands etc. Brothel prostitution was legalized in Victoria in 1984, the Australia capital territory in 1992, in Queensland in 1999 and in New South Wales in 1999. The proponents of legalization have upheld Victoria and New-South-Wales models as good practices in various national and international fora. Legalization and de-criminalization are viewed as providing safety to prostituted women and solutions to their health hazards.

Unfortunately, even two decades after legalization of prostitution in Victoria there are studies that clearly reveal that this experiment has been a failure and its objectives have remained unfulfilled. In legalized brothels the prostituted women, and not the male customers, are examined for sexually transmitted diseases on a regular basis. It is a retrograde step and mark return to a time when the state itself took a role in providing disease-free women for men's sexual pleasure. One of the primary objects of legalization has been to protect the women from sexually transmitted diseases like HIV/AIDS, but studies have revealed that practices in legal brothels expose women to far greater health hazards. They face greater risks of unwanted pregnancy and sexually transmitted diseases because men often do not use condoms. A study in Victoria found that 40 per cent of clients had enjoyed prostituted women without using condoms.[2]

Safety of Women

Legalization according to its proponents ensures the safety of women in prostitution. But facts prove otherwise. Marry Sullivan's research on the Occupational Health and Safety Codes for brothels developed in Australia by state governments and prostitutes' rights organization documents the kind of violence that exists in such industry. The OHSC code suggests that women exercise their *"intuition to work out whether the buyers are likely to be violent. But the prostituted women may be fined by their employers if they refuse to service clients whom the women considered to be dangerous."*[3]

Indeed, legalization makes men more demanding of practices, which women do not like and makes women further powerless to resist them because of greater competition. It gives more power and muscle to the brothel owners.[4]

Street Prostitution

It has been argued by the proponents of legalization that it would discourage street prostitution and the street prostitutes, for safety reasons will choose to work in legal brothels. But this, however, does not happen in practice. Street prostitution and problems associated with this have remained the same and sometimes have increased following legalization. Research estimates that 80 per cent of street prostitutes in Victoria are addicts and 80 to 90 per cent are homeless. Local councils and state government have undertaken new legislation and initiatives to deal with this growing problem.

In New South Wales a local council has set up *"Safe houses"* which allows women to take their male buyers picked from the tolerance zones. But safe houses and sex workers' centres under the control of local government are better understood as state run brothels. Another problem with the creation of tolerance zone is that local authorities are encouraging aggressive sexual behaviour of males and their tendency to abuse women in those areas.

South Australian MP Steve Condous visited New South Wales in July 2000 on a survey of brothels. He was shocked to find sharp increase in street prostitution—*"street prostitution had become so bad that it led to a street protest by St. Kilda residents in 2001."*[5] By contrast Swedish law introduced on 1st January, 1999 prohibited sexual services and there is evidence that it had led to a major reduction of the prostitutes in the streets.

Increase in Organized Crime

A significant objective of legalization of prostitution is to control involvement of crime gangs in running the brothels and exploiting the prostitutes. But in reality wherever prostitution has been legalized, the illegal sector has grown much larger than the legalized sector. In Victoria, it has been estimated by the police that the number of illegal brothels is nearly 400, four-times more than the legal brothels.[6] New South Wales police in 2000 reported about 40 shootings, as part of a struggle between rival groups for control of prostitution. A Dutch academic reported that in Holland the brothels trade is dominated by illegal immigrants imported by Polish and Russian Mafia.[7] It is a fact that legalization and decriminalization has accounted for the growth of prostitution industry. Legalization institutionalizes and legitimizes the sex industry pimps masquerade as *"foremen"* and *"legal enterprises"* and rationalizes the marketing of prostitutes locally or transnationally.

To meet the growing demands for more sex workers, brothel keepers and other captains of sex industry resort to trafficking in women and children. Traffickers sell women to both legal and illegal brothels. Trafficked women can work legally in brothels with work permits if traffickers apply on their behalf for refugee status. Many of the trafficked women are so debt-bonded that their earnings out of commercial sex go towards repayment of debt. This makes them more vulnerable and beholden to the traffickers.

Child Prostitution

Further in countries like the Netherlands child prostitution has increased dramatically since 1990s. Similarly, in Australia child prostitution has increased sharply in Victoria as compared to other states, where prostitution has not been legalized. A study carried out by Christ Church School of Medicine, New Zealand revealed that nearly 2000 Christ Church prostitutes were under the age of 12. Girls as young as 12 years have been picked up by the police.[8]

Some of the female activists and organizations working for the economic and human rights of the prostitutes would like to call prostitution a profession and argue that women have the right to choose the profession of their liking. However, prostitution is not a profession selected among other options by today's career women. Large numbers of street workers are homeless and live below the poverty line. Even women who work in call or escort services have no control over the income because they are at the mercy of the pimps. Many complete their innings in profession without any savings.

A disturbing fact is that the average age of entry into prostitution in many developed and developing countries is coming down. In India Action research by the Institute of Social Sciences in collaboration with National Human Rights Commission revealed that majority of the victims were children. Children are preferred because of the clients' fear of contracting sexually transmitted diseases. The hard reality is that the overwhelming majority of the prostitutes are not there by choice, but due to destitution, deprivation, ostracism, deception etc. Many have been the victims of sexual violence either at home or at street, and many have been purchased from their starving parents by the pimps. Even before they reach their puberty some of them are administered steroids to make malnourished children artificially plumpy just as cattle are fattened to yield more milk. The question of free choice just does not arise. Further there is now greater demand for trafficked women and children because in many western countries there is shortage of white prostitutes. In US for example 70 per cent of the prostitutes are non-white.

In Germany, law makers thought that they would be able to amass huge tax revenue when they legalized prostitution in 2002. But because of the criminal nature of the profession many of the brothel owners and the staff did not pay off and it was estimated by the Federal officers that the government has lost over 2 billions Euro a year from the unpaid tax revenue from the sex industry. Again in countries like Germany, the Netherlands and Australia normalization of prostitution has not occurred following legalization. Free women have not signed up for benefits or for unions. The reason lies in the basic fact that prostitution is not like any other job. Women are mostly engaged in prostitution when they are forced to or have no other options. Even where prostitution is legal, a significant number of women are being trafficked. Women and children under the control of mafia and criminals are in no position to register themselves to authorities or join a union. Again many women join prostitution as a temporary means of making money and hope that as soon as the debt is paid off and a certain amount of money is saved for the poverty stricken families, they will go home. They seldom tell the friends and relatives what they are doing to earn money. They naturally do not want to register with the authority and create a permanent record of being a prostitute. Unionism of sex workers is indeed very often incompatible with the coercive and abusive nature of prostitution.

Further, commercial sexual exploitation has another demeaning aspect. It teaches men that female bodies can be traded, used and discarded. It aggravates gender inequality in all areas of society and encourages sexual violence and harassment in domestic life as well as in work place. Indeed, prostitution is an insult to self-respect of women and violates their basic human rights. In a joint study on sex trafficking done by Coalition Against Trafficking in women and children funded by Ford Foundation, most of the 146 women interviewed strongly stated that prostitution should not be legalized and warned that legalization would aggravate risks and harm for women from already violent pimps and customers.

In 1999 Sweden passed a law, which makes a criminal offence for any person who seeks casual sexual favour in exchange of payment. A law levelled equally at both client and the seller along with evenhanded enforcement would be a better solution than decriminalization. It is callous on the part of the government to abdicate its responsibility to provide decent livelihood option for women and children and pull them out of the inferno of prostitution. Instead of legalizing prostitution, the state should take steps to create alternative livelihood options for women and sex workers and punish those who seek to exploit women with the intent of financial gain. Very often under the laws of most of the countries the prostitute is penalized and the male client goes scot-free. In India under the Prevention of Immoral Traffic Act there are provisions of punishment of traffickers, brothel owners as well as the clients but seldom they are visited with any kind of punishment. Only victims are revictimized. This is unfair and iniquitous. Instead of cashing in on the economic benefits of sex industry by taxing it, government should step forward to provide to prostituted women economic resources from seizures of the assets of the traffickers, brothel-keepers and other captains of the sex industry.

NOTES

1. Dr. Syeeda Hameed, *"Silence Around the Sex Work: Women's Future Service"* in http://southasia.onworld.net/article/view/123869/1/70.
2. Louie, R., (1998), *Project Client Call*, Melbourne Macfarlane Burnett Centre for Medical Research.
3. Sullivan Mary, (2003), *Making Sex Work in Victoria*, Ph.D. Thesis, Department of Political Science, University of Melbourne.
4. Barclay, Ingrid, (2001), *Interactive Process in Brothel Prostitution*, Honours Thesis, University of Melbourne.
5. Voice of the Voiceless, *Newsletter* of NATSAP, Vol. 2, February 2006, Issue 2.
6. Murphy Padraic, (2002), Licensed brothels call for blitz on illegal sex shops, *The Age*, 3 June.
7. Voice of the Voiceless, *Newsletter*.
8. *Ibid*.

Landmark Supreme Court Judgements Related to Trafficking in Women and Children

I. Vishal Jeet vs. Union of India and Others AIR 1990 SC 14120

(a) Directions given to the Central Government and various State Governments to set up Appropriate Committees for monitoring and evaluation of welfare and rehabilitation schemes for sex-workers and their children.

(b) However, directing the CBI to conduct a nation-wide inquiry into all those cases in which the police personnel are hand-in-glove with traffickers, pimps and brothel-owners, is not practically feasible.

Judges

S.R. Pandian and K. Jayachandra Reddy, JJ.

Order

1. This writ petition under Article 32 of the Constitution of India at the instance of an Advocate is filed by way of a Public Interest Litigation seeking issuance of certain directions, directing the Central Bureau of Investigation (1) to institute an enquiry against those police officers under whose jurisdiction Red-Light Areas as well as Devadasi and Jogin traditions are flourishing and to take necessary action against such erring police officers and law breakers, (2) to bring all the inmates of the red-light areas and also those who are engaged in "flesh trade" to protective homes of the respective States and to provide them with proper medical aid, shelter,

education and training in various disciplines of life so as to enable them to choose a more dignified way of life and (3) to bring the children of those prostitutes and other children found begging in streets and also the girls pushed into "flesh trade" to protective homes and then to rehabilitate them.

2. The averments made in the writ petition on the basis of which these directions are prayed for can be summarized thus:

3. Many unfortunate teen-aged female children (hereinafter referred to as "the children") and girls in full bloom are being sold in various parts of the country, for paltry sum even by their parents finding themselves unable to maintain their children on account of acute poverty and unbearable miseries and hoping that their children would be engaged only in household duties or manual labour. But those who are acting as pimps or brokers in the "flesh trade" and brothel-keepers who hunt for these teenaged children and young girls to make money either purchase or kidnap them by deceitful means and unjustly and forcibly inveigle them into "flesh trade". Once these unfortunate victims are taken to the dens of prostitutes and sold to brothel-keepers, they are shockingly and brutally treated and confined in complete seclusion in a tiny claustrophobic room for several days without food until they succumb to the vicious desires of the brothel-keepers and enter into the unethical and squalid business of prostitution. These victims though unwilling to lead this obnoxious way of life have no other way except to surrender themselves retreating into silence and submitting their bodies to all the dirty customers including even sexagenarians with plastic smile.

4. The petitioner has cited certain lurid tales of sex with sickening details alleged to have been confessed by some children and girls either escaped or rescued from such abodes of ill fame. After giving a brief note on Devadasi system and Jogin tradition, the petitioner states that this system and tradition, which are still prevailing in some parts of the country, should be put to an end. The ultimate plea of the petitioner is that the young children and girls forcibly pushed into "flesh trade" should be rescued and rehabilitated. With

this petition, the petitioner has filed 9 affidavits said to have been sworn by 9 girls who claim to be living in the brothel houses, pleading for rescue and a list of names of 9 girls who are mortally afraid to swear the affidavits. Be it noted that no counter has been filed by anyone of the respondents.

5. The matter is one of great importance warranting a comprehensive and searching analysis and requiring a humanistic rather than a purely legalistic approach from different angles. The questions involved cause considerable anxiety to the Court in reaching a satisfactory solution in eradicating such sexual exploitation of children. We shall now examine this problem and address ourselves to the merits of the prayers.

6. No denying the fact that prostitution always remains as a running sore in the body of civilization and destroys all moral values. The causes and evil effects of prostitution manning the society are so notorious and frightful that none can gainsay it. This malignity is daily and hourly threatening the community at large slowly but steadily making its way onwards leaving a track marked with broken hopes. Therefore, the necessity for appropriate and drastic action to eradicate this evil has become apparent but its successful consummation ultimately rests with the public at large.

7. It is highly deplorable and heart-rending to note that many poverty stricken children and girls in the prime of youth are taken to "flesh market" and forcibly pushed into the "flesh trade" which is being carried on in utter violation of all cannons of morality, decency and dignity of humankind. There cannot be two opinions-in-deed there is none that this obnoxious and abominable crime committed with all kinds of unthinkable vulgarity should be eradicated at all levels by drastic steps.

8. Article 23 which relates to Fundamental Rights in Part III of the Constitution and which has been put under the caption "Right against exploitation" prohibits "traffic in human beings and beggar and other similar forms of labour" and provides that any contravention of Article 23(1) shall be an offence punishable in accordance with law. The expression "traffic in human beings" is evidently a very wide expression

including the prohibition of traffic in women for immoral or other purposes. Article 35(a)(ii) of the Constitution reads that notwithstanding anything in this Constituion, Parliament shall have, and the legislature of a State shall not have, power to make laws for prescribing punishment for those acts which are declared to be offences under this part. The power of legislation, under this article, is given to the Parliament exclusively, for, otherwise the laws relating to fundamental rights would not have been uniform throughtout the country. The power is specifically denied to the State legislatures. In implementation of the principles underlying Article 23(1) the Suppression of Immoral Traffic in Women and Girls Act, 1956 (SITA for short) has been enacted under Articles 35 with the object of inhibiting or abolishing the immoral traffic in women and girls.

9. In this connection, it is significant to refer Article 39, which relates to Directive Principles of State Policy under Part IV of the Constitution. Article 39 particularizes certain objectives. Clause (f) of Article 39 was substituted by Forty-Second Amendment Act, 1976. Among the objectives mentioned under Clauses (e) and (f) of Article 39, we will confine ourselves only to certain relevant objectives under those two clauses, which are sufficient for the purpose of this case. One of the objectives under Clause (e) of Article 39 is that the State should, in particular, direct its policy towards securing that the tender age of children are not abused. One of the objectives under Clause (f) is that the State should, in particular, direct its policy towards securing that childhood and youth are protected against exploitation and against moral and material abandonment. These objectives reflect the great anxiety of the Constitution-makers to protect and safeguard the interests and welfare of the children of our country. The Government of India has also, in pursuance of these constitutional provisions of Clauses (e) and (f) of Article 39, evolved a national policy for the welfare of the children.

10. It will be apposite to make reference to one of the principles, namely, principle No. (9) formulated by the Declaration of the Rights of the Child adopted by the General

Assembly of the United Nations on November 20, 1959. The said principle reads thus:

The Child shall be protected against all forms of neglect, cruelty and exploitation. He shall not be the subject of traffic, in any form.

11. Before the adopting of SITA, there were enactments in some of the States for suppression of immoral traffic, but they were not uniform nor were they found to be adequately effective. Some States did not have any law on the subject.

12. With the growing danger in society to healthy and decent living with morality, the world public opinion congregated at New York in a convention for suppression of traffic in persons for exploitation for immoral purpose. Pursuant to the signing of that convention on May 9, 1950 our Parliament has passed an Act called "Suppression of Immoral Traffic in Women and Girls Act, 1956" which is now changed as "The Immoral Traffic (Prevention) Act, 1956" to which certain drastic amendments are introduced by the Amendment Acts of 46 of 1978 and 44 of 1986. This Act aims at suppressing the evils of prostitution in women and girls and achieving a public purpose, viz. to rescue the fallen women and girls and to stamp out the evils of prostitution and also to provide all opportunity to these fallen victims so that they could become decent members of the society. Besides the above Act, there are various provisions in the Indian Penal Code such as Sections 366-A (dealing with selling of minor for purposes of prostitution etc.) and 373 (dealing with the offence of buying minor for proposes of prostitution etc.). The Juvenile Justice Act, 1986 which provides for the care, protection, treatment, development and rehabilitation of neglected or delinquent juveniles contains a specific provision, namely Section 13 which empowers a police officer or any other person or organization authorized by the State Government in this behalf to take charge of any neglected juveniles and bring them before the Board constituted under this Act which Board under Section 15 has to hold an enquiry and make such orders in relation to the neglected juveniles as it may deem fit.

13. In spite of the above stringent and rehabilitative provisions of law under various Acts, it cannot be said that

the desired result has been achieved. It cannot be gainsaid that a remarkable degree of ignorance or callousness or culpable indifference is manifested in uprooting this cancerous growth despite the fact that the day has arrived imperiously demanding an objective multi-dimensional study and a searching investigation into the matter relating to the causes and effects of this evil and requiring most rational measures to week out the vices of illicit trafficking. This malady is not only a social but also a socio-economic problem and, therefore, the measures to be taken in that regard should be more preventive rather than punitive.

14. In our view, it is neither practicable and possible nor desirable to make a roving enquiry through the CBI throughout the length and breadth of this country and no useful purpose will be served by issuing any such direction, as requested by the petitioner. Further, this malignity cannot be eradicated either by banishing, branding, scourging or inflecting severe punishment on these helpless and hapless victims most of whom are unwilling participants and involuntary victims of compelled circumstances and who, finding no way to escape, are weeping or wailing throughout.

15. This devastating malady can be suppressed and eradicated only if the law enforcing authorities in that regard take very severe and speedy legal action against all the erring persons such as pimps, brokers and brothel-keepers. The Court in such cases have to always take a serious view of this matter and inflict condign punishment on proof of such offences. Apart from legal action, both the Central and the State Governments who have got an obligation to safeguard the interest and welfare of the children and girls of this country have to evaluate various measures and implement them in the right direction.

16. Bhagwati, J. (as he then was) in *Lakshmi Kant Pandey* vs. *Union of India* while emphasizing the importance of children has expressed his view thus:

It is obvious that in a civilized society the importance of child welfare cannot be over-emphasized, because the welfare of the entire community, its growth and development, depend on the health and well-being of its children. Children are a "supremely important national asset" and the future well-being of the nation depends on how its children grow and develop.

17. We, after bestowing our deep and anxious consideration on this matter feel that it would be appropriate if certain directions are given in this regard. Accordingly, we make the following directions:

(1) All the State Governments and the Governments of Union Territories should direct their concerned law enforcing authorities to take appropriate and speedy action under the existing laws in eradicating child prostitution without giving room for any complaint of remissness or culpable and indifference.

(2) The State Governments and the Governments of Union Territories should set up a separate Advisory Committee within their respective zones consisting of the Secretary of the Social Welfare Department or Board, the Secretary of the Law Department, sociologists, criminologists, members of the women's organizations, members of Indian Council of Child Welfare and Indian Council of Social Welfare as well as the members of various voluntary social organizations and associations etc., the main objects of the Advisory Committee being to make suggestions of:

   (a) The measures to be taken in eradicating the child prostitution, and
   (b) The social welfare programmes to be implemented for the care, protection, treatment, development and rehabilitation of the young fallen victims, namely the children and girls rescued either from the brothel houses or from the vices of prostitution;

(3) All the State Governments and the Governments of Union Territories should take steps in providing

adequate and rehabilitative homes manned by well-qualified trained social workers, psychiatrists and doctors.

(4) The Union Government should set up a committee of its own in the line, we have suggested under direction No. (2) the main object of which is to evolve welfare programmes to be implemented on the national level for the care, protection, rehabilitation etc. etc. of the young fallen victims, namely the children and girls and to take suggestions of amendments to the existing laws or for enactment of any new law, if so warranted for the prevention of sexual exploitation of children.

(5) The Central Government and the Governments of States and Union Territories should devise a machinery of its own for ensuring the proper implementation of the suggestions that would be made by the respective committees.

(6) The Advisory Committee can also go deep into Devadasi system and Jogin tradition and give their valuable advice and suggestions as to what best the Government could do in that regard.

(7) The copies of the affidavits and the list containing the names of 9 girls are directed to be forwarded to the Commissioner of Police, Delhi for necessary action.

18. We may add that we are not giving an exhaustive list of the members for the constitution of the committee. Therefore, it is open to the concerned Government to include any member or members in the committee, as it deems necessary.

19. We hope and trust that the directions given by us will go a long way towards eradicating the malady of child prostitution, Devadasi system and Jogin tradition and will also at the same time protect and safeguard the interests of the children by preventing the sexual abuse and exploitation.

20. So far as the remaining prayer regarding rehabilitation of the children of prostitutes is concerned, we

understand that a similar issue is raised in a separate writ petition bearing W.P. No. 824/88 pending before this Court and this Court is seized of the matter and also has given an interim direction on 15.11.1989 for setting up a committee to go into the question from various angles of the problems taking into consideration the different laws relevant to the matter and to submit its report. (Vide *Gaurav Jain* vs. *Union of India and Others*). Therefore, we are not expressing any opinion on this prayer regarding the rehabilitation of the children of prostitutes.

21. With the above directions, the Writ Petition is disposed of.

II. Kumari Sangeeta *vs.* State and Anr 1995(101) CrLJ 3923 (Delhi)

Immoral Traffic (Prevention) Act, Section 17(5)—Constitution and Composition of Tribunals—The word "may" is to be construed as meaning "shall", and therefore, it is mandatory for the Magistrate to seek the assistance of a panel of five respectable persons while discharging his duties under Section 17(2) of the Act.

Judge

Monoranjan Mallick, J.

Order

1. These are three Revision Petitions Nos. 219/94, 227/94 and 10/95 preferred by Miss Sangita, Mrs. Usha Singh, Mrs. Pooja and Rekha. Besides the above, Mrs. Usha also filed Criminal Writ Petition No. 872/94. All the aforesaid petitions are being taken up together as they raise the same pleas and legal issues, which can be disposed of by a common judgment and order.

2. Brief facts which led to the presentation of the present petitions are as under: that Inspector P.L. Suri, S.H.O. PS Kamla Market was present at G.B. Road along with a lady constable

and staff in connection with his usual patrolling duty during the night of June 12, 1994. He received secret information that certain minor girls were indulging in prostitution in premises No. 5216, G.B. Road, Delhi. On receipt of the said information, he organized a raiding party and included therein two members of the public known as Rajesh Chawla r/o 2860/3, and Mrs. Sneh Srivastava r/o 107/1, Railway Colony, Thomson Road, Special Police Officer of PS Kamla Market. The above said premises were searched which resulted in the recovery of nine girls from the said premises including the present petitioners. All of them were produced before the learned Metropolitan Magistrate who after conducting an enquiry under Section 17 of the Immoral Traffic (Prevention) Act, 1956 hereinafter referred to as the Act for the sake of convenience ordered the detention of the petitioners, i.e. Usha Singh, Sangita, Pooja and Rekha for a period of three years in a protective home through his judgment and order dated August 16, 1994.

3. The petitioners on being dissatisfied with the above said order approached the Court of Sessions. The appeals were dismissed *vide* order dated October 17, 1994.

4. It is in the above circumstances that the petitioners are before this Court.

5. Learned counsel for the petitioners have assailed the legality and validity of the judgment and order passed by the Courts below, *inter alia,* on the following grounds: that the raiding party was not constituted in accordance with the provisions of Section 13 and Section 15(6A) of the Act inasmuch as it did not include two lady Police Officers. The interrogation was not done in the presence of a lady member of a recognized welfare institution. The constitution of the tribunals was also not valid and legal inasmuch as it was in flagrant disregard of the mandatory provisions of Section 17(5) of the Act. There is absolutely no evidence on record to show and prove that there was sexual exploitation or abuse of the petitioners for commercial purposes. The case of the petitioners does not fall within the domain of Section 2(g) of the Act. Hence no action could have been taken against the petitioners.

6. Learned Public Prosecutors have urged to the contrary.

7. It was been urged for and on behalf of the petitioners that the learned Magistrate who was working as a tribunal for the purposes of limited jurisdiction was not assisted at the relevant time by a panel of five respectable persons as envisaged by Section 17(5) of the Act. It thus as a corollary whereof rendered nugatory the entire proceedings before the learned Magistrate since a duty has been cast on the shoulders of the Magistrate to have the assistance of the panel of five respectable persons while discharging his functions under sub-sec.(2) of Section 17. Thus, the learned Magistrate was left with no option but to seek the assistance of the said panel comprised five persons as provided under Section 17(5) while discharging his functions under the said section. The learned PPs, on the other hand, have contended that it was not incumbent on the Magistrate to seek the assistance of a panel of five persons as spoken of under Section 17(5) of the Act inasmuch as the word used therein is "may" which gave an ample option and latitude to the Magistrate and left to his judicious discretion to have the services of those five persons or to ignore the same.

8. Since we are concerned with the construction of Section 17 of the Act it would be just and proper to examine the provisions of the said section before embarking upon a detailed discussion. In view of the above I am inclined to reproduce Section 17 of the Act in extenso. It is in the following words.

> "17. (1) When the special police officer removing a person under sub-sec (4) of Section 15 or a police officer rescuing a person under sub-sec. (1) of Section 16, is for any reason unable to produce him before the appropriate Magistrate as required by sub-sec. (5) of Section 15, or before the Magistrate issuing the order under sub-sec. (2) of Section 16, he shall forthwith produce him before the nearest Magistrate of any class, who shall pass such orders as he deems proper for his safe custody until he is produced before the appropriate Magistrate, or, as the case may be, the Magistrate issuing the order:

Provided......

(2) When the person is produced before the appropriate Magistrate under sub-sec. (5) of Section 15 or the Magistrate under sub-sec. (2) of Section 16, he shall, after giving him an opportunity of being heard, cause an inquiry to be made as to the correctness of the information received under sub-sec. (1) of Section 16, the age, character and antecedents of the person and the suitability of his parents, guardian or husband for taking charge of him and the nature of the influence which the conditions in his home are likely to have on him if he is sent home, and, for this purpose, he may direct a probation officer appointed under the Probation of Offenders Act, 1958, (20 of 1958), to inquire into the above circumstances and into the personality of the person and the prospects of his rehabilitation.

Provided......

(4) Where the Magistrate is satisfied, after making an inquiry as required under sub-sec. (2),

(a) That the information received is correct;
(b) That he is in need of care and protection; and
(c) He may, subject to the provisions of sub-sec(5), make an order that such person be detained for such period, being not less than one year and not more than three years, as may be specified in the order, in a protective home, or in such other custody as he shall, for reasons to be recorded in writing, consider suitable:

    Provided that such custody shall not be that of a person or body of persons of a religious persuasion different from that of the person and that those entrusted with the custody of the person including the persons in charge of a protective home, may be required to enter into a bond which may, where necessary and feasible, contain undertakings based on directions relating to the proper care, guardianship, education, training and medical and psychiatric treatment of the person as well as supervision by a person appointed by the court, which will be in force for a period not exceeding three years.

(5) In discharging his functions under sub-sec.(2), a Magistrate may summon a panel of five respectable persons, three of whom shall, wherever practicable, be women to assist him and may, for this purpose, keep a list of experienced social workers, in the field of suppression of immoral traffic in persons."

9. Learned counsel for the petitioners Mr. Mukul Rohatgi, Senior Advocate, Sodhi Teja Singh and Mr. T. Gaur, on the basis of the provisions of law alluded to above, have argued with great zeal and fervour that no doubt it is true that the legislators in their wisdom have used the word "may" while authorizing a Magistrate to summon a panel of five persons in order to assist him in the due discharge of his duties a tribunal, however, the word "may" has been used in the sense of "shall" making it obligatory on the part of the Magistrate to have the services of five respectable persons while performing his functions and duties under Section 17 of the Act. According to them there is no escape from the said conclusion keeping in view the context in which the word "may" has been used.

10. Learned Public Prosecutors, Mr. H.J.S. Ahluwalia and Ms. Meera Bhatia have urged to the contrary.

11. Thus the pertinent question whereon hinges the fate of the present cases which comes to the tip of the tongue is as to whether the legislators have used the word "may" in the sense of "shall" and as such a duty was cast on the shoulders of the learned Magistrate to summon a panel of five respectable persons to assist him and to advise him in the due discharge of his functions under Section 17 of the Act.

12. It is a well-established principle of law that the word "may" and the word "shall" are interchangeable terms. It cannot be deduced ipso facto from use of word "may" in a particular statute that it has been used in the sense of directory conferring an ample discretion on the part of the authority to take recourse to particular course of action or not. Much would depend upon the context in which the word "may"

has been used and the intention of the legislature which they want to convey through a particular enactment. It is true that ordinarily whenever the words "shall" and "must" are used they issue a mandate and a duty is cast thereby on the shoulders of an authority to carry out the said obligations. In the other hand, if it appears from the context that the legislators, have used the word "may" in the sense of "shall" keeping in view the statute as a whole and with regard to its nature and object in that eventually it would be appropriate for the Courts to construe the word "may" as "shall". It has also been held time and again that in case the word "may" as "shall". It has also been held time and again that in case the word "may" occurs in a statute concerning the rights and interests of the public and if some benefit is proposed to be conferred on the persons affected by the said statute in that eventuality the word "may" should be construed as "shall" and would have a mandatory meaning.

13. Admittedly the present Act is meant to prevent immoral traffic in the human beings. The said Act was enacted by the Parliament in pursuance of the International Convention signed at New York on the 9th day of May 1950. Furthermore, Act 23 of our Constitution deals with right against exploitation. It lays down traffic in human beings and beggar and other similar forms of forced labour are prohibited and any contravention of this provision shall be an offence punishable in accordance with law. Article 35 casts a duty on the shoulders of the Parliament to make laws as soon as possible after the commencement of the Constitution. Thus, the present Act is a piece of social legislation. It is meant to ameliorate the lot of the persons of this country who are being exploited by others. Hence the present Act is meant for the benefit of these persons who are suffering and being exploited at the hands of others. Consequently according to well established principles of interpretation the word "may" which occurs in Section 17(5) of the Act is to be read as "shall" and as such, whatever, is contemplated therein cannot be ignored. I am tempted here to refer to the enthralling commendatory on the *Law of Interpretation of Statutes* by Maxwell, 1940 Edn. Page 246, in support of my above view:

"Statutes which authorize persons to do acts for the benefit of others, or, as it is sometimes said, for the public good or the advancement of justice, have often given rise to controversy when conferring the authority in terms simple enabling and not mandatory. In enacting that they "may" or "shall, if they think fit", or "shall have power", or that "it shall be lawful" for them to do such acts, a statute appears to use the langauge of mere permission, but it has been so often decided as to have become an axiom that in such cases such expressions may have—to say the least—compulsory force, and so would seem to be modified by judicial exposition. On the other hand, in some cases, the authorized person is invested with a discretion, and then those expressions seem, divested of that compulsory force, and probably that is the prima facie meaning......Again, Section 13 of the Weights and Measures Act, 1889 (c. 21), which provides that an inspector "may take in respect of the verification and stamping of weights, measures, and weighing instruments the fee: specified", has been held to be obligatory and to impose on the inspector a duty to take the fees in all cases."

14. Crawford in his famous book *"The Construction of Statutes"* has got to say the following at page 519 in this regard:

"Ordinarily the words "shall" and "must" are mandatory, and the word "may" is directory, although they are often used interchangeably in legislation. This use without regard to their literal meaning generally makes it necessary for the counts to resort to construction in order to discover the real intention of the legislature. Nevertheless, it will always be presumed by the court that the legislature intended to use the words in their usual and natural meaning. If such a meaning, however, leads to absurdity, or great inconvenience, or for some other reason is clearly contrary to the obvious intention of the legislature, then words which ordinarily are mandatory in their nature will be construed as directory, or *vice versa.* In other words, if the language of the statute, considered as a whole and with the due regard to its nature and object, reveals that the legislature intended the words "shall" and "must" to be directory, they should be given that meaning. Similarly, under the same circumstances, the word "may" should be given a mandatory meaning, and especially where the statute concerns the rights and interests of the public, or where third persons have a claim *de jure* that a power shall be exercised, or whenever something is directive to be done for the sake of justice or the public good, or is necessary to sustain the statute's constitutionality."

15. Yet, the construction of mandatory words as directory and directory words as mandatory should not be lightly adopted. The opposite meaning should be unequivocally evidenced before it is accepted as the true meaning, otherwise, there is considerable danger that the legislative intent will be wholly or partially defeated.

16. I would also like to cite a few lines from *Corpus Juris Secundum,* Vol. 82, Art. 380, page 880......" 'may' construed as mandatory. Where, from a consideration of the whole statute, and its nature and object, it appears that the intent of the legislature was to impose a positive duty rather than a discretionary power, the word 'may' will be held to be mandatory. A mandatory construction will usually be given to the word 'may' where public interests are concerned, and the public or third persons have a claim *de jure* that the power conferred should be exercised, or whenever something is directed to be done for the sake of justice of the public good; but never for the purpose of creating a right. Accordingly, in a proper case the word 'may' will be construed as 'must' or 'shall'. Such a construction is warranted only where it is necessary to effectuate a manifest legislative intent, and, if no imperative reason exists for a mandatory construction, the word 'may' will be construed as permissive. The word 'may' will be construed as 'shall', when the statute can thereby by upheld, if construction to the contrary would render it.

17. To the same effect are the observations of their Lordships of the Supreme Court as reported in *Shri A.C. Aggarwal, Sub-Divisional Magistrate, Delhi* vs. *Ms. Ram Kali,* (1968) 1 SCR 205: (1968 Cr LJ 82), wherein their Lordships had had an occasion to construe the words appearing 'may take cognizance' under Section 190(1)(c) of the Code of Criminal Procedure. Their Lordships opined that the Magistrate is bound to take cognizance of any offence brought to his notice under Section 190(1)(c) of the Code of Criminal Procedure. The words 'may take cognizance' in the context means 'must take cognizance'. He has no discetion in the matter; otherwise that section will be violative of Article 14 of the Constitution.

18. Their Lordships gave vent to the same view in *State (Delhi Admn.)* vs. *I.K. Nangia,* (1980) 1 SCC 258: (AIR 1979 SC 1977)......"Normally, the word 'may' imply what is optional, but for the reasons stated, it should in the context in which it appears, mean 'must'. There is an element of compulsion. It is a power coupled with a duty." Their Lordships cited with approval the observations of Lord Kairns in *Julius* vs. *Lord Bishop of Oxford,* (1974-80) 5 AC 214 ......" There may be something in the nature of the thing empowered to be done, something in the object for which it is to be done, something in the title of the person or persons for whose benefit the power is to be exercised, which it is to be done, something in the title of the person or persons for whose benefit the power is to be exercised, which may couple the power with a duty, and make it the duty of the person in whom the power is reponsed to exercise that power when called upon to do so."

19. There is another side of the picture. A close scrutiny of Section 17(4) reveals that when the Magistrate has satisfied himself that the information with regard to a particular person is correct and that such person is in need of care and protection then he will pass an order subject to the provisions of sub-sec. (5) that such person be detained for such period being not less than one year and not more than three years as may be specified in the order in a Protective Home. It implies thereby that an order under the said section can be made only subject to the provisions of sub-sec. (5) of Section 17 of

the Act. Sub-section (5) of Section 17 which has already been adverted to above provides that the Magistrate while discharging the functions under Section 17 would be assisted by five respectable persons out of whom whenever it is practicable there would be women to assist him.

20. In view of the above it can be safely inferred therefrom that the legislature while using the word 'may' wanted to use it in the mandatory sense otherwise they would not have subjected the exercise of powers under Section 17(2) to Section 17(5). It is axiomatic that nothing can be made subject to which is discretionary.

21. Learned Public Prosecutors have contended that after the amendment of Section 17 in the year 1986 the legislature introduced an enquiry by a Probation Officer with regard to the circumstances, character and antecedents of the women and girls and the prospects of their rehabilitation. Thus, the Magistrate was left free to adopt either of the two modes, i.e. he could have an enquiry conducted through the Probation Officer under Section 17(2) of the Act, as was the case in the instant case, or could have summoned a panel of five respectable persons as contemplated by Section 17(5) while discharging his functions. The Magistrate took a recourse to the procedure provided under Section 17(2). Thus he need not have followed the mode provided under Section 17(5) of the Act. I feel the learned Public Prosecutors have construed amiss the provisions of Section 17(2) and Section 17(5). A close scrutiny of the said sub-sections leaves one in no doubt that every function of the learned Magistrate whichever is to be performed by him is subject to the provisions of sub-sec.(5) of Section 17. Had it not been so the legislators would not have provided that every function under the said section to be performed by a Magistrate would be subject to the provisions of sub-sec. (5) (*vide* sub-sec. (4) of Section 17). To the same effect are the observations of a Division Bench of the Allahabad High Court as reported in 1963 ILR 543 (*sic*), *Smt. Ram Devi* vs. *State* ...... "The word 'may' occurring in sub-sec.(3) Section 17 of the Suppression of Immoral Traffic in Women and Girls Act has been used in the sense of 'shall', i.e. in the sense of being imperative with the result that in

discharging his functions under sub-sec. (2) of Section 17 the Magistrate has to summon a panel of five respectable persons.

22. The panel of five respectable persons is summoned in order to assist the Magistrate discharging all his functions under sub-sec. (2) of Section 17 of the Act and not only part of those functions and that the panel is an integral part of the tribunal.

23. The next contention raised by the learned counsel for the petitioners is that no offence was being committed by the petitioners. In any case there is no evidence to the effect that the petitioners were living or carrying on or were being made to carry on prostitution in a brothel at the time of the raid. Hence the impugned order is liable to be set aside.

24. A perusal of the relevant provisions of the Act goes a long way to show that the purpose and the object of the Act is not to abolish the prostitute or the prostitution. There is no provision under the Act which makes the prostitution *per se* a criminal offence of punishes a person because he is indulging in prostitution. What is punishable under the Act is sexual exploitation or abuse of persons for commercial purposes and to earn the bread thereby except where a person is carrying on prostitution in the vicinity of the public place (*vide* Section 7) or when a person is found soliciting or seducing another person (*vide* Section 8).

25. It is thus crystal clear from above that the prostitution by itself is not an offence except when it is committed in the vicinity of public place or somebody seduces or solicits a person for the purpose of prostitution. Learned counsel for the petitioners thus contend that in the instant case no evidence has been placed on record that the petitioners were indulging in prostitution as defined under Section 2(f) of the Act. There is no evidence to show and prove that the petitioners were seducing any person for the purposes of prostitution. There is no evidence again on record that the petitioners were running brothels. The learned Magistrate it appears was swayed while passing the impugned order by the fact that the petitioners belonged to a particular caste. To my mind, no order could have been passed against the petitioners for the rescue (*sic*) from their rooms simply because they belonged

to Badya caste whose profession is stated to be dancing and singing.

26. The second factor which weighted with the learned Magistrate was that on being medically examined they were found to have had sexual intercourse very recently, such as within a week before their medical examination. To my mind as I have already observed above, sexual intercourse by itself is not an offence. Thus, the learned Magistrate was wrong in coming to his conclusion that the petitioners were indulging in prostitution as defined under the Act.

27. Section 16 of the Act deals with the rescue of person. It provides "where a Magistrate has reason to believe from information received from the police or from any other person authorized by the State Government in this behalf or otherwise, that any person is living, or it carrying on or is being made to carry on prostitution in a brothel, he may direct a Police Officer not below the rank of a Sub-Inspector to enter such brothel, and to remove therefrom such person and produce him before him." It is manifest from above that a person can be removed from his hearth and home only in those discerning few cases when he is living or carrying on or is being made to carry on prostitution in a brothel. The respondents for the best reasons known to them have not placed anything on record to make the case of the petitioners fall within the domain of Section 16 of the Act.

28. The above view was also given vent to by a Division Bench of the Allahabad High Court as reported in *Smt. Ram Devi's case* (*supra*) ...... "From this it would follow that Section 16 can only apply if some person is gaining by any acts of prostitution committed by a girl or when one or more prostitutes carry on the profession for mutual gain. There is thus nothing in the Act which punishes or makes liable for action a women, who carries on prostitution for her own gain, unaided by others own who carries it on for the mere pleasures or fun of it."

29. The other contention put forward by the learned counsel for the petitioners is that even the raising party was not constituted in accordance with the mandate of Section 13

of the Act. Hence the entire proceedings in the instant case were an exercise in futility as the non-compliance of the said provisions rendered them to be nugatory. Since the point raised by the learned counsel for the petitioners requires a close examination of the relevant provision of law, alluded to above, the same can be adverted to with profit. Section 13 of the Act lays down:

> "(1) There shall be for each area to be specified by the State Government in this behalf a special police officer appointed by or on behalf of that government for dealing with offences under this Act in the area.
>
> (2) The special police officer shall not be of below the rank of an Inspector of Police.
>
> (3) For the efficient discharge of his functions in relation to offences under this Act:
>
> (a) The special police officer of an area shall be assisted by such number of subordinate police officers (including women police officers wherever practicable) as the State Government may think fit;"

Section 15(6A) envisages "the special police officer or the trafficking police officer, as the case may be, making a search under this section shall be accompanied by at least two women police officers, and where any women or girl removed under sub-sec. (4) is required to be interrogated, it shall be done by a women police officer and if no women police officer is available, the interrogation shall be done only in the presence of a lady member of a recognized welfare institution or organization."

30. Learned counsel for the petitioners on the basis of the above provisions of law have found fault with the constitution of the raiding party and have argued that a duty has been cast on the shoulders of the Special Police Officer to include in the raiding party at least two women police officers. Admittedly learned counsel contends there were no two

women police officers in the raiding party. The raiding party consisted of a women constable and a lady member of the public. Thus the constitution of the raiding party fell far short of the requirement of the provisions of law, alluded to above.

31. The contention of a learned counsel I feel does not hold much water. A close scrutiny of Section 13(3)(a) reveals that it provides that women police officers be included in the raiding party as and when it is practicable. Thus, it has been, I feel, left to the discretion of the special police officer which leads the raiding party to include women police officers as and when they are available. The police officer, I feel, in view of the above was not bound to include women police officers if the same were not available.

32. A careful perusal of sub-sec. (6A) of Section 15 of the Act reveals that the Special Police Officer would be accompanied by at least two women police officers. However, again it has been left to the discretion of the Special Police Officer to include two women police officers at the time of the search and at the time of the interrogation. This intention of the legislature is crystal from the subsequent last lines of sub-sec. (6A) inasmuch as it provides that if no women police officer is available in that eventuality interrogation shall be done only in the presence of a lady member of a recognized welfare institution or organization.

33. There is another aspect of the matter. Admittedly the raiding party in the instance case consisted of Inspector P.L. Suri who was a Special Police Officer, SI Uday Singh and a lady constable Ms. Julia, Smt. Sneh Srivastava, a Special Police Officer of PS Kamla Market, and Shri Rajesh Chawla, residents of 107/1 and 2860/3, Thomson Road, New Delhi. Thus the raiding party had two women police officers. Hence even if the contention of the learned counsel is taken to be correct even then they cannot find fault with the constitution of the raiding party.

34. The next limb of the argument in support of the above contention is that the constitution of the raiding party was not in accordance with law inasmuch as all the members of the raiding party were not above the rank of the Head

Constable, i.e. not below the rank of Assistant Sub-Inspector of Police as required *vide* Notification No. F. 5/67/88-Home (P)/Estt. Dated December 14, 1988. The learned counsel in this connection has led me through the abovesaid notification. It is in the following words:

> "In exercise of the powers conferred by sub-section (1) of Section 13 of the Immoral Traffic (Prevention) Act, 1956, read with Government of India, Ministry of Home Affairs, Notification No. 37/1/57-P-II dated 26th April, 1958, the Administrator of the Union Territory of Delhi is pleased to appoint all Assistant Commissioners of Police, working as Sub-Divisional Police Officers, all Station House Officers, and all the Assistant Commissioners of Police of the Crime Branch, Palam Airport and Railways, as Special Police Officers within the said territory for purposes of the said Act. He is further pleased to direct under sub-section (3)(a) of the said Section 13 that the subordinate police officers (not below the rank of Assistant Sub-Inspector of Police) shall assist their respective officers so appointed as Special Police Officers."

35. The learned counsel on the basis of the above Notification has contended that it is mandatory in view of the above Notification that all the members of the raiding party should not be less than the Assistant Sub-Inspectors of Police in rank. Admittedly, according to the learned counsel there was one lady police constable in the raiding party. Thus all the members of the raiding party were not above the rank of Head Constables. Thus the said raiding party can be no stretch of imagination be called to be legal and validly constituted raiding party.

36. The contention of the learned counsel I feel is without any substance. A careful perusal of the said Notification shows that there is no mandate that all the members of the raiding party should not be below the rank of assistant Sub-Inspectors of police. What is required by the said Notification is that a

Special Police Officer would be assisted by an officer not below the rank of Assistant Sub-Inspector of Police. The raiding party consisted of an Inspector of Police known as Inspector P.L. Suri and a Sub-Inspector of Police known as S.I. Uday Singh a lady constable. Thus the Inspector of Police who was a Special Police Officer was being assisted by a Sub-Inspector of Police. Thus the constitution of the raiding party cannot be found fault within the said score.

37. In the circumstances stated above the petitioners are entitled to succeed. The petitions are allowed. The impugned order dated August 16, 1994 passed by the learned Magistrate and the order dated October 17, 1994 passed by the learned Additional Sessions Judge are hereby set aside. The petitioners be set at liberty in case they are not required to be detained in connection with any other case.

Petition allowed.

III. Gaurav Jain *vs.* Union of India & Ors. AIR 1997 SC 3021

Various directions given to the Union and State Governments by the Supreme Court for rehabilitation and ameliorating the pitiful plight of Sex-workers and their children.

Judges

K. Ramaswamy and D.P. Wadhwa, JJ.

Order

1. "Frailty, the name is woman", was the ignomity heaped upon women of Victorian Era by William Shakespeare in his great work 'Hamlet'. The history of sociology has, however, established the contrary, i.e., 'fortitude', thy name is women; 'caress', thy name is women; 'self-sacrifice', thy name is women; tenacity and successful pursuit, their apathetical is women. Indira Gandhi, Margaret Thatcher, Srimavo Bhandarnaike and Golda Meir are few illustrious women

having proved successful in democratic governance of the respective democratic States. Amidst them, still, a class of women is trapped as victims of circumstances, unfounded social sanctions, handicaps and coercive forms in the flesh trade, optimized as 'prostitutes', (for short, 'fallen women'). Seeking their redemptions, a few enlightened segments are tapping the doors of this Court under Article 32 of the Constitution, through a public spirited advocate, Gaurav Jain who filed, on their behalf, the main writ petitions claiming the right to be free citizens; right not to be trapped again; readjusted by economic empowerment, social justice and self-sustenance thereby with equality of status, dignity of person in truth and reality and social integration in the mainstream are their *magna carta.* An article "A Red light trap: Society gives no chance to prostitutes' offspring" in *'India Today'* dated July 11, 1988 is founded as source material and has done yeoman's service to ignite the sensitivity of Gaurav to seek improvement of the plight of the unfortunate fallen women and their progeny. Though Gaurav had asked for establishing separate educational institutions for the children of the fallen women, this Court after hearing all the State Governments and Union Territories which were then represented through their respective standing counsel, observed on November 15, 1989 in *Gaurav Jain* vs. *Union of India,* that "segregating children of prostitutes by locating separate schools and providing separate hostels" would not be in the interest of the children and the society at large. This Court directed that they "should be segregated from their mothers and be allowed to mingle with others and become a part of the society". Accepting the suggestion from the Bar and rejecting the limited prayer of the petitioner, this Court had ordered that "Children of prostitutes should, however, not be permitted to live in inferno and the undesirable surroundings of prostitute homes". This was felt particularly so in the case of young girls whose body and mind are likely to be abused with growing age for being admitted into the profession of their mothers. While this Court did not accept the plea for separate hostels for children of prostitutes", it felt that "accommodation in hostels and other reformatory homes should be adequately available to help segregation of these children from their mothers living in prostitute homes as soon as they are identified". In that view, instead of disposing of the writ petition with a set of directions, this Court constituted a Committee comprising Shri V.C. Mahajan, R.K. Jain, Senior Advocates and others including M.N. Shroff, Advocate, as its Convener, and other individuals named in the Order; the Court directed the Committee to submit its report giving suggestions for appropriate action. Accordingly, the report was submitted. Arguments were heard and judgment was reserved but could not be delivered. Resultantly, it was released from judgment. We have re-heard the counsel on both sides. The primary question in this case is: what are the rights of the children of fallen women, the modules to segregate them from their mothers and others so as to give them protection, care and rehabilitation in the mainstream of the national life? And as a facet of it, what should be the scheme to be evolved to eradicate prostitution, i.e., the source itself; and what succor and sustenance can be provided to the fallen victims of flesh trade? These are primary questions we angulated for consideration in this public interest litigation.

2. The Preamble, an integral part of the Constitution, pledges to secure 'socio-economic justice' to all its citizens with stated liberties, 'equality of status and of opportunity', assuring 'fraternity' and 'dignity' of the individual in a united and integrated Bharat. The fallen women too are part of citizenry. Prostitution in society has not been an unknown phenomenon; it is of ancient origin and has its manifestation in various forms with varied degrees unfounded on so-called social sanctions etc. The victims of the trap are the poor, illiterate and ignorant sections of the society and are the target group in the flesh trade; rich communities exploit them and harvest at their misery and ignominy in an organized gangsterism, in particular, with police nexus. It is of grave social concern, increasingly realized by enlightened public-spirited sections of the society to prevent gender exploitation of girl children. The prostitute has always been an object and was never seen as complete human being with dignity of

person; as if she has had no needs and aspirations of her own, individually or collectively. Their problems are compounded by coercion laid around them and torturous treatment meted out to them. When they make attempts either to resist the prostitution or to relieve themselves from the trap, they succumb to the violent treatment and resultantly many a one settle for prostitution. Prostitute is equally a human being. Despite that trap, she is confronted with the problems to bear and rear the children. The limitations of trade confront them in bringing up their children, be it male or female. Their children are equally subjected to inhuman treatment by managers of brothels and are subjected to discrimination, social isolation; they are deprived of their right to live normal life for no fault of their own. In recent times, however, there has been a growing body of opinion, by certain enlightned sections of the society advocating the need to no longer treat the fallen women as a criminal or as an object of shocking sexual abuse; they are victims of circumstances and hence should be treated as human beings like others, so as to bring them into the mainstream of the social order without any attached stigma. Equally, they realize the need to keep their children away from the red light area, particularly girls children and have them inducted into respectable and meaningful avocations and/or self-employment schemes. In no circumstances, they should continue to be in the trap of flesh trade for commercial exploitation. They need to be treated with humanity and compassion so as to integrate them into the social mainstream. If given equal opportunity, they would be able to play their own part for peaceful rehabilitation, live a life with happiness purposefully, with meaningful right to life, culturally, socially and economically with equality of status and dignity of person. These constitutional and human rights to the victims of fallen track of flesh trade need care and consideration of the society. This case calls upon to resolve that human problem with caress and purposeful guidelines, lend help to ameliorate their social-economic conditions, eradicate social stigma and to make available to them equal opportunities for the social order.

3. Equally, the right of the child is the concern of the society so that fallen women surpass trafficking of her person from exploitation; contribute to bring up her children; live a life with dignity; and not to continue in the foul social environment. Equally, the children have the right to equality of opportunity, dignity and care, protection and rehabilitation by the society with both hands open to bring them into the mainstream of social life without pre-stigma affixed on them for no fault of her/his. The Convention on the Rights of the Child, the Fundamental Right in Part III of the Constitution, Universal Declaration of Human Rights, the Directive Principles of the State Policy, are equally made available and made meaningful instruments and means to ameliorate their conditions—social, educational, economical, and cultural, and to bring them into the social stream by giving the same opportunities as had by other children. Thus, this case calls for a careful and meaningful consideration with diverse perspectives, to decide the problems in the light of constitutional and human rights and directions given to the executive to effectuate them on administrative side effectively so that those rights become real and meaningful to them.

4. Let us, therefore, first consider the fights of the fallen women and their children given by the Constitution and the Directive Principles; the Human Rights and the Convention on the Right of Child, before considering the social ignominy attached to them and before looking for the remedy to relieve them from the agnoy and make them equal participants in normal social order. Article 14 provides for equality in general. Article 21 guarantees right to life and liberty. Article 15 prohibits discrimination on the grounds of religion, race, caste, sex or place of birth, or of any of them. Article 15(3) provides for special protective discrimination in favour of woman and child relieving them from the moribund of formal equality. It states that "nothing in this article shall prevent the State from making any special provision for women and children". Article 16(1) covers equality of opportunity in matters of public employment. Article 23 prohibits traffic in human beings and forced labour and makes it punishable under Suppression of Immoral Traffic in Women and Girls

Act, 1956, which is renamed in 1990 as the Immoral Traffic (Prohibition) Act (for short, the 'ITP Act'). Article 24 prohibits employment of children in any hazardous employment or in any factory or mine unsuited to their age.

5. Article 38 enjoins the State to secure and protect, as effectively as it may, a social order in which justice—social, economic and political, shall inform all the institutions of national life. It enjoins, by appropriate statutory or administrative actions, that the State should minimize the inequalities in status and provide facilities and opportunities to make equal results. Article 39(O) provides that the children should be given opportunities and facilities to develop in a healthy manner and youth are protected against exploitation and against moral and material abandonment. Article 46 directs the State to promote the educational and economic interests of the women and weaker sections of the people and that it shall protect them from social injustice and all forms of exploitation. Article 45 makes provision for free and compulsory education for children, which is now well settled as a fundamental right to the children up to the age of 14 years; it also mandates that facilities and opportunities for higher educational avenues be provided to them. The social justice and economic empowerment are firmly held as fundamental rights to every citizen.

6. Article I of the Universal Declaration of Human Rights provides that all human beings are born free and equal in dignity and rights. They are endowed with reason and conscience and should act towards one another in a spirit of brotherhood. Article 2 provides that everyone, which includes fallen women and their children, is entitled to all the rights and freedoms set forth in the Declaration without any distinction of any kind such as race, colour, sex, language, religion, political or other opinion, national or social origin, property, birth or other status. Article 3 provides that everyone has the right to life, liberty and security of person. Article 4 enjoins that no one shall be held in slavery or servitude; slavery and the slave trade shall be prohibited in all their forms. The fallen victim in the flesh trade is no less than a slave trade. Aricle 5 provides that no one shall be

subjected to torture or to cruel, inhuman or degrading treatment or punishment. The fallen/trapped victims of flesh trade and subjected to cruel, inhuman and degrading treatment, which are obnoxious, abominable and an affront to Article 5 of the Universal Declaration and Article 21 of the Constitution of India.

7. Equally, Article 6 declares that everyone has the right to recognition everywhere as a person before the law. The victims of flesh trade are equally entitled before the law to the recognition as equal citizens with equal status and dignity in the society. Article 7 postulates that all are equal before the law and are entitled, without discrimination, to equal protection of the law. So denial of equality of the rights and opportunities and of dignity and of the right to equal protection against any discrimination of fallen women is violation of the Universal Declaration under Article 7 and Article 14 of the Indian Constitution.

8. Article 8 of the Universal Declaration provides that everyone has the right to an effective remedy by the competent national tribunals for acts violating the fundamental rights granted by the Constitution or the law. The Supreme Court of India, which is the sentinel on the *qui vive,* is enjoined to protect equally the rights of the poor, the deprived, the degraded women and children trapped in the flesh trade, kept in inhumane and degrading conditions, and to grant them the constitutional right to freedoms, protection, rehabilitation and treatment by the social engineering, in law. Constitution and appropriate administrative measures so as to enable them to work hand-in-hand to live life with dignity and without any stigma due to their past conduct tagged to them by social conditions, unfounded customs and circumstances which have become blot on the victims and their children. They too are entitled to full equality, fair and adequate facilities and opportunities to develop their personality with fully-grown potentiality to improve their excellence in every walk of life. Article 51-A of the Constitution enjoins duty on every citizen to develop the scientific temper, humanism and the spirit of inquiry and reform and to strive towards excellence in all spheres of individual and collective

activity so that the nation constantly rises to higher levels of endeavour and achievement.

9. Preamble to the Declaration of the Rights of the Child adopted by the UND on November 20, 1959, provides that the child by reason of his or her physical or mental immaturity needs special safeguards and care including her appropriate legal protection before as well as after birth. Recalling the provisions of Declaration on Social and Legal Principles relating to Protection and Welfare of the Children with Special Reference to Foster or Placement and Adoption Nationally and Internationally: the General Assembly Resolution 41/85 of December 3, 1986; the United Nations adopted Standard Minimum Rules for the Administration of Juvenile Justice (The Beijing Rules) dated November 29, 1985. India is a signatory to the Declaration and has the same and effectively participated in bringing the Declaration in force. Article 3(1) postulates that in all actions concerning children, whether undertaken by public or private social welfare institutions. Courts of law, administrative authorities or legislative bodies, the best interest of the child shall be the primary consideration. Article 3(2) enjoins to ensure the child such protection and care as is necessary for his or her well-being, taking into account the rights and duties of his or her parents, legal guardians, or other individuals legally and all the appropriate measures in that behalf shall be taken by the State. Article 3(3) postulates that the State shall ensure the availability of institutional services and facilities responsible for the care or protection of children, and shall conform with the standards established by competent authorities, particularly in the areas of safety, health, in the number and suitability of their self as well as competent supervision. Article 4 obligates by appropriate legislative, administrative or other measures, implementation of the rights recognized in the Convention. The State has undertaken to implement economic, social and cultural rights, such measures to the maximum extent of the available resources and where needed within the framework of international co-operation.

10. Article 6 postulates that State Parties recognize that every child has the inherent right to life which is already

granted by Article 21 of the Constitution of India which has been interpreted expensively by this Court to make the right to life meaningful, socially, culturally, economically, even to the deprived segments of the society with dignity of person and in pursuit of happiness. Article 6(2) enjoins to ensure development of the child and Article 7(2) postulates that the State shall ensure implementation of these rights in accordance with law and their obligations. Article 9(3) envisages that the State shall respect the right of the child who is separated from her parents to maintain personal relations and contact with her parents on regular basis. Article 14(2) provides that the State shall respect the rights and duties of the parents, and when applicable, legal guardians, to provide direction to the child in the exercise of his or her right in a manner consistent with the evolving capacities of the child. Article 17(2)(c) enjoins the State to encourage the development of appropriate guidelines for the protection of the child from information and material injurious to his or her well-being bearing in mind the provisions of Articles 13 and 18. Article 18(1) provides that the State shall use their best efforts to ensure recognition of the principle that both parents have common responsibilities for the upbringing and development of the child. Parents and State have the primary responsibility for the upbringing and development of the child. The best interests of the child will be their basic concern. Sub-para (2) postulates that for promoting the rights set forth in this Convention, parents, legal guardian or the State in the performance of their child-rearing responsibilities, shall ensure the development of institutions, facilities and services for the care of children.

11. Article 19(1) provides that the State Parties shall take all appropriate legislative, administrative, social and educational measures to protect the child from all forms of physical or mental violence, injury or abuse, neglect or negligent treatment, maltreatment or exploitation including sexual abuse, while in the care of parents, legal guardians or any other person who has the care of the child. Equally, Sub-para (2) of Article 19 postulates protective measures, as may be appropriate, should include effective procedure for the establishment of social programmes to provide necessary

support for the child and for those who have the care of the child as well as for other forms of prevention etc. Article 20 which is material for the purpose postulates as under:

(a) A child temporarily or permanently deprived of his or her family environment, or in whose own best interest cannot be allowed to remain in that environment, shall be entitled to special protection and assistance provided by the State.
(b) State Parties shall in accordance with their national laws ensure alternative care for such a child.
(c) Such care could include, *inter alia,* foster placement, Kafala in Islamic Law, adoption, or if necessary placement in suitable institutions for the care of children. When considering solutions, due regard shall be paid to the desirability of continuity in a child's upbringing and to the child's ethic, religious, cultural and linguistic background.

12. Article 28 recognizes the right of the child to education and with a view to achieving this right progressively and on the basis of equal opportunity, the State shall in particular: (a) make primary education compulsory and available free to all; (b) encourage the development of different forms of secondary education, including general and vocational education, make them available and accessible to every child and take appropriate measures such as the introduction of free education and offering financial assistance in case of need; (c) make higher education accessible to all on the basis of capacity by every appropriate means; (d) make educational and vocational information and guidance available and accessible to all children; and (e) take measures to encourage regular attendance at schools and the reduction of drop-out rates. Article 29 envisages that the State Parties agree that the education of the child shall be directed to: (a) the development of the child's personality, talents and mental and physical abilities to their fullest potential; (b) the development of respect for human rights and fundamental freedoms and for the principles enshrined in the Charter of

the United Nations; (c) the development of respect for the child's parents, his or her own cutlural identity, langauges and values, for the national values of the country in which the child is living, the country from which he or she may originate, and for civilizations different from his or her own; (d) the preparation of the child for responsible life in a free society, in the spirit of understanding, peace, tolerance, equality of sexes, and friendship among all peoples, ethnic, national and religious groups and persons of indigenous origin; and (e) the development of respect for the natural environment.

13. Article 32 recognizes the right of the child to be protected from economic exploitation and from performing any work that is likely to be hazardous or to interfere with the child's education or to be harmful to the child's health or physical, mental, spiritual, moral or social development. Articles 34, 36 and 37(a) are equally relevant and read as under:

> (34) State Parties undertake to protect the child from all forms of sexual exploitation and sexual abuse. For these purposes, States Parties shall in particular take all appropriate national, bilateral and multilateral measures to prevent:
>
> (a) The inducement or coercion of a child to engage in any unlawful sexual activity;
> (b) The exploitative use of children in prostitution or other unlawful sexual practices;
> (c) The exploitative use of children in pornographic performances and materials.
>
> * * *
>
> (36) State Parties shall protect the child against all other forms of exploitation prejudicial to any aspects of the child's welfare:
> (37) State Parties shall ensure that:

(a) No child shall be subjected to torture or other cruel, inhuman or degrading treatment or punishment. Neither capital punishment nor life imprisonment without possibility of release shall be imposed for offences committed by persons below 18 years of age;

Article 8 of the Declaration on the Right to Development provides that the State shall undertake at the national level, all necessary measures for the realization of the right to development and shall ensure, *inter alia*, equality of opportunity for all in their access to basic resources, education, health services, food, housing, employment and the fair distribution of income. Effective measures should be undertaken to ensure that women have an active role in the development process. Appropriate economic and social reforms should be carried out with a view to eradicating all social injuries.

14. The Convention on the Elimination of All Forms of Discrimination Against Women, 1979 enjoins by Article 1, prohibition of discrimination of women. Article 5 enjoins to modify social and patterns of conduct of men and women with a view to achieving elimination of prejudices and customary and all other practices which are based on the idea of the inferiority or the superiority of the sexes or on stereotyped roles for men and women. Article 12 prescribes discrimination against women in the field of health care in order to ensure on the basis of equality of men and women, access to health care services, including those related to family planning. Article 13 prescribes discrimination and directs that the State Parties shall eliminate discrimination against women in other areas of economic and social life in order to ensure on the basis of equality of men and women, the same rights, in particular, the right to family benefits, the right to participate in recreational activities, sports and all aspects of cultural life. Article 16(d) enjoins the State to ensure on the basis of equality of men and women, the same rights and responsibility as parties, irrespective of their marital status, in matters relating to their children; in all cases the interests

of the children shall be paramount. In *Madhu Kishwar* vs. *State of Bihar,* this Court considered the provisions of the Convention on the Elimination of All Forms of Discrimination Against Women, 1979 (CEDAW) and held the same to be integral scheme of the Fundamental Rights and the Directive Principles. Article 2(e) of CEDAW enjoins the State Parties to breathe life into the dry bones of the Constitution, international Conventions and the Protection of Human Rights Act, to prevent gender-based discrimination and to effectuate right to life including empowerment of economic, social and cultural rights. Article 2(f) read with Articles 3, 14 and 15 of the CEDAW embodies concomitant right to development as an integral scheme of the Constitution of India and the Human Rights Act. Section 12 of the Protection of Human Rights Act charges the National Commission with duty to ensure proper implementation as well as prevention of violation of human rights and fundamental freedoms.

15. Human Rights are derived from the dignity and worth inherent in the human person. Human rights and fundamental freedom have been reiterated by the Universal Declaration of Human Rights. Democracy, development and respect for human rights and fundamental freedoms are interdependent and have mutual reinforcement. The human rights for women, including girl child are, therefore, inalienable, integral and indivisible part of universal human rights. The full development of personality and fundamental freedoms and equal participation by women in political, social, economic and cultural life are concomitants for national development, social and family stability and growth—cultural, social and economical. All forms of discrimination on ground of gender is violative of fundamental freedoms and human rights. It would, therefore, be imperative to take all steps to prohibit prosecution. Eradication of prostitution in any form is integral to social weal and glory of womanhood. Right of the child to development hinges upon elimination of prostitution. Success lies upon effective measures to eradicate root and branch of prostitution.

16. Section 2(a) of the Immoral Traffic (Prevention) Act, 1956 (in short, the 'ITP Act') defines 'brothel' to mean any

house, room, conveyance or place which is used for purpose of sexual exploitation or abuse, for the gain of another person or for the mutual gain of two or more prostitutes. The essential ingredient, therefore, is a place being used for the purpose of sexual exploitation or abuse. The phrase 'for the purpose to indicates that the place being used for the purpose of the prostitution may be a brothel provided a person uses the place and ask for girls, where the person is shown girls to select from and where one does engage or offer her body for promiscuous sexual intercourse for hire. In order to establish prostitution, evidence of more than one customer is not always necessary. All that is essential to prove is that a girl/lady should be a person offering her body for promiscuous sexual intercourse for hire. Sexual intercourse is not an essential ingredient. The inference of prostitution would be drawn from diverse circumstances established in a case. Sexuality has got to be established but that does not require the evidence of more than one customer and no evidence of actual intercourse should be adduced or proved. It is not necessary that there should be repeated visits by persons to the place for the purpose of prostitution. A single instance coupled with the surrounding circumstances may be sufficient to establish that the place is being used as a brothel and the person alleged was so keeping it. The prosecution has to prove only that in a premises a female indulges in the act of offering her body for promiscuous sexual intercourse for hire. On proof thereof, it becomes a brothel.

17. The Juvenile Justice Act, 1986 (for short, the 'JJ Act') was enacted to provide for the care, protection, treatment, development and rehabilitation of neglected or delinquent juveniles and for the adjudication of such matters relating to disposition of delinquent juveniles. The pre-existing law was found inadequate to tic over social knowledge, instrument, delinquency or improvement of the child. The Act sought to achieve a uniform legal framework for juvenile justice in the country as a whole so as to ensure that no child, in any circumstance, is lodged in jail and police lock-up. This is being ensured by establishing Juvenile Welfare Boards and Juvenile Courts to deal adequately with the subject. The object of the

Act, therefore, is to provide specialized approach towards the delinquent or neglected juvenile to prevent recurrence of juvenile delinquency in its full range keeping in view the developmental needs of the child found in the situation of social maladjustment. That aim is secured by establishing observation homes, juivenile houses, juvenile homes or neglected juvenile and special homes for delinquent or neglected juveniles. The JJ Act is consistent with the right of the child to development; the established norms and standards for the administration of juvenile justice and special mode of investigation, prosecution, adjudication and disposition of the juvenile. The JJ Act provides for care, treatment and rehabilitation by developing appropriate linkage and co-operation between formal system of juvenile justice and voluntary agencies engaged in the welfare of the neglected or socially mal-adjusted children; it specifically defines the areas of the responsibilities etc. Section 2(a) defines 'begging'. Section 2(b) defines 'Board' to mean a Juvenile Welfare Board constituted under Section 4. Terms 'Brothel', 'prostitute', 'prostitution' and 'public place' have been adopted as defined in ITP Act. 'Competent authority' or 'Juvenile Court' as the case may be, is defined under Section 2(d). Section 2(f) defines 'fit person' or 'fit institution' to mean any person or institution (not being a police station or jail) found fit by the competent authority to receive and take care of a juvenile entrusted to his or its care and protection on the terms and conditions specified by the competent authority. 'Guardian' in relation to a juvenile has been defined under Section 2(g). 'Juvenile' has been defined under Section 2(h) to mean a boy who has not attained the age of sixteen years or a girl who has not attained the age of eighteen years. 'Juvenile Court' and 'Juvenile Home' have been defined in Sections 2(i) and 2(j) respectively. 'Neglected Juvenile' which is more relevant for the purpose of this case, has been defined in Section 2(1) to mean a juvenile who (i) is found begging; or (ii) is found without having any home or settled place of abode and without any ostensible means of subsistence and is destitute; (iii) has a parent or guardian who is unfit or incapacitated to exercise control over the juvenile; or (iv) lives in a brothel or with a prostitute or frequently goes to any place used for the purpose of prostitution, or is found to associate with any prostitution or any other person who leads an immoral, drunken or depraved life; (v) who is being or is likely to be abused or exploited for immoral or illegal purposes or unconscionable gain. 'Prostitution' means the sexual exploitation or abuse of persons for commercial purposes and the expression 'prostitute' shall be construed as it is defined under Section 2(O) of ITP Act. After the amendment to the ITP Act, 'prostitution' means sexual exploitation or abuse of person for commercial purpose.

18. Therefore, prostitution is not confined, as in the ITP Act, to offering of the body to a person for promiscuous sexual intercourse. Normally, the word 'prostitution' means an act of promiscuous sexual intercourse for hire or offer or agreement to perform an act of sexual intercourse or any unlawful sexual act for hire as was the connotation of the Act. It has been brought within its frame, by amendment, the act of a female and exploitation of her person by an act or process of exploitation for commercial purpose making use of or working up for exploitation of the person of the women taking unjust and unlawful advantage of trapped women for one's benefit or sexual intercourse. The word 'abuse' has a very wide meaning everything, which is contrary to good order established by usage amounts to abuse. Physical or mental maltreatment also is an abuse. An injury to genital organs in an attempt of sexual intercourse also amounts to 'sexual abuse'. Any injury to private parts of a girl constitutes abuse under the JJ Act. 'Public place' means any place intended for use by, or accessible to the public and includes any public conveyance. It is not necessary that it must 'be public property.' Even if it is a private property, it is sufficient that the place is accessible to the public. It must be a place to which the public, in fact, resorts or frequents.

19. The Probation Officer is kept in-charge for enforcement of the provisions of the Act. Section 4 of the J.I. Act deals with 'Juvenile Welfare Boards' under Chapter III titled 'Competent Authority and Institutions for Juvenile'. It postulates that the State Government by offical notification

may constitute for any area specified in the notification, one or more Juvenile Welfare Boards for exercising the powers and discharging the duties conferred or imposed on such Board in relation to neglected juveniles under the JJ Act. The power of the Juvenile Courts, defined in Section 5, have been reiterated in Section 7. Section 9 deals with 'Juvenile Homes'. It enjoins the State Government to establish and maintain as many juvenile homes as may be necessary for the reception of neglected juveniles under the JJ Act. Every juvenile home to which a neglected juvenile is sent under the JJ Act shall not only provide the juvenile with accommodation, maintenance and facilities for education, vocational training and rehabilitation, but also to provide him with facilities for the development of his character and abilities and give him necessary training for protecting himself against moral danger of exploitation and shall also perform such other functions as may be prescribed to ensure all-round growth and development of his personality. Sections 10 and 11 deal with establishment of special or observation homes for delinquent juveniles, details of which needs no elaboration. Section 12 touches upon the need for after-care organizations. Under Section 13 in Chapter III, if any police officer or any other person or organization authorized by the State Government in this behalf, by general or special order, is of opinion that a person is apparently a neglected juvenile, such police officer or other person or organization may take change of that person for bringing him before a Board for rehabilitation, care and protection of the child. Section 14 deals with special procedure to be followed when neglected juvenile has parents. Section 15 regulates inquiry regarding the neglected juvenile, the details of which are not material. The question, therefore, is: what procedure is efficacious to prevent prostitution, bring the fallen women and their children into the social mainstream by giving care, protection and rehabilitation?

20. Three Cs, viz., counselling, cajoling and coercion are necessary to effectively enforce the provisions of ITP Act and JJ Act. By order dated May 2, 1990, this Court, after hearing the counsel, passed an order to set up an Advisory Committee to make suggestions for eradicating child prostitution and to

point out social aspects for the care, protection, treatment, development and rehabilitation of the young victims, children and girls prostitutes from red-light area and get them free from the abuses of prostitution; to amend the existing law or to enact a new law, if so warranted; to prevent sexual exploitation of children and to take various measures for effective enforcement thereof. It is seen that the Committee constituted by this Court under the Chairmanship of Shri V.C. Mahajan travelled far and wide to have a look into the field of operation of the Governmental agencies and has suggested nodal programme for the eradication of the twin facets of prostitution, viz., protection, care and rehabilitation of the fallen women and negelected juveniles. The Committee has opined that the problem of child prostitution does not stand by itself and is a component of overall phenomenon in the country. It highly concentrates or identified red-light areas as well as on areas, which are not so clearly identified. Though the problem of prostitution is mainly found in large cities, but in the urban areas and some rural areas, the problem gives frequent recurrence. Among the fallen women, and child prostitutes constitute major bulk of the component. Child prostitutes constitute 12 to 15 per cent of prostitutes in any area. On account of the social sanctions, women are exploited by the monstrous customs of Devdasis, Jogins and Venkatansis known by other names in different parts of the country. The unfounded social and religion-based sanctions are only camouflage; their real motive is to exploit the unfortunate women. Most of them belong either to Scheduled Castes or Backward Classes coming from socio-economically lower groups. They are prevalent highly in Karnataka, Maharashtra and Andhra Pradesh. The specific areas in major cities are identified as red light areas as well as some semi-urban but rural areas. The number of red light areas having increased in recent times, brothel based prostitution is on the vane but there is an increasing trend towards decentralized mode of prostitution. 86 per cent of the fallen women hail from Andhra Pradesh, Karnataka, Tamil Nadu West Bengal, Bihar, Maharashtra, Uttar Pradesh, Assam, Gujarat, Goa, Madhya Pradesh, Kerala, Meghalaya, Orissa, Punjab, Rajasthan and Delhi. Delhi receives prostitutes from about 70 districts in the country; Bombay from 40 districts; Bangalore from 70 districts; Calcutta from 11 districts, Hyderabad from 3 districts etc. There is growing evidence that the maximum number of prostitutes get into flesh trade either voluntarily or by organized gangster force women and girls by offering rosy future to innocent fallen women and trap them often with the connivance of the police.

21. The Committee has also identified ten types of prostitutes like Street walkers, religious prostitutes, prostitutes in brothel, singing and dancing girls, bar nude, massage parlour and some are call girls. Comprehensive study conducted by another Committee in six metropolitan cities, viz., Delhi, Bombay, Calcutta, Madras, Hyderabad and Bangalore, reveals the age group of the prostitutes below 20 years of age are 75%, 21 to 30 years are 40%, 30 to 35 years are 18% and above 35 years 12%. At the time of induction into the prostitution, 9% are below 15 years; 24.9% between 16 to 18 years, 27.7% between 19 to 21 years; and 32.9% are above 22 years. At the time of entry, therefore, 15% of the fallen girls are in the category of neglected juveniles; about 25% are minors between the age group of 16 to 18 years. The major reasons for induction of prostitution are poverty and unemployment or lack of appropriate rehabilitation etc. All about social stigma; 16% due to family tradition and 9% due to illiteracy. 94.6% prostitutes are Indians while 2.6% are Nepalis and 2.7% are Bangladesis, 84.36% are Hindus; 18.8% are Muslims and 3.5% are Christians. In terms of caste classification Dalits and Tribes constitute 36%, Other Backward Classes 24% and others 40%. In terms of marital status, only 10.6% of the prostitutes are married; 34.4% are unmarried and 54.2% are divorcee or widows. In terms of education level; 70% of them are illiterates while 4% only are literates. Only 24% of the prostitutes are educated at primary and secondary level while 1.4% have higher qualifications. Therefore, prostitution is primarily due to ignorance illiteracy, coercive trapping or scare of social stigma. In India, they enter into the prostitution between the age of 16 to 19 years and

lose market by the time they became 35 years of age. Thereafter such persons either manage brothels or develop contact with high heads. Recent trend is that ladies from higher levels of income are initiated into the prostitution to sustain sufficient day-to-day luxurious style of life so as to ensure continuous economic support for their well-being.

22. The Mahajan Committee report indicates that in two villages in Bihar and some villages in West Bengal, parents send their girl children to earn in prostitution and the girls in turn send their earnings for maintenance of their families. It further indicates that certain social organizations have identified the poverty as the cause for sending the children for prostitution in expectation of regular remittance of income from prostitution by the girls who have already gone into the brothels. It is also an inevitable consequence that over years the fallen women are accustomed to certain life-style and in terms of expenditure they need certain amount of money for their upkeep and maintenance. When they bear children, it becomes additional burden for them. They are led or caught in the debt traps. The managers of the brothel are generally ladies. They do not allow the girls to bear children. In case of birth against their wishes, the unforutnate are subjected to cruelty in diverse forms. In the process of maintaining the children, again they land themselves in perpetually growing burden of debt without any scope to get out from the bondage. Thereby, this process lends perpetuality to slavery to the wile of prostitution. To support their children for education etc. 44% of them desire to leave the red-light traps and 43% of them express their despondence languishing between hope and despair. Most of those who want to leave, have given the reasons to save their children from prostitution and protection of the future of their children, fear of contacting the venereal diseases, the fear of their children following the path; some of them expressed dislike to the profession, social stigma and their yearning is to start new life. Those who want to remain in prostitution have given absence of alternative source of income, their social non-acceptability, family customs, poverty, ill-health and their

despondence as the reasons and, thus, they want to continue in the prostitution as the last resort for their livelihood. They do not like to remain in red-light area and the profession but lack of alternative source of livelihood is the prime cause of their continuation in the profession.

23. If alternatives are available and society is inclined to receive them, they will gladly shed off their past and start with a clean slate as a fresh lease of life with renewed vigorous hope and aspiration to live a normal life, with dignity of person; respect for the personality, equality of status; crave for fraternity and acceptability in the social mainstream. Therefore, it would be imperative to provide a permanent cure to the malady. There would be transition from the liberation from the prostitution to start with fresh lease of life. This period should be taken care of by providing behavioural corrections by constant interaction, counselling, cajoling and coercion as the last resort for assurance of social acceptability inculcating faith in them. An avenue to earn sufficient income for rehabilitation rekindles their resolve to start with fresh lease of life, without which their craving to shed off the past and to start with a new lease of life would remain a distant dream and a futile attempt. Therefore, the Rubicon has to be bridged between the past and the hope to make them realize their desire as normal citizenry, by providing opportunity and facilities. Provision of opportunities and facilities is input of the constitutional guarantee to the disadvantaged, deprived and denied people. The directive principles of the Constitution are particular Articles 38 and 39; and all relevant related Articles enjoin the State to provide them as impregnable inbuilt right to life guaranteed by Article 21 and equality of opportunities with protective discrimination guaranteed in Article 14 the genus and its species, Articles 15 and 16 the Preamble, the arch of the Constitution by legislative and administrative measures.

24. Therefore, it is the duty of the State and all voluntary non-government organizations and public spirited persons to come into their aid to retrieve them from prostitution, rehabilitate them with a helping hand to lead a life with

dignity of person, self-employment through provisions of education, financial support, developed marketing facilities as some of the major avenues in this behalf. Marriage is another object to give them real status in society. Acceptance by the family is also another important input to rekindle the faith of self-respect and self-confidence. Housing, legal aid, free counselling assistance and all other similar aids and services are meaningful measures to ensure that unfortunate fallen women do not again fall into the trap of red-light area contaminated with foul atmosphere. Law is a social engineer. The Courts are part of the State steering by way of judicial review. Judicial statesmanship is required to help regaining social order and stability. Interpretation is effective armory in its bow to steer clear the social malady, economic reorganization as effective instruments remove disunity, and prevent frustration of the disadvantaged, deprived and denied social segments in the efficacy of law, and pragmatic direction pave way for social stability, peace and order. This process sustains faith of the people in rule of law and the democracy becomes useful means to the common man to realize his meaningful right to life guaranteed by Article 21.

25. V.C. Mahajan Report states that an organization by name Prerana, selected Kamathipura red-light area, Bombay, where 14 lanes are in the occupation of the Managers of the brothels and have located a centre for counseling. Therein, they organize regular counselling and service centre for the fallen women and do work for the children. The national plan of action for the girl child in the SAARC Decade of the Girl Child (1991-2000) was launched as a project for the welfare and development of the girl children including adolescent girls and street children in particular. An inter-departmental monitoring committee was also set up under this plan in some of the red-light areas. The provisions of Integrated Child Development Services Scheme were extended. A number of voluntary agencies have also been involved in the care, rehabilitation and advocacy to retrieve prostitutes including child prostitutes. The rehabilitation and welfare organization is to be initiated.

26. Women found in the flesh trade, should be viewed more as victims of adverse socio-economic circumstances rather than as offenders in our society. Prostitution in five star hotels is a licence given to persons from higher echelons. The commercial exploitation of sex may be regarded as crime but those trapped in custom oriented prostitution and gender oriented prostitution should be viewed as victims of gender oriented vulnerability. That could be arrested by not only law enforcing agencies but by constant counseling and interaction by the NGOs impressing upon them the need to shed off the path and to start with a new lease of life. The ground realities should be tapped with meaningful action imperatives, apart from the administrative action, which aims at arresting immoral traffic of women under ITP Act through inter-State or Interpol arrangements and the nodal agency like the CBI is charged to investigate and prevent such crimes. We are concerned in this case more with the rehabilitation aspect than with prevention of the crime. Therefore, we emphasize on the review of the relevant law in this behalf, effective implementation of the scheme to provide self-employment, training in weaving, knitting, painting and other meaningful programmes to provide the fallen women the regular source of income by self-employment or, after vocational education, the appropriate employment generating schemes in governmental, semi-governmental or private organizations.

27. The customary initiation of women in the practice of Devdasis, Jogins and Venkatasin is prevalent in Andhra Pradesh, Karnataka and Maharashtra areas: in particular the practice of prostitution is notorious. It is an affront to the human dignity and self-respect but the pursuit of customary beliefs traps the fair sex into this glorified self-sacrifice and ultimately leads to prostitution service in the temples and charitable institutions etc. which is a crime against humanity, violation of human right and obnoxious to Constitution and Human Rights Act. They are void under Article 13 of the Constitution of India and punishable under the law. They are antithetical to the Constitutional scheme. Fundamentalists and

proponents of these practices are constitutional criminals. The unfounded customs cannot have legal sanction. On the other hand, penal enactments provide for abolition thereof. Instead of progressive outlook, regressive unfortunate tendency, of late, is raising its ugly head to glorify these ignominious practices which is leading not only to abetment of commission of the crime, but also misleading the unfortunate illiterate and weaker sections of the society, to be taken in seriously by the later by their false promises or false theories such as God's ordain which finds easy acceptance by the poor and illiterate and is acted upon. Every right thinking person should condemn such attempts apart from keeping and helping strict implementation of the law prohibiting initiation of the nasty practice wherein the eldest girl child in particular families, is offered as Devadasi or Jogin or Venkatasin, by whatever local name they are called. They are making the lives of the girl miserable: in the guise of prosperous future and custom, the girl is detained in prostitution for no fault of her. This is prevalent in particular in six districts of Karnataka, viz. Raichur, Bijapur, Belgaum, Dharwar, Bellary and Gulbarga, where their number is identified as 21,306. In Andhra Pradesh, in five districts, namely Medak, Karimnagar, Nizamabad, Nalgonda and Warangal, such girls are known as Jogins. Nizamabad District has the largest number of Jogins as per the survey conducted in 1996, as many as 16,300 Jogins were found in that State. Similarly, in Maharashtra, they are found in large number, in particular in Marathawada and Vidarbha regions. The common features of such women are that predominantly they are from Scheduled Castes, Scheduled Tribes and Other Backward Classes. The eldest girl in every family is being offered as Devadasi, Jogin or Venkatasin. Sometimes, they do redeem the pledge made to the Gods or Goddesses, etc. Original families of these Devadasis, Jogins or Venkatasins were by and large poor. They are primarily agricultural labourers having no access to credit facilities or literacy. The eldest girl in each family is driven to prostitution. The system has been in existence for years as a result of lack of awareness about the exploited segments of the Devadasis etc. Many families, which dedicated their girls, do so due to the pursuit of customary practices.

28. Economic rehabilitation is one of the factors that prevent the practice of dedication of the young girls to the prostitution as Devadasis, Jogins or Venkatasins. Their economic empowerment and education gives resistance to such exploitation; however, economic programmes are necessary to rehabilitate such victims of customs or practices. They are being rehabilitated with the help of vocational training centres set up in Maharashtra giving preferential admission into educational training institutes; they are admitted into informal adult education. In Maharashtra, educational training centres have been opened for Devadasis. In Karnataka, Devadasi women have been assisted under DWCRA schemes in various districts, in particular six district, where an extensive Devadasi rehabilitation programme is in full force. The Karnataka State Women's Development Corporation and the Karnataka State Scheduled Castes and Scheduled Tribes Development Corporation are implementing this programme in the aforesaid six districts where the phenomena of Devadasi system is being observed: training is imparted in hand-weaving, 50% subsidy is given in weaving; good work-shed is given to them free of cost; income assistance like micro-business enterprises, rope and basket making etc. are being provided to Devadasi women for rehabilitating them. Training in production of soap, chalk-making, Khadi and weaving activities is being imparted in Andhra Pradesh. Karnataka State also has taken the lead in forming self-help group of Devadasis; a thrift and saving programme is being implemented in some areas. Social Welfare Departments should undertake these rehabilitation programmes for the fallen victims of social practice so that the foul practice is totally eradicated and the fallen women are redeemed from the plight and are not again trapped into the proposition. In Andhra Pradesh, the State Government is providing housing sites or house facilities to Devadasi women; they are getting free treatment in hospitals. Devadasi women aged about 60 years and above are being given pension. In

order to improve literacy, adult literacy programmes are being organized for them. The NGOs in these three States are playing important role in implementation of various programmes and they are largely concentrating on generating awareness among these persons and their economic rehabilitation. It would, therefore, be meaningful if rehabilitation programmes are launched and implementation machinery is set not only to eradicate the fertile source of prostitution but also for successful rehabilitation of the fallen women who are the victims of circumstances to regain their lost respect to the dignity of person to sustain equality of status, economic and their social empowerment.

29. Children of the world are innocent, vulnerable and dependent. They are all curious, active and full of hope. Their life should be full of joy and peace, playing, learning and growing. Their future should be shaped in harmony and co-operation. Their childhood should mature, as they broaden their perspectives and gain new experience. Abandoning the children, excluding good foundation of life for them, is a crime against humanity. The children cannot wait till tomorrow; they grow everyday; along with them grows their sense of awareness about the surroundings. Tomorrow is no answer; the goal of their present care, protection and rehabilitation is the need of the hour. We have already dealt with the rights assured to them by the Constitution, the Directive Principles and the Convention on the Right of the Child. The United Nations Declaration on the Rights of the Child made on November 20, 1959, has formulated and given 10 principles in that behalf. Principle No. 1 provides that the child shall enjoy all the rights set fourth in the Declaration. All children, without any exception whatsoever, shall be entitled to these rights, without distinction or discrimination on account of race, colour, sex, langauge, religion, political or other opinion, national or social origin, property, birth or other status, whether himself or of his family. Principle No. 2 postulates that the child shall enjoy special protection, and shall be given opportunities and facilities, by law and by other means to enable him to develop physically, mentally, morally, spiritually

and socially in a healthy and normal manner and in conditions of freedom and dignity. Principle No. 3 postulates that the child shall be entitled from his birth to a name and a nationality. Principle No. 4 postulates among other things that the child shall enjoy the benefits of the social security. He shall be entitled to grow and develop in health; to this end, special care and protection shall be provided to him. Principle No. 5 provides that the child who is physically, mentally or socially handicapped shall be given special treatment, education and care required by that particular condition. This is more relevant for the purpose of this case. Principle 6 postulates that the child for the full and harmonious development of his personality needs love and understanding. A child of tender years shall not, save in exceptional circumstances, be separated from his/her mother. Society and the public authorities shall have the duty to extend particular care to children without a family and to those without adequate means of support. Payment of State and other assistance towards the maintenance of children of large families is desirable.

30. Principle No. 7 provides that the child is entitled to receive education, which shall be free and compulsory, at least in the elementary stages. He/She shall be given an education which will promote his/her general culture, and enable him/her on a basis of equal opportunity to develop his/her abilities, his/her individual judgment, and his/her sense of moral and social responsibility and to become a useful member of the society. The best interests of the child shall be the guiding principles of those responsible for his education and guidance that responsibility lies in the first place with his parents. The child shall have full opportunity for play and recreation, which should be directed to the same purposes as education; society; and the public authorities shall endeavour to promote the enjoyment of this right. Principle No. 8 postulates that the child shall in all circumstances be among the first to receive protection and relief. Principle 9 is most important in this behalf, which provides that the child shall be protected against all forms of neglect, cruelty and exploitation. He shall not be the subject of traffic, in any form. The child shall not be

admitted to employment before an appropriate minimum age; he shall in no case be caused or permitted to engage in any occupation or employment, which would prejudice his health or education, or interfere with his physical mental or moral development. Principle No. 10 postulates that the child shall be protected from practices, which may foster racial, religious and any other form of discrimination. He shall be brought up in a spirit of understanding, tolerance, and friendship among peoples, peace and universal brotherhood and in full consciousness that his energy and fallates should be devoted to the service of his fellow men.

31. The Government of India has adopted the National Policy for Children by Resolution No. 1-14/74-CDD dated August 22, 1974. The main purpose of the policy is that the nation's children are supremely important asset. Their nurture and solicitude are our responsibility. Children's programme should find a prominent part in our national plans for the development of human resources, so that our children grow up to become robust citizens, physically fit, mentally alert and morally healthy, endorses with the skills and motivations needed by the society. They participate in equal measure in democratic governance of the State of useful citizens. Equal opportunities for development to all children during the period of growth should be our aim; for this we would serve our larger purpose of reducing inequality and ensuring social justice. To care for, plan out needs of the children and successful implementation is, therefore, our duty, as citizen, be an Administrator, a Magistrate or a Judge.

32. Among the diverse programmes, Programme No. 4 of India for children postulates that the children of the weaker sections of the society need special protection. The programme of informal education for pre-school children from such sections will also be taken up. Programme No. 5 postulates that children who are not able to take full advantage of formal school education shall be provided other forms of education suited to their requirements. Programme No. 7 directs to ensure equality of opportunity; special assistance shall be provided to all children belonging to the weaker sections of the society, such as children belonging to the Scheduled Castes

and Scheduled Tribes and those belonging to the economically weaker sections, both in urban and rural areas. Programme No. 8 envisages that children who are socially handicapped, who have become delinquent or have been forced to take to begging or are otherwise in distress, shall be provided facilities for education, training and rehabilitation and will be helped to become useful citizens. Programme No. 10 provides that no child under 14 years of age shall be permitted to be engaged in any hazardous occupation or be made to undertaken heavy work. Programme No. 11 postulates that facilities shall be provided for special treatment, education, rehabilitation and care of children who are physically handicapped, emotionally disturbed or mentally retarded. Programme No. 13 provides that special programmes shall be formulated to spot out and encourage and assist gifted children, particularly those belonging to the weaker sections of society. Programme No. 14 envisages that existing laws should be amended so that in all legal disputes, whether between parents or institutions, the interests of children are given paramount consideration. Programme No. 15 provides that in organizing services for children, efforts would be directed to strengthen family ties so that full potentialities of growth of children are realized within the normal family, neighbourhood and community environment. Priority sectors have been provided in this behalf and paragraph 4(c) provides maintenance, education and training of orphan and destitute children. They require special care, education, training and rehabilitation of handicapped children, in Clause (e) thereof, role of voluntary organizations is emphasized. Paragraph 6 thereof postulates that the Government shall endeavour that adequate resources are provided for child welfare programmes and approriate schemes are undertaken.

33. India has a tradition of voluntary action, which shall be the endeavour of the State to encourage and strengthen voluntary actions so that State and NGOs complement each other. Paragraph 7 postulates legislative and administrative action in that behalf and paragraph 8 emphasizes people's participation in implementation of this proramme. It would, thus, be seen that the constitutional imperatives of the national

policy of the children and the international principles for the development of children are of the paramount need and consideration is for the child development. The handicapped children and those from weaker sections are given special attention by the State and voluntary agencies.

34. The question, therefore, is: What action is to be taken to rescue, rehabilitate and bring the children of fallen women into the mainstream of the society? As stated earlier, three Cs (CCC) are necessary for successful implementation, to rescue and rehabilitate the children of the fallen women living in the red-light area. Counselling, cajoling by persuasion and coercion, as the last resort, are the three Cs for successful implementation of them: 65.3% of the fallen women have children and usually they are in the age group of one to ten years. Generally, they prefer to keep their children away from them while they are in the act of intercourse except those children who are very young. Out of 71% children of illiterate fallen women 39% are literate while 58% of the total have had primary or secondary or higher education. They show keen interest to educate their children. The children tend to spend their time at study or leisure; though girl children tend to be engaged in household jobs as is usual among poorer classes. The children face the problems mainly due to (i) lack of father figure to provide security, care and guidance; (ii) increased responsibilities of mother; (iii) economic hardships (iv) lack of facilities to meet basic needs; (v) unhealthy social environment; (vi) mal-nutrition; (vii) coercive attempts by managers of brothels; (viii) taunting due to dislike by surrounders; and (ix) lack of proper counselling and guidance; motivation and opportunity gaps.

35. Many prostitutes themselves are child prostitutes (for short, the 'CP'); they and the children of the prostitutes (for short, the COP') need to be removed from the red-light area. Generally, the police resort to IPC and ITP Act in this behalf but the forceful rescue of CP or COP in reality is not successful in their rehabilitation. In this behalf, it is necessary to take aid of the definition of "neglected child" defined in JJ Act. It is already seen and is reiterated for continuity that 'neglected juvenile' means one found in begging; or found without having

any home or settled place of abode and without any ostensible means of subsistence and is destitute; or has a parent who is unfit or incapacitated to exercise control over the juvenile; or lives in a brothel or with a prostitute or frequently goes to any place used for the purpose of prostitution or is found to associate with any prostitute or any other person who leads, an immoral, drunken or depraved life or who is being or is likely to be abused or exploited for immoral or illegal purposes or unconscionable gain. The JJ Act makes distinction between 'delinquent juvenile' and 'neglected juvenile' attributing to a delinquent juvenile an act or omission punishable by law to identify him as a delinquent juvenile. A neglected juvenile is one who is of the age of 16 years in the case of a boy and 18 years in the case of a girl, or whose parents are unfit because of being living in prostitution, or the child born to a prostitute, or one who frequents or associates with prostitution becomes a neglected juvenile. A child brought to associate with a prostitute or is engaged in the prostitution or the profession of prostitution or another juvenile who leads an immoral or depraved life or one who is likely to be abused or exploited for immoral or illegal purposes for unconscionable gain is also a juvenile. The crime is not attached for identifying him/her as neglected juvenile; it is so in the case of a delinquent juvenile under the Act. They are to be kept in the juvenile home as a place of safety.

36. An institution established or certified by a State Government under Section 9 of the JJ Act is a juvenile home. The object of the Act is not to punish the juvenile but to rehabilitate him/her, be it a delinquent juvenile or neglected juvenile. In the latter case, it is one of the obligations of the State to provide for care and concern of the State to establish a juvenile home under Section 9 of the JJ Act. Section 4 of the JJ Act enjoins the State to constitute, by a notification, for any area specified in the notification, one or more Juvenile Welfare Boards for exercise of the powers and discharging the duties conferred or imposed, under the JJ Act on such Board in relation to neglected juveniles.

37. The Board shall consist of a Chairman and such other members as the State Government thinks fit to appoint, of

whom not less than one shall be a woman; and every such member shall be vested with the powers of a Magistrate under the Cr.P.C. The Board shall function as a Bench of Magistrates and shall have the powers conferred by the Cr.P.C. as the case may be on a judicial Magistrate of the first class or Metropolitan Magistrate in Metropolitan cities. Even, in certain cases a delinquent juvenile who commits an offence like begging, being the neglected juvenile, is covered as a neglected juvenile and should not be treated as delinquent juvenile since he began begging due to destitution or was forced to beg by organised gangsters. Therefore, all types of juvenile defined within the ambit of neglected juvenile, though attached with certain acts or omission, are punishable under law they still remain to be neglected juvenile and should be dealt with by the Welfare Board and he brought within the protective umbrella of the juvenile home established under Section 9, Establishment of juvenile home. Thus, it is a mandatory duty of the State to provide teeth to the provisions of the Constitution, the Directive Principles, the Convention on the Right of the Child read with principles of United Nations Declaration and National Policy of the Government of India referred to hereinbefore, and are protected by the JJ Act.

38. Every child who is found to be neglected juvenile should be dealt by the Board and should be brought within the protective umbrella of the juvenile home. The attribution as 'neglected children' is not social stigma; the purpose is to identify the children as juveniles to be dealt with under the JJ Act which is more a reformative and rehabilitated centre rather than for punishing the child as criminal; and mend their behaviour and conduct. In an appropriate case, where the treatment of bringing the neglected juvenile into the national mainstream takes long time, the definition coupled with age prescription, should not be strictly interpreted to deny the ameliorative care, consideration and rehabilitation of the neglected juveniles. The benefit of reformation, rehabilitation and bringing them into the mainstream after the passing of the age prescription under the Act, is the goal sought to be achieved. Lest, it has the effect of throwing the

neglected juvenile into the vile of prostitution or exploitation him for organized crimes by the organized gangsters taking advantage of his immaturity and despondence; that would be deleterious to the child's development and would widen the deep gap between hope and reality in the operation of the provisions hereinbefore referred to. The definition of 'neglected juvenile', therefore, shoud be interpreted broadly, which is an important function for the purpose of identifying the groups of children who need care and attention and protection for rehabilitation. Their withdrawal from the protective umbrella of the JJ Act foils the goals set out; besides all measures to bring the neglected juvenile into the mainstream of the social status end up in failure and frustration.

39. Even if the economic capacity of the mother of neglected juvenile in the red-light area to educate and to bring him up would not relieve the child from social trauma: it would always be adverse to keep the neglected juvenile in the custody of the mother or the manager of the brothel; thus, the child prostitute is unsafe and insecure. So, they should be rescued, cared for and rehabilitated. As stated earlier, the three C's, namely, counselling, cajoling and coercion of the fallen women to part with the child or child prostitute herself from the manager of the brothel is more effective, efficacious and meaningful method to rescue the child prostitute or the neglected juvenile. The income criteria, therefore, is not a factor not to rescue the child prostitute or the neglected juvenile for rehabilitation.

40. It is of necessity to remember that the arms of law are long enough to mould the law to operate on the even keel. The coercive power with the law enforcement agency to rescue the child prostitute or the neglected juvenile may not necessarily end up as a successful means. It would be last resort when all avenues fail. on the other hand, involvement of the non-governmental organizations in particular women organizations which are more resourceful for counselling and cautioning, would make deep dent into the thinking mould of the fallen victims and would be a source of success for their retrieval from the prostitution or sending the neglected

juvenile to the juvenile homes for initial treatment, psychologically and mentally, and will yeild place to voluntariness to surrender guardianship of the child prostitute or neglected juvenile to the Welfare Board or to the NGOs to take custody of child prostitute or the neglected juvenile for, care, protection and rehabilitation.

41. The V.C. Mahajan Committee report states that the resort to Sections 14 and 17 of JJ Act has met with resistance by the mothers and in the case of child prostitute, by the managers of the brothels. The coercive method adopted on one occasion by the Delhi Police pursuant to a complaint under Section 13 of the JJ Act on March 7, 1990, led to frustration of the entire operation, when on an early morning, the prostitutes were taken by surprise by tap on the doors and children were taken into custody, on the pretext of being examined by the doctors. Total 450 juveniles were taken into custody but no prior arrangement was made with the doctors for their examination. The children were not given custody immediately. The children were taken into custody; 112 children below 16 years were kept in the custody of the police. Their examination went on up to March 23, 1990 by which time, the agitated mothers and the managers of the brothels resorted to pressure techniques. Ultimately, it all ended in a fiasco. All were released by the managers of juvenile home. This would indicate apathy on the part of police in proper implementation and lack of prior planning, understanding and concerted action between the law enforcement agency, the NGOs and public-spirited persons and doctors. Instead of doing good, it does harm. It, therefore, gives a stark lesson that until proper arrangements are made and concerted action taken *ad hoc* attempt to enforce law results in defeat of the purpose of the JJ Act. On the other hand, if the NGOs in particular women members of the NGOs pursue and counsel the mothers of the children or managers of child prostitutes to have them into custody and if proper care and treatment is given, rehabilitation is the sure road to the successful results; it would be a success rather than frustration of the enforcement of the JJ Act. It is, therefore, clear imperative that proper planning, constant counselling and persuasion are the

appropriate means, rather than abrupt to *ad hoc* coercive steps, unless it becomes the last resort, for successful enforcement of the scheme.

42. The question then is: what is the proper method required to rehabilitate the neglected juvenile or child prostitute taken into custody under the JJ Act for enduring results? It is rather unfortunate that the juvenile homes established and being run by the Government are not effectively been managed and *yielding* expected results. They become ornament for the statistical purpose defeating the constitutional objectives and international Conventions, which are part of the municipal law. This Court on May 2, 1990 had directed the enforcement agencies to bring the prostitute, neglected juveniles for the rehabilitation in the juvenile homes manned by well-qualified and trained social workers. The child prostitutes rescued from the red-light areas should be shifted into the juvenile homes. They should ensure their protection in the homes. The officers in charge of the juvenile homes, the welfare officers and the probation officers should coordinate the operation and enforce it successfully. They should be made responsible for the protection of the child prostitutes or the neglected juveniles kept in the juvenile homes for psychological treatment in the first instance relieving them from the trauma under which they were subjected to while in the brothels and red-light areas. The special police authorities should be established to coordinate with the social welfare officers of the State Government and public spirited persons, NGOs locally available, and see that the juvenile homes are entrusted to efficient and effective management, the child prostitutes or neglected juveniles are properly protected and psychologically treated, education imparted and rehabilitation succeeded. They should also be provided with proper accommodation maintenance facilities for education and other rehabilitation facilities.

43. V.C. Mahajan Committee's report specifies at page 31 that since its inception till November 1989, 102 boys and 34 girls were admitted by a responsible institute, a non-statutory body in Pune run on voluntary basis to impart education to the destitute children in general and

neglected juveniles and child prostitutes in particular, with all facilities; it is run by Bal Sangopan Centre run by Shreemant Dagausheth Halwai Ganpat Trust which gets fund from the Ministry of Welfare, Government of India under the scheme for children in need of care and protection. Similar homes are also being run for 75 children at Kolhapur and Bombay. As a policy, the Trust does not keep girls above 12 years in the institute. On the other hand, it has tied up with Hinge Shree Sikshan Sansthan at Pune for placement of the girls above 12 years into their custody but the Trust continues to be the parent institution, paying their fees and holding the overall responsibility to bring up the girls above 12 years. The report also states that the mothers are allowed to visit the children once in month and they are allowed to take them home for brief spells during festivals and other special occasions. There is another institution, viz., 'Nihar' run by 'Vanchit Vikas' institute at Pune. It is founded on the basis of the felt needs of the neglected juveniles. Social workers of Pune Corporation co-operate with them. There are special health reforms available to prostitutes; the workers come into frequent contact with the prostitute mothers and their children. Gradually, they are getting acquainted with the situation and awareness is generated of the disadvantages to keep the children with them while remaining in red-light area. The motivation yielded positive results in helping the children rescued from the mothers and their placement in the home. The institute is run through donations. It is being run for the past 15 years. Much progress has been made in the struggle to rehabilitate the neglected juveniles. Therein, they have established a school for 23 children being used in that 'Nihar'. Most of the children are in the age group of 5 to 10 years. They take only female children with the female staff to attend to the needs of the children. Their basic requirements of food, clothing and shelter are taken care of the 'Nihar'. Health, education and overall development is also taken care of. The children are enrolled in Zila Parishad Schools. Residential staff helps them to take them to the schools and bring them home. On Saturdays, teachers spend their time in 'Nihar' teaching music and playing games with the children. On Sundays, teachers come from Pune and spend time with the children and keep them in their studies. The mothers of the children visit once in a month. The management does not allow the mothers to take the children except for short duration. The prostitute mothers themselves have realized the advantage to keep their children away from vile environment and are happy with educational progress of their children. Similarly, "Devadasi Nirandhar Mukti Kendra, Ganghiganj" is running a centre by name "Devadasi Chhatra Vasti Graha" at Pune from October 1986. It is a residential institution for the children of the Devadasis. 80% of them are the Devadasi children while 20% are children from socio-economic backward classes. Funds for this institution are granted by the Department (contd. on col. 2), of Social Welfare, Government of Maharashtra. It has on its roll, 75 boys and girls. As on the date of the visit by the Committee on July 7, 1990, 57 boys and 8 girls (total 65) were found in the institute. Similar institutions are being run elsewhere; the details of which are not material. They have been elaborated in the Report of V.C. Mahajan Committee.

44. The above facts do indicate that the NGOs are actively involved in the field of rehabilitating and educating the children of the fallen women as neglected juveniles not brought within the net of JJ Act. The mothers have their legitimate aspirations to bring their children into the mainstream of the nation. What needs to be done is proper, efficient and effective co-ordination and management in particular entrustment to the NGOs, which would yield better results than the management solely by the Governmental agencies. The motivation by the NGOs makes a deeper dent into the mind of the prostitute mothers or child prostitutes to retrieve them from the flesh trade and rehabilitate the children as useful citizens in the mainstream of the society. V.C. Mahajan Committee has given details of the Child Development and Care Centres (for short, the 'CDCC') in Annexure IV to the Report. It states how the management needs to be done, as under:

Child Development and Care Centres (for brevity CDCC)

(A scheme for Children of Prostitutes and Children Associating with Prostitutes and Prostitution)

Various factors have led to the perpetuation of prostitution, which in turn has given rise to a large population of prostitutes' children. Their mothers' nature of work, status, income, etc. often leave the children wanting in attention and care for their overall development. However, it is not enough to perceive them as more victims of neglect. Their cause has to be taken up to prevent them from taking to prostitution or its promotion and curbing their proneness to delinquency. It is believed that children's energies have to be tapped and channelised. The Child Development and Care Centres are envisaged to provide Localized services through which the larger interests of these children can be attended to. Such Centres are to be situated in:

(i) The Vicinity of red-light areas,
(ii) The vicinity of other areas identified as having a concentration of prostitutes,
(iii) Those areas where there is a concentration of communities among whom prostitution is the traditional occupation of the women and girls.

These Centres will be run by voluntary organization with Government Fund and have Advisory and Monitoring Committees at Central, State and Local levels.

(Emphasis supplied)

Objectives

The scheme would:

(i) Provide welfare and developmental services for children of prostitutes and other children associating with prostitutes and prostitution by making them socially productive beings;

(ii) Try to wean them away from their surroundings by referring them to suitable residential institutions as and when necessary;
(iii) Try to reach out to the mothers (through their children) and counsel them on different issues related to their personal lives, their occupational lives and their children; and
(iv) Operate as an information dissemination and conscientious point, particularly for the higher age group (12-18 years).

Services/Facilities

Keeping in view the total care and development of the child, the following services/facilities would be provided:

(i) Creche (day and night)
(ii) Pre-school education (Balwadi): The objective of pre-school education, besides the physical, emotional and social development of the children, is to prepare them mentally to attend formal schools in future. This, it is hoped, will increase the enrolment in schools.
(iii) Non-formal education/functional literacy
(iv) Counselling (personal and career)
(v) Nutritional inputs
(vi) Health Care
(vii) Library
(viii) Toy-bank
(ix) Recreation
(x) Outings and Educational Trips
(xi) Skill Development
(xii) 'Save for the Child' Scheme: Mothers are anticipated to be spending Rs. 100 (at least per child per month) when the child stays with her. When the child is placed in the custody of a residential institution, she no longer has to spend on the scheme, therefore, start an account in the name of the child in any

nationalized bank and deposit Rs. 100 every months. If at the end of one year it is found that she has been regular in depositing the amount, the CDCC will start contributing an equal share. By the time the child is out of the institution he/she will have some immediate financial support.

Note: Suggestion by the Court: The Government of India should extend the Thrift Scheme of Women for these fallen women as well.

(xiii) After school educational help the children complete their homework, prepare help lessons for schools. Teachers would also help them with any difficulties faced in school. By this measure, the rate of school dropout can be checked.

Suggestions and Directions of the Court: Special coaching should be arranged for these children.

(xiv) De-institutionalized Help: Some of the mothers may be agreeable to part with their children or have different priorities for the children. Money may not be their problem. In such cases the CDCC may enlist their children as recipients of de-institutionalized care services. It would ensure that the minimum needs of the child are met by the mother and his/her development is in no way impeded. It would be binding on the mother to provide the child with the basic minimum facilities for the child's overall growth and development. This would be a means of getting the mother to provide for the child instead of institutionalizing him/her. Here, in the process, the CDCC would operate as a catalytic and monitoring agency.

The CDCC will also follow up the cases of those children whose mothers are placed in Protective Homes. In case they are endangered in any way by separation from mother, the CDCC will adopt necessary steps to help them.

The CDCC would be paid a nominal sum for its services and also for spending on some of the items required by the child for its growth, in case the mother is unable to meet such expenditure. The mother will be liable to make regular reports to the CDCC to facilitate its monitoring function.

Suggestions and Directions of the Court: All necessary funds should be provided by the Appropriate Government i.e., either the Central Government or the State Government, as the case may be.

(*Note*: This arrangement will work for the traditional communities, with either a CDCC or any other voluntary organization functioning as a catalytic and monitoring agent.)

The CDCC would function as a nodal agency in the field and would co-ordinate with Government departments to bring as many programmers to its group of beneficiaries as possible. Further, they would arrange referal services in the following areas as and when the need is felt for the benefit of a child:

(i) Institutionalized care—arrange sponsorship foster care
(ii) Skill Development
(iii) Health
(iv) On the job training
(iii) Training for Entrepreneurship

Eligibility of Beneficiaries

Children of any age between 0-18 years who are either:

(i) Children of prostitutes, or
(iii) Children associated with prostitution or prostitute, may be benefited from this scheme.

In all deserving cases the scheme should extend services to those children above 18 years, only if it is clearly seen that they are not yet able to feed for themselves and would be benefited by further support. Those older than 18 years would be assisted as special cases.

Coverage

There would be no limit to the number of children being covered by the Centre. Being a service oriented centre it is likely that only groups of children will come to the Centre during the day asking for any of the services.

Only in the case of creches and balwadis there would be regular attendance where not more than 25-30 children should be enrolled at any given time and when the member increases separate groups be formed and benefit of service extended.

Organization

The following are some of the general conditions for eligibility for applying for the scheme:

(i) The applicant should be a voluntary, non-governmental organization, registered under an appropriate Act or a regularly constituted branch of a registered welfare organization.

(ii) The organization seeking assistance should be a non-profit and secular organization in a way that its services would be open to all without any discrimination of religion, caste, creed, language or sex.

(iii) The organization should have a regularly constituted managing committee with its functions and their responsibilities clearly laid down in its Bye-laws.

(iv) The organization should preferably have had some experience in managing child development programmes or experience of working on the issues related to prostitution.

Programme

Though it is viewed as a localized service centre, its community outreach aspect must be active. By reaching the prospective target group and acquainting them with the services available, the utilization of the CDCC can be availed.

The staff at the Centre would organize health camps and awareness generation camps from time to time.

While providing the services of the children, efforts of the staff at the Centre would be to counsel the mothers and children and encourage the latter to join educational institutions. It should assist them in getting admitted into the educational institutions. Teachers attached to the CDCC would help the school going children in completing their homework and coping with other difficulties. During school hours the teacher would hold functional literacy classes for the elder children who are uneducated.

By way of extending further support to this group of uneducated and unskilled children, the Centre's staff will have to counsel them regularly.

As it is advisable to remove the children from the vicinity of the red-light area by about 6 years of age, the staff will have to convince the mothers and arrange for their placement in residential institutions. Regular meetings are to be held with the mothers to discuss about the health and nutritional needs of their children and to make them conscious about the environment. Efforts should be directed towards making them interested in the activities of the CDCC. They must be kept informed about the progress of their children and of their current activities, problem and future plans. They must be allowed to participate in planning and execution of programmes.

The Centre must follow up cases of women who are placed in Protective Homes. Their children must be immediately enlisted in the list of beneficiaries at the Centre. Depending upon their situation care and protection must be extended to them such that the separation from mother does not:

(i) Hamper their education,
(ii) Make them emotionally and physically insecure,
(iii) Render them neglected and uncared for,
(iv) Expose them to greater risks of delinquency.

In case a child is affected in any of these ways, the Centre must step in and to give him/her emotional support and to place him/her in a residential institution. The mother must be involved in the process and the Centre must be in touch with her at the protective Home.

The CDCC will involve the local level youth clubs or any other organizations and with support from them:

(i) Mobilize the local community,
(ii) Organise activities for the beneficiary group.

Working Hours of the CDCC

1. Creche (day and night): as per decision of the Local Committee
2. Balwadi ...... 9.00 a.m. to 1.00 p.m.
3. Non-formal Education ...... 1.00 p.m. to 4.00 p.m.
4. After School Education ...... 4.00 p.m. to 6.00 p.m.

Timings of the other facilities to be fixed according to local situation.

Staff

1. Programme Co-ordinator	1
2. Special Worker-cum-Counseller	2
3. Teacher	1
4. Balwadi Teacher	1
5. Helper-cum-Office Assistant	1
6. Ayah-cum-Cook	2
7. Chowkidar	1

Advisory and Monitoring Committees

To ensure effective implementation of the scheme advisory and Monitoring Committees will be set up at various levels. There would be a Central Committee with State and Local Committees under it. While there will be a State Committee in every State, there may be as many Local Committees as the number of CDCCs operative in the respective State. A single Committee may be adequate in case there are more than one CDCC in the same city/town. Members of the Committees:

Central Committee (Seven Members)

(i) Chairperson, Central Social Welfare Board.
(ii) Representative of the Department of Women and Child Development.
(iii) Representative of the Ministry of Welfare.
(iv) Retired Police Officer.
(v) Three Social Workers.

State Committee (Seven Members)

(i) Chairperson, State Social Welfare Advisory Board.
(ii) Representative of the Department of Women and Child Development.
(iii) Representative of the Department of Social Welfare.
(iv) Retired Police Officer.
(v) Three Social Workers.

Local Committee (Seven Members)

(i) Programme Coordinator CDCC.
(ii) Representative of Mothers
(iii) Representative of Community
(iv) Representative of Local Club, if any
(v) Secretary or Representative of the Voluntary Organization implementing the scheme
(vi) Two Social Workers.

These Committees will run the scheme with the assistance from the Government. No separate office needs to be maintained. The necessary office work can be done at the offices of the Chairperson.

CSWB (in the case of the Central Committee) and Chairperson SSWAB (in the case of the State Committee). The

CDCC would help in the office work of the Local Committee. For this, the respective organizations will receive a token Administrative Assistance Grant.

Meeting of the Committee can be organized by the respective organizations. There must be quarterly meetings of the Central and State Committees. The Local Committees must, however, meet once in every month. The Local Committee is to send its minutes of meeting held and reports of activities to the State and Central Committees.

The Central Committee will function as the central co-ordinating body, with regular feedback from the State and Local Committees. Besides regular meetings, the Committee may call emergent meetings to discuss any urgent matter.

These Committees will co-ordinate the functioning of any ICDS Centres being run in lieu of the CDCC (in case a voluntary organization is not available to run and manage a CDCC) and execute the same functions as it does in the case of CDCC.

45. We are of the view that the suggestions require earnest examination to give force and content to them. The rescue and rehabilitation of the child prostitutes and children should be kept under the nodal Department, namely, Department of Women and Child Development under the Ministry of Welfare and Human Resource, Government of India. It would devise suitable schemes for proper and effective implementation. The institutional care, thus, would function as an effective rehabilitation scheme in respect of the fallen women or the children of fallen women even if they have crossed the age prescribed under the JJ Act. They should not be left to themselves, but should be rehabilitated through self-employment schemes or such measures as are indicated hereinbefore. The juvenile homes should be used only for a short stay to relieve the child prostitutes and neglected juveniles from the trauma they would have suffered; they need to be rehabilitated in the appropriate manner. The details are required to be worked out by meaningful procedure and programmes. In the light of the directions already given by this Court from time to time to the Central

Government, State Governments and Union Territory Administrators, adequate steps should be taken to rescue the prostitutes, child prostitutes and the neglected juveniles as indicated hereinabove; they should take measures to provide them adequate safety, protection and rehabilitation in the juvenile homes manned by qualified trained social workers or homes run by NGOs with the aid and financial assistance given by Government of India or State Government concerned. A nodal Committee with the public spirited NGOs, in particular women organizations/woman members should be involved in the management. Adequate encouragement may be given to them; the needed funds should be provided and timely payments disbursed so that the scheme would be implemented effectively and fruitfully.

46. The Minister of Welfare, Government of India will constitute a Committee consisting of the Secretary in charge of Department of Women and Child Development as the Chairperson and three or four Secretaries from the concerned State Governments, to be nominated by the Minister of Welfare. They would make an in-depth study into these problems and evolve such suitable schemes as are appropriate and consistent with the directions given above. The Committee should be constituted within one month from the date of the receipt of this judgment. The Committee should finalize the report within three months thereafter. As soon as the report is submitted, the same may be communicated to all the State Governments and the concerned Ministries for their examination. Within two months from date of the communication, the Minister of Welfare, Government of India, in coordination with the Prime Minister Office should convene a meeting presided over by the Prime Minister, with Minister of Welfare, Home Minister, Human Resource Minister, the concerned Ministers of the State Governments and their Secretaries as well to discuss the problem and take decisions. The Committee should finalize the report with further suggestions or amendments, if suggested in the conference. Thereafter, the report should be finalized and then direction would be given to the State Governments for effective

implementation of the schemes. The nodal Department would enforce and regularly be supervised by the Ministry of Welfare, Government of India. A permanent Committee of Secretaries should be constituted to review the progress of the implementation on annual basis, and to take such other steps as may be expedient in the effective implementation of the schemes. Periodical progress as to funding and enforcement of the scheme should be submitted to the Registry of this Court. If further directions would be needed, liberty is given to the parties to approach this Court. In that view of the matter, it is believed and hoped that the above law and directions would relieve the human problem by rehabilitation of the unfortunate fallen women caught in the trap of prostitution; their children would be brought into the mainstream of the social order; these directions would enable them to avail the equality of opportunity and of status, with dignity of person which are the arch of the Constitution.

47. My learned brother D.P. Wadhwa, J. has disagreed to the directions given to the Union of India etc. In the first part of the Order on the ground, as seems to me, that in view of the relief sought for in the writ petitions and the directions given by this Court on the earlier occasions there is no scope for the relief being granted now and directions given in the concluding part of the Order. Brother Wadhwa, J. thus agrees with the directions given at pages 78 to 81 relating to the prostitutes' children and the children of the fallen women. Directions at pages 38-39 and 43 to 45 of this Order pertain to the prevention of induction of women, in various forms, into prostitution; their rescue from the vile flesh trade; and rehabilitation through various welfare measures so as to provide them with dignity of person, means of livelihood and socio-economic empowerment. In that behalf, my learned brother has not concurred for the reasons given in the separate Order proposed to be delivered by him. That has necessitated me to have a re-look into the precedents on Public Interest Litigation *vis-a-vis* the scope, ambit and power of the Court to grant relief in matters arising from real and true public interest litigation in which the condition of *locus standi* has

been relaxed and public-spirited persons, not motivated by pressure tactics for ultimate ends, are encouraged to work for the poor, under-privileged or weaker segments of the society who are otherwise unable to avail of judicial process for grant of general relief to such a group of persons.

48. In *Labourers working on Salal Hydro Project* vs. *State of Jammu & Kashmir* offspring of a labourer in a letter addressed to this court enclosing a clipping of the newspaper *"Indian Express"* dated August 26, 1982—it was brought to the notice of this Court that a large number of migrant workmen were subjected to exploitation and violation of various welfare laws made for them. Intervention was sought to prohibit exploitation and to grant different relief to them. The letter was treated by this Court as a writ petition under Article 32. Directions were issued to the Labour Commissioner (Centre) to enquire into and submit a report; the Central Government was also directed to file their affidavit. After receipt of the report and filing of the counter-affidavits, this Court found, as a fact, from the evidence that the workmen were denied of the minimum wages and other welfare benefits. Accordingly, directions were given. This decision, therefore, is an authority of the proposition that a Public Interest Litigation is not of adversary character but one of performance of the constitutional duty; therein new procedure was adopted for collecting evidence from acceptable source. In *Dr. Upendra Baxi (II)* vs. *State of U.P.*, Dr. Upendra Baxi, a noted humanist and champion of Human Rights, had addressed a letter to this Court that a writ peition may be entertained in public interest to protect the girls living in the Government Protective Homes at Agra who were being denied right to live with basic human dignity by the State of Uttar Pradesh which was running the Home. In that case, it was held that the public interest litigation is not a litigation of an adversary undertaken for the purpose of holding the State Government or its officers responsible for making reparation. Public interest litigation involves a collaborative and cooperative effort by the State Government and its officers, the lawyers appearing in the case and the Bench for the purpose of making Human Rights

meaningful for the weaker sections of the community in ensuring the socio-economic justice to the deprived and vulnerable sections of the humanity in the country. Directions, therefore, were accordingly issued; details thereof are, however, not material for the purpose of this case. What is material is that the power of this Court is wide to grapple with new situations; it can get the evidence collected with cooperation of the counsel for the parties and the State and mete out justice to protect the constitutional rights guaranteed to all the citizens in particular, the vulnerable weaker segments of the society. *Vincent Panikur-langara* vs. *Union of India,* related to manufacture of drugs and involved examination of evidence to determine the character of the action taken by the Government on the basis of advice tendered to it to prohibit the manufacture and trade of drugs in the interest of patients who required the drugs for that treatment. This Court pointed out that the statutory bodies and the Government are bound to respond and join the proceedings pending before the Court. They are not litigants; yet they do not have the choice of keeping away from the Court like private parties in ordinary litigations opting to go *ex parte*. Since the matter involves technical aspects *vis-a-vis* health of the public and is of national importance, this Court ensured co-operation of all the parties and *suo motu* extended the opportunity of hearing and inviting the named statutory authorities to assist the Court. In that behalf, it was held that the public interest litigation is not a normal litigation with adversaries fitted against one another.

49. As already seen, in *Bandhua Mukti Morcha case* [1984(3) SCC 161: AIR 1984 SC 802], this Court has evolved a new procedure supplementing the existing procedure to meet the new situation and to render justice in public interest litigations. It directed the Labour Commissioner (Central) to investigate into and collect the evidence and submit the report to the Court, as dealt with at pages 189-90 (of SCC): (at pp. 815-816 of AIR). In *Rural Litigation and Entitlement Kendra* vs. *State of U.P.* this Court dealt with a public interest litigation relating to ecological imbalances created due to mining operations and denudation of forest. In paragraphs 16 and 17, this Court

at pages 515-16 [of (Supp) SCC]: (at p. 2195 of AIR) had pointed out that the writ petitions before the Court were not inter-parties disputes and had been raised by way of public interest litigation and the controversy before the Court was as to whether for social safety and for creating a hazardless environment for the people to live in, mining in the area should be permitted or stopped. This Court had directed stoppage of twining activity since it created ecological imbalance and denudation of the forest. In *M.C. Mehta* vs. *Union of India*, a Constitution Bench of this Court was to consider the scope of the public interest litigation to grant compensation to the victims of hazardous or dangerous activities when deaths or injuries were caused to them on account of the accident during the operation of such activities. This Court had held that the law should keep pace with changing socio-economic norms; where a law of the past does not fit in the present context, the Court should evolve new law in a public interest litigation. The power of this Court is very wide to devise appropriate procedure and to issue directions, orders or rules. This Court is competent to grant a remedial assistance by way of compensation in exceptional cases. The Court has incidental and ancillary power in exercise of which it can devise new methods and strategy in securing enforcement of fundamental rights particularly in public interest litigation or social action cases. Directions were accordingly granted in that case. In *Bandhua Mukti Morcha* vs. *Union of India* the writ petition under Article 32 was filed to release bonded labourers in the country by way of letter addressed to this Court. In that behalf, this Court had taken assistance of the parties, got the evidence collected and then issued appropriate directions for release of the bonded labour. In this behalf, it was held at page 169 (of SCC) : (at p. 815 of AIR) that when the poor come before the Court, particularly for enforcement of their fundamental rights, it is necessary to depart from the adversarial procedure and to evolve a new procedure which will make it possible for the poor and the weak to bring the necessary material before the Court for the purpose of securing enforcement of their fundamental rights. It must be remembered that the problems of the poor, which are now coming before the Court, are qualitatively different from those, which have hitherto occupied the attention of the Court and they need a different kind of lawyering skill and a different kind of judicial approach. If we blindly follow the adversarial procedure in their case, they would never be able to enforce their fundamental rights and the result would be nothing but a mockery of the Constitution. We have, therefore, to abandon the *laissez faire* approach in the judicial process particularly where it involves a question of enforcement of fundamental rights; we should forge new tools, devise new methods and adopt new strategies for the purpose of making fundamental rights meaningful for the large masses of the people. And this is clearly permissible by the language of Clause (2) of Article 32 because the Constitution-makers while enacting that clause, have deliberately and advisedly not used any words restricting the power of the Court to adopt any procedure which it considers appropriate in the circumstances of a given case for enforcing the fundamental right. In *Santhal Pargana Antyodaya Ashram* vs. *State* of *Bihar* (1987) Supp. SCC 141 in a public interest litigation, this Court obtained a report of the Committee appointed by the Court, accepted the report and gave directions to release and rehabilitate the bonded labourers identified by the Committee and to implement the Committee's recommendations, as far as possible, were issued to the State Government. The State Governments were directed to carry out the statutory obligations under the Bonded Labour System Act, 1976.

50. It would, thus, be the established procedure of this Court under Article 32 that the public interest litigation is not adversarial. It is one of collaboration and cooperation between the State and the Court. This Court as the sentinel on the *qui vive,* is constitutionally obligated to enforce the fundamental rights of all the citizens of the country and to protect them from exploitation and to provide guidance and direction for facilities and opportunities to them for securing socio-economic justice, empowerment and to free the handicapped persons from the disabilities with which they

suffer from and to make them realize and enjoy the fundamental rights ensured to them under the Constitution. In that behalf, this Court is entitled and empowered under Article 32 to adopt such procedure as is expedient in a given fact situation and deal with the matter appropriately. Therefore, the rigour of the pleadings or the relief's sought for the adversarial litigation, has been softened; new methods, tools and procedures were evolved to mete out justice and to enforce the fundamental rights. Obviously, therefore, when a limited relief to establish separate schools for the children of the fallen women was sought for by the petitioner—Gaurav Jain, this Court did not confine to the same. It, instead, enlarged the scope and directed the authorities as an interim measure to have those children admitted in the general schools to make the children overcome the disabilities had from foul atmosphere and to generate the feeling of oneness and desegregation. In addition, this Court appointed V.C. Mahajan Committee to enquire into and submit a report. The report was accordingly submitted after extensive travelling to far and wide parts of the country; it studied not only the problem of the children of the fallen women but also the root cause of the menace of child prostitution and the prostitution as such and the need for its eradication. The prevailing conditions have been pointed out in the Report and beneficial actions already taken by some of the Social Action Groups have been pointed and also noted as illustrated hereinabove. They have also dealt with the problems of the children. The State Governments and the Central Government were supplied with the copies of the Report and they have not even objected to the recommendations; in fact, they cannot be objected to since it is a fact prevailing, unfortunately, in the country. Therefore, the relief cannot be restricted to the pleadings or to the scope of the directions earlier issued; the Court can take cognizance from indisputable or the undisputed facts from the Report of V.C. Mahajan Committee and other reports and articles published in recognized Journals and act upon it. Placing reliance thereon, the directions given in the Order, aim not only at giving benefits to the children but also to root out the very source of the problem as has been pointed out in the first part of the Order, it is for the Government to evolve suitable programme of action. My learned brother has very graciously agreed to the second part of the order relating to the setting up of juvenile homes for the prostitute children and children of fallen women.

51. By operation of Article 145(6), to the extent both of us have agreed, the Order constitutes as binding precedent. It is to remember that this Court being composed of large number of Judges has evolved its own procedure to transact Court management of its judicial work and to decide cases/ causes sitting in appropriate Division Benches constituted by the Chief Justice of India as per the Supreme Court Rules. Any observation made by one of the Judges has persuasive obiter. When there is a dissent, the majority of opinion forms a binding precedent. Any difference of opinion between a Bench composed of two Judges, in an adversarial litigation requires resolution by a larger Bench of three Judges and/or if further reference is made to a Constitution Bench, it is to deal with the controversy and majority opinion forms precedent. As stated earlier, public interest litigation is not adversarial in nature but is one of cooperation and coordination between the three wings of the State and the coordination and it is the constitutional duty of this Court to ensure enjoyment of the fundamental rights by all citizens and in particular the poor and deprived social segments and in case of violation thereof, to prevent the same by giving appropriate directions in that behalf. In aid thereof, this Court has been armed by Article 142 to pass such orders as may be necessary for doing complete justice in a cause or pending matter before it. An order so made shall be enforceable throughout the Territory of India. Normally, if it were an adversarial dispute, we would have referred the matter to three Judge Bench in respect of the first part of the directions, namely, to prevent prostitution; to rehabilitate fallen women and to provide them facilities and opportunities by evolving suitable measures by all the Governments for enforcement of their economic empowerment and social integration with

dignity of person which are fundamental rights to the unfortunate fallen women, i.e., the victims of circumstances. It is seen that this matter is pending for nearly a decade. If a reference is made to a three Judge Bench, it may further be delayed. Since "delay defeats justice" it may amount to everyday denial of the fundamental rights to large number of fallen women.

52. I put a caveat upon myself and I am aware that Article 142 would be used to enforce final judgment or order which, in given special or exceptional circumstanes, would include directions of this type to mitigate injustice and to elongate enforcement of fundamental and human rights. Article 142 speaks of doing complete justice in a cause. The arm of the Court is long enough to reach injustice wherever it is found and to mete out justice. Denial of the constitutional rights to the unfortunate fallen women outrage's the quest for justice and pragmatism of constitutional ethos which constrain me to avail Article 142 of the Constitution of India to direct the Union of India as well as all State Governments to evolve, after in-depth discussion at Ministerial level conference, such procedures and principles or programmes, as indicated in this Order, as guidance would help rescue and rehabilitate the fallen women. Otherwise, the fundamental and human rights remain pious platitudes to these miserable souls crushed in the cruel flesh trade with grinding poverty in the evening of their lives. Generally, Article 142 may not be invoked before the difference of opinion is resolved in an adversarial litigation and in a keenly contested matter of even public interest litigation, in particular, of recent type cases. However, in the cases of the type in hand, where there would be no controversy on human problems of most unfortunate women which reqire their careful planning, rescue and rehabilitation, the exercise of the power under Article 142, even by a single member of the Bench, may be appropriate and efficacious to enforce fundamental and human rights of large number of neglected and exploited segments of the society. Society is responsible for a woman's becoming victim of circumstances.

The society should make reparation to prevent trafficking in women, rescue them from red light areas and other areas in which the women are driven or trapped in prostitution. Their rehabilitation by socio-economic empowerment and justice is the constitutional duty of the State. Their economic empowerment and social justice with dignity of person are the fundamental rights and the Court and the Government should positively endeavour to ensure them. The State in a democratic polity includes its three constitutional organs—the Legislature, the Executive and the Judiciary. Legislature has already done its duty. The Executive and the Judiciary are required to act in union to ensure enforcement of fundamental and human rights of the fallen women. I am also conscience that (*sic*) Union of India as well as the State Governments are sensitive to the conscience of their constitutional duty under Article 23 and are desirous to have the prostitution eradicated from the root with the aid of ITP Act, IPC and other appropriate legislative or executive actions. Sequential rehabilitation of the fallen women rescued from the red-light areas and other areas requires enforcement. The observations made in this Order, the constitutional provisions, the human rights and other International Conventions referred to in the Order and the national policy would aid the Union of India and the State Governments as foundation and guide them to discuss the problems in Ministerial and Secretarial level Conferences and as suggested in this Order to evolve procedures and principles to ensure that the fallen women also enjoy their fundamental and human rights mentioned in the Order.

53. Before parting with the case, we place on record the valuable assistance and yeoman's service rendered by V.C. Mahajan Committee.

54. The directions are accordingly given. The writ petitions are directed to be posted after the compliance report as regards the action taken in that behalf, is furnished by the Union of India for appropriate orders.

D.P. Wadhwa, J.

55. This writ petition under Article 32 of the Constitution was filed by Mr. Gaurav Jain, advocate of this Court as public interest litigation after he had read a report appearing in the 'India Today', a national magazine of July 11, 1988. The petitioner had prayed as under:

In the circumstances, it is therefore most respectfully prayed that this Hon'ble Court may graciously be pleased to:

(a) Issue an appropriate writ, in the nature of *mandamus* Order or direction, directing the respondents to provide separate schools with vocational training, hostels with the medical check-up facilities in each respondent State and Union territory and such other places where this Hon'ble Court may direct, for the children of prostitutes, up to the age of sixteen years to rescue them, from falling into the infernal existence and the same immoral and deprived way of life by indulging in the vice profession of prostitution, pimps, drug-pushers and bootleggers and other hazardous employments.

(b) Pass any other order/orders, which this Hon'ble Court may deem fit and proper in the circumstances of the case.

56. By order dated February 20, 1989 the petitioner was directed "to suitably amend the writ petition and confine claim in the petition to the relief of setting up of juvenile homes as provided under Section 9 of the Juvenile Justice Act, 1986". Then on the next date, that is, March 13, 1989 the prayer for amendment was allowed and it was directed that prayer in the writ petition shall stand substituted "by what has now been indicated in the application for amendment".

57. By order dated November 15, 1989 while the Court noted submission of Mr. V.C. Mahajan, advocate of the petitioner that separate schools and hostels be provided for the children of the prostitutes, the Court did not find itself inclined to accept such a submission. The Court was of the

view that segregating prostitutes' children by locating separate schools and providing separate hostels would not be in the interest of such children. The Court by this very order constituted a Committee headed by Mr. V.C. Mahajan, Senior Advocate to consider the problems faced by the children of the prostitutes. This order of the Court is reported in 1990 Supp SCC 709: AIR 1990 SC 292. This Committee examined the matter keeping the following objects in view:

(i) Viability of having separate schools and hostels,
(ii) Existing laws relating to the target groups, and
(iii) Possibility of evolving a scheme for these children, workable at the national level.

58. The Committee has since submitted its report. In its report the Committee has made various recommendations for the rehabilitation of the children of prostitutes. I do not find that the question of eradication of prostitution was an issue involved in these proceedings or subject matter of Committee's deliberations. The Committee in its report, which runs into over 100 pages, has only referred in two paragraphs, while examining target group, as to who are the prostitutes. Apart from this I do not find there is any discussion in the report of the Committee towards eradication of prostitution. As to what should be the scheme to be evolved to eradicate prostitution, i.e. the source itself; the basics; and what succor and sustenance can be provided to the fallen victims of flesh trade was not a question agitated in the proceedings. Certainly no one can dispute that evil of prostitution must be curbed. It is the mandate of the Constitution, which prohibits traffic in human beings. Keeping that object in view and in pursuance to International Conventions for the Suppression of Traffic in persons and of the Exploitation of the Prostitution of others signed at New York on May 9, 1950, the Parliament enacted the Suppression of Immoral Traffic in Women and Girls Act, 1956. The Act was amended in 1978 to make good some inadequacies in the implementation of the Act and in the light of the experience gained during the period the Act was being implemented. Despite the amendments of the Act it was felt

that enforcement of the Act had not been effective enough to deal with the problems of immoral traffic in all its dimensions. Suggestions had been made to Government by voluntary organizations working for women, advocacy groups and various individuals urging the enlargement of the scope of the Act, to make penal provisions more stringent and to provide for certain minimum standards for correctional treatment and rehabilitation of the victims. The Act was, therefore, further amended in 1986 making it more wide based. The Act is now called as Immoral Traffic (Prevention) Act, 1956. I need not detail other objects of the Act as all the discussions would not be relevant in these proceedings.

59. I am not entering into the scope and width of public interest litigation but when the issue has not been squarely raised, concerned parties not informed, pleadings being not there, it may not be correct to embark upon that task and to give interpretation of the law applicable thereto and that too without hearing the parties when the issue is so profound certainly involving hearing of the Union of India and State Governments with respect to their problems.

60. Thus considering the substratum of the judgment prepared by my learned brother relating to children of the prostitutes and establishment of the juvenile homes I would concur with the directions being issued by him in his order. I would, however, record my respectful dissent on the question of prostitution and the directions proposed to be issued on that account and also, in the circumstances of the case, what my learned brother has to say on the directions proposed to be issued referring to the provisions of Articles 142 and 145(5) of the Constitution.

IV. Ms. Khushi Harkishan Malhotra *vs.* State of Maharashtra 2006 (112) CrLJ 0612 (Bom)

(a) A person who is a victim of trafficking for prostitution can not be detained in a Protective Home on the orders of a

Magistrate without following the procedure laid down in Section 17 of the the Immoral Traffic (Prevention) Act, 1956.

(b) State Government given strict directions to immediately remedy the appalling conditions and stop the rampant corruption in Protective Homes.

(c) State Government directed to expeditiously set up Special Courts as mandated under Section 22 of the Immoral Traffic (Prevention) Act, 1956 to ameliorate the plight of many victims who are languishing in Protective Homes pending Magisterial inquiry.

Judges

A.S. Oka and S.R. Borulkar, JJ.

Order

1. The submissions of the Counsel appearing for the parties were heard on the last date and the Judgment was reserved. Today these Petitions are kept for dictation of the Judgment.

2. With a view to appreciate the submissions made by the Counsel appearing for the parties, it will be necessary to refer to the facts of the case. It appears that on receiving specific information, the police raided a room in Hotel 'Holiday Inn' in Mumbai. With the help of the bogus customer, police entered the said room. In the said room, a woman by the name of Sarika was found. Certain articles found in the room were seized by the police. It appears that there were two other ladies in the room including the petitioner in these Petitions. According to the police the Petitioner disclosed that she was working as prostitute. According to the case of the police, earlier the Petitioner was taken in custody in connection with C.R. No. 18 of 2004 registered with Khar Police Station in connection with the offence punishable under Section 4, 5, 7(1)(b) of the Immoral Traffic (Prevention) Act, 1956 (hereinafter referred to as the said Act of 1956). It is alleged that the petitioner was handed over the custody of her relatives on 2nd June 2004 and again on 5th August 2004 she

was found in hotel Holiday Inn. The offence was registered under Sections 4, 5, 7(1)(b) of the said Act of 1956 against the two accused persons, viz. Mishtakim Ahmed *alias* Robbin Azim Ahmed Shaikh and Chetan Laxmidas Sohani. The accused persons were arrested and were produced before the learned Additional Chief Metropolitan Magistrate, 37th Court, Mumbai on 6th August 2004 and the application for remand was moved by the Sub-Inspector of Social Services Branch of Crime Branch, CID, Mumbai. It appears that the Petitioner was also brought before the learned Magistrate. While passing the order on remand application, the learned Additional Chief Metropolitan Magistrate passed an order directing that the Petitioner should be kept in Navjeevan Mahila Sudhar Griha at Mumbai and shall be produced before him on 7th August 2004. He directed that the girls be examined under Section 15 of the said Act of 1956.

3. It appears that an application was filed on August 2004 by one Advocate Shri Jaiswal on behalf of the Petitioner praying that she may be set free. The said application was rejected by the learned Additional Chief Metropolitan Magistrate by order dated 17th August 2004. It appears that on 13th August 2004 an application was made before the learned Magistrate for grant of time in favour of the Probation Officer for submission of the report. In a separate report dated 13th August 2004 submitted by the Senior Inspector of Police, it was stated that office bearers of Navjeevan Mahila Vastigriha, Mumbai were making enquiry as regards the Petitioner. It appears that on 30th August 2004 an application was made on behalf of the Petitioner praying that she may be released as she has been confined to Protective Home for a period of more than 21 days. By order dated 10th September 2004, the learned Magistrate rejected the said application. An Appeal was preferred before the Sessions Court by the Petitioner for challenging the order of the learned Magistrate. In the said Appeal, an application for bail was filed on behalf of the Petitioner by her Advocate. The said application came to be rejected by order dated 1st October 2004.

4. Writ Petition No. 2037 of 2004 was filed by the Petitioner *inter alia* praying for direction to set aside the order passed by the Sessions Court on 1st October 2004. A prayer was also made for compensation. The prayer for interim relief was made directing that the Petitioner should be set free. In the said Petition only State of Maharashtra was made party. On 20th October 2004 the learned A.P.P. pointed out to this Court that on 10th October 2004 the Petitioner had escaped from the custody of the Superintendent of the Navjeevan Mahila Vastigriha. When this submission was made. The Counsel appearing for the Petitioner took time to enable him to take instructions. The Petitioner was directed to remain present in the Court on 26th October 2004.

5. On 3rd November 2004 this Court directed that it was necessary to take investigation as to the reasons why the instances of about eight girls having escaped from Navjeevan Mahila Vasatigriha have taken place. This Court directed to the Superintendent of the said institution to remain present in this court. By order dated 24th November 2004, this court noted that the Superintendent of Navjeevan Mahila Vasatigriha and the Superintendent of Government Rehabilitation of Girls (Special home) Deonar, Mumbai submitted a report accepting that large number of inmates have escaped from the custody. The report also indicates that intimation in that behalf was not only given to the concerned police stations but also to the Government agencies. For various reasons the report discloses that it will be difficult to stop such instances. Therefore, this Court issued notice to the Secretary of Women and Child Welfare Department, Mantralaya, Mumbai. In the subsequent order, this Court noted that in a short span of seven months in the year 2004, about 141 inmates succeeded in escaping from Navjeevan Mahila Vasatigriha. From Special Rehabilitation Centre at Deonar about 94 inmates escaped.

6. There is a detailed report submitted by the Additional Chief Secretary (Services) of the Government of Maharashtra dated 20th June 2005. In the said report steps taken by the

Government have been highlighted. The said steps are as under:

(i) To build good infrastructure, a Swadhar project is being set up at Deonar. This will fulfil the need of a bigger and airy campus. Also the ancillary units attached to it will provide counselling, recreation. vocational, medical, networking facilities in better manner. The construction is likely to start in September 2005 after finalizing the tenders.

(ii) On the issue of the establishment of the Special Courts, the State Government has sought the views of Hon'ble High Court as to how many Special Courts are needed and the requirement of the additional staff and the additional expenditure therefor.

(iii) The Proposal to create additional posts including that for the security at Navjeevan Mahila Vastigriha, Chembur is under consideration. However, the required additional staff has been posted to this home on working arrangement by pooling of the staff. Now these two institutions are having exclusive female staff. The department has taken a special care to post the sensitized staff.

(iv) The instructions have been issued to the concerned authority to get the electricity connection required for water supply.

(v) The Revised Maher Scheme has been extended to the residents of Navjeevan Mahila Vastrigriha. Under this scheme, an assistance of Rs. 250 per month is granted to these women for out of pocket expenses.

(vi) I would further submit to the Hon'ble High Court that the Department of Women and Child Development is in the process of framing rules under Immoral Trafficking (Prevention) Act, 1956. This will ensure the strict implementation of the Act. The victims of commercial sexual exploitation are often looked as offenders but the rules will help to change this scenario and take stringent action against those who are responsible for exploiting them.

The report also discloses that there are large number of vacant posts in the said Navjeevan Mahila Vasatigriha. There is one more report dated 13th July 2005 placed on record by the Chief Secretary of the State Government. In the said report, the programme for taking action has been set out. The material particulars in the said report are as under:

Proposed	*Time*
1. Creation of addition in Navjeevan Mahila Sudhar Griha	1 year
2. Granting approval for appointing private guards	6 months
3. Setting up special Court for trying the cases under the said Act of 1956	6 months
4. For framing rules under the said Act of 1936	6-8 months
5. For construction Swadhar Griha Deonar	1-½ years

7. There are Affidavits filed by the Registrar General of this Court setting out the pendency of the cases under the said Act of 1956. The affidavit discloses that 1265 cases are pending in the Court of Metropolitan Magistrates in Bombay and about 44 cases are pending in the Sessions Court at Bombay. As stated earlier, now there is a proposal initiated by the State Government to set up a Special Court for the offences under the said Act of 1956.

8. Writ Petition No. 1710 of 2005 is filed by the same Petitioner. In the said Petition very serious allegations have been made against the Officers of Navjeevan Mahila Vasatigriha. It is stated that the Incharge of the said Navjeevan Mahila Vasatigriha informed the Petitioner that she has been ordered to be enlarged on bail on payment of Rs. 10,000. A case is made out that accordingly the Petitioner managed to collect the said amount and paid the said amount to him and was permitted to leave the said Sudhar Griha. A contention is raised that the Petitioner has not escaped and was permitted to leave. A contention raised in this, Petition is that the detention of the Petitioner in the said Navjeevan Mahila

Vasatigriha was illegal as procedure under the said Act of 1956 is not followed.

9. The learned Counsel for the Petitioner in both the Petitions submitted that there was no order passed by the Competent Court authorizing detention of the Petitioner in the said institution. He pointed out that no specific orders were passed under sub-sections 3 and 4 of Section 17 of the said Act of 1956. He submitted that the Petitioner was mislead by the Incharge of the said Institution and therefore, she believed that she has been enlarged on bail on payment of Rs. 10,000. He submitted that he is in a position to substantiate the said allegation.

10. The learned P.P. submitted that the allegations, which are made in the Writ Petition No. 1710 of 2005 are patently false. He relied upon the affidavit of one Dilip Vana Hivrale who is present at District Welfare and Child Welfare Officer. He was working as the Superintendent of Navjeevan Mahila Vasatigriha at the relevant time. He stated in the Affidavit that he requested 'Prerna', a Non-Government Organization in Mumbai to conduct confidential enquiry on the question of rehabilitation of the Petitioner. The said organization contacted their counterpart at Delhi, i.e. 'Prayas' a Non-Government Organization. The report submitted on confidential enquiry reveals that the Petitioner is likely to re-enter into immoral traffic. He stated in the Affidavit that on 25th February 2005 when he was sitting in his office at about 10:00 a.m. three unknown persons entered his office. One of them whipped out knife and assaulted him on his back. He reiterated that the Petitioner escaped from the said Navjeevan Mahila Vasatigriha. The learned A.P.P. fairly conceded that except for the order passed by the learned Magistrate on 6th August 2004 on remand report, no further order has been passed by the learned Magistrate. He candidly stated that it is observed that the learned Metropolitan Magistrates in Mumbai are not following the procedure incorporated under Section 17 of the said Act of 1956 and therefore, necessary directions are required to be issued.

11. With a view to appreciate the submissions, it will be necessary to refer to the relevant provisions of the said Act of 1956.

Section 2 contemplates establishment of two institutions by the name 'corrective institution' and 'protective home' Corrective institution is one where the persons who are in need of correction are detained. Protective home is one where persons who are in need of care and protection are kept. Sections 3 to 9 are the penal provisions. Section 10A gives power to the Court to detain the female offender in corrective home in lieu of sentence of imprisonment. Section 15 gives power to Special Police Officer or Trafficking Police Officer to search the premises without warrant when there is a reasonable ground for believing that an offence has been committed or being committed. Section 16 deals with rescuing the persons from brothel. Section 17 is the material provisions for these Petitions, which reads thus:

"17. Intermediate custody of (persons) removed under Section 15 or rescued under Section 16:

(1) When the special police officer removing a person under sub-section (4) of Section 15 or a police officer rescuing a person under sub-section (1) of Section 16, for any reason unable to produce him/her before the appropriate Magistrate as required by sub-section (5) of section 15, or before the Magistrate issuing the order under sub-section (2) of Section 16, he shall forthwith produce him/her before the nearest Magistrate of any class, who shall pass such orders as he deems proper for his/her safe custody until he/she is produced before the appropriate Magistrate, or, as the case may be, the Magistrate issuing the order:

Provided that no (person) shall be:

(i) Detained in custody under this sub-section for a period exceeding ten days from the date of order under this sub-section; or
(ii) Restored to or placed in the custody of a person who may exercise a harmful influence over him/her.

(2) When the (person) is produced before the Magistrate.

12. Sub-section 1 of Section 17 of the said Act of 1956 provides that whenever special police officer removes a person

under Section 15 or a person is removed under Section 16, he or she is required to be produced before nearest Magistrate of any class. The said Magistrate is enjoined to pass such order as he deems fit for the safe custody of the women or the person until the person is produced before the appropriate Magistrate. The said Section puts a restriction that detention cannot be allowed for a period exceeding ten days. Sub-section 2 provides that appropriate Magistrate shall after giving the person opportunity of being heard cause an enquiry to be made as to correctness of the information received under Section 16(1), the age, character and antecedents of the person and the suitability of said person's parents, guardian or husband for taking charge of the person. He may direct a Probation Officer to enquire into the above circumstances. Sub-section 3 authorizes the Magistrate to pass an order for safe custody of the person pending the enquiry under Sub-section 2. Proviso of Sub-section 3 lays that no person shall be in custody for the period exceeding three weeks from the date of such order. A Sub-section 4 deals with the power of the Magistrate after enquiry is completed under Sub-section 2. If the learned Magistrate is satisfied that the information is correct and the person is in need of care and protection, he may authorize the detention of such person for such period being not less than one year and not more than three years in Protective Home or in such other custody. Sub-section 5 provides that while discharging function under Sub-section 2 the learned Magistrate may summon five respectable persons, three of whom wherever practicable, be women to assist him. Order under Sub-section 4 is made an appealable order by virtue of Sub-section 6.

13. As conceded by the learned A.P.P. only judicial order which is passed in the matter of the Petitioner is dated 6th August 2004. That order is surprisingly passed on remand report seeking police custody of the accused. It is not the case of the State that the Petitioner was an accused. The said order dated 6th August 2004 directs that the Petitioner shall be kept in Navjeevan Mahila Vastigriha and she will be produced before any Court on 7th August 2004. There is nothing on record to show that the Petitioner was produced before the Court on or after 7th August 2004. It appears that

an application was moved on behalf of the Petitioner for release of the Petitioner. The said application was rejected by an order dated 17th August 2004. Only observation made by the learned Magistrate is that the Petitioner needs protection under the said Act of 1956. It appears that as the Petitioner was under wrong impression that there is order passed under Sub-section 4 of Section 17 of the said Act of 1956. An appeal was preferred to the Session Court. An application for bail was made in the said Appeal which came to be rejected by order dated 1st October 2004.

14. The sum and substance of the aforesaid discussion is that neither the learned Magistrate nor the learned Sessions Judge applied his mind to provisions of Section 17 of the said Act of 1956. While passing the orders for keeping the Petitioner in protective home for a period of one day, there is no order passed by the learned Magistrate for holding enquiry under Sub-section 2 of Section 17 of the said Act of 1956. Even assuming that he ordered enquiry, he could have passed an order detaining the Petitioner only for a period of three weeks. Admittedly, there is no order passed under Sub-section 4 of Section 17 of the said Act of 1956. Thus, without their being any judicial order, the Petitioner was kept with the said protective home from 6th August 2004 onwards though there was no order passed either under Sub-section 3 or 4 of Section 17 of the said Act of 1956. In any event, the Petitioner could not have been kept in the protective home after 27th August 2004. Thus, the fact that the Petitioner escaped on 10th October 2004 becomes irrelevant. Therefore, I have no adjudicated upon the allegation regarding payment of Rs. 10,000 by the Petitioner. The Petitioner could not have been detained after 27th August 2004 even assuming that there was order passed under Sub-section 3 of Section 17 of the said Act of 1956.

15. The impression which one gathers from the orders passed by the learned Magistrate and the learned Sessions Judge is that the Petitioner is an accused. Going by the case of the prosecution, the Petitioner really appears to be a victim. In my view, the learned Magistrate was duly bound to strictly follow the procedure laid down by the provisions of Section 17 of the said Act of 1956. The order of the Sessions

Court rejecting the Bail Application of the Applicant dated 1st October 2004. The said order is passed by ignoring that the Petitioner could not have been detained after 27th August 2004. The entire episode shows sad state of affairs. The approach of the Courts below ought to have been very cautious considering the fact that the Court was dealing with an victim and not accused. The Court should have shown more sensitivity. In fact a mechanical approach has been adopted by the Court.

16. The reports, which are submitted by the State Government in Writ Petition No. 2037 of 2004 deserve to be accepted. It is expected that the State Government will act on the reports and will establish a Special Court under Section 22A of the said Act of 1956. As more than 1500 cases are pending in the city of Mumbai, establishment of Special Courts is a matter of great necessity and urgency.

17. Hence, Petitions are disposed of by passing the following order:

(i) It is declared that detention of the Petitioner after 27th August 2004 in the Navjeevan Mahila Vasatigriha is illegal and therefore, the Petitioner is set at liberty unless the Petitioner is required in connection with any other offence.

(ii) The reports submitted by the State Government in Criminal Writ Petition No. 2037 of 2004 are accepted.

(iii) A copy of this order be forwarded to the Secretary of Law and Judiciary Department of the State Government and learned Chief Metropolitan Magistrate, Mumbai. The learned Chief Metropolitan Magistrate, Mumbai is expected to circulate a copy of the Judgment to all the Magistrates in the city. The learned Chief Metropolitan Magistrate will consider assigning the cases under the said Act to specified Courts till establishment of the Special Courts. This will facilitate passing of appropriate orders and holding of enquiry as contemplated by Section 17 of the said Act of 1956. Parties to act upon an authenticated copy of this order.

Order accordingly.

Index